AGING AND RETIREMENT

SAGE FOCUS EDITIONS

1. **POLICE AND SOCIETY**, edited by David H. Bayley
2. **WHY NATIONS ACT**, edited by Maurice A. East, Stephen A. Salmore, and Charles F. Hermann
3. **EVALUATION RESEARCH METHODS**, edited by Leonard Rutman
4. **SOCIAL SCIENTISTS AS ADVOCATES**, edited by George H. Weber and George J. McCall
5. **DYNAMICS OF GROUP DECISIONS**, edited by Hermann Brandstatter, James H. Davis, and Heinz Schuler
6. **NATURAL ORDER**, edited by Barry Barnes and Steven Shapin
7. **CONFLICT AND CONTROL**, edited by Arthur J. Vidich and Ronald M. Glassman
8. **CONTROVERSY**, edited by Dorothy Nelkin
9. **BATTERED WOMEN**, edited by Donna M. Moore
10. **CRIMINOLOGY**, edited by Edward Sagarin
11. **TO AUGUR WELL**, edited by J. David Singer and Michael D. Wallace
12. **IMPROVING EVALUATIONS**, edited by Lois-ellin Datta and Robert Perloff
13. **IMAGES OF INFORMATION**, edited by Jon Wagner
14. **CHURCHES AND POLITICS IN LATIN AMERICA**, edited by Daniel H. Levine
15. **EDUCATIONAL TESTING AND EVALUATION**, edited by Eva L. Baker and Edys S. Quellmalz
16. **IMPROVING POLICY ANALYSIS**, edited by Stuart S. Nagel
17. **POWER STRUCTURE RESEARCH**, edited by G. William Domhoff
18. **AGING AND SOCIETY**, edited by Edgar F. Borgatta and Neil G. McCluskey
19. **CENTRE AND PERIPHERY**, edited by Jean Gottmann
20. **THE ELECTORATE RECONSIDERED**, edited by John C. Pierce and John L. Sullivan
21. **THE BLACK WOMAN**, edited by La Frances Rodgers-Rose
22. **MAKING BUREAUCRACIES WORK**, edited by Carol H. Weiss and Allen H. Barton
23. **RADICAL CRIMINOLOGY**, edited by James A. Inciardi
24. **DUAL-CAREER COUPLES**, edited by Fran Pepitone-Rockwell
25. **POLICY IMPLEMENTATION**, edited by John Brigham and Don W. Brown
26. **CONTEMPORARY BLACK THOUGHT**, edited by Molefi Kete Asante and Abdulai S. Vandi
27. **HISTORY AND CRIME**, edited by James A. Inciardi and Charles E. Faupel
28. **THE FUTURE OF EDUCATION**, edited by Kathryn Cirincione-Coles
29. **IMPROVING SCHOOLS**, edited by Rolf Lehming and Michael Kane
30. **KNOWLEDGE AND POWER IN A GLOBAL SOCIETY**, edited by William M. Evan
31. **BLACK MEN**, edited by Lawrence E. Gary
32. **MAJOR CRIMINAL JUSTICE SYSTEMS**, edited by George F. Cole, Stanislaw J. Frankowski, and Marc G. Gertz
33. **ANALYZING ELECTORAL HISTORY**, edited by Jerome M. Clubb, William H. Flanigan, and Nancy H. Zingale
34. **ASSESSING MARRIAGE**, edited by Erik E. Filsinger and Robert A. Lewis
35. **THE KNOWLEDGE CYCLE**, edited by Robert F. Rich
36. **IMPACTS OF RACISM ON WHITE AMERICANS**, edited by Benjamin P. Bowser and Raymond G. Hunt
37. **WORLD SYSTEM STRUCTURE**, edited by W. Ladd Hollist and James N. Rosenau
38. **WOMEN AND WORLD CHANGE**, edited by Naomi Black and Ann B. Cottrell
39. **ENVIRONMENTAL CRIMINOLOGY**, edited by Paul J. Brantingham and Patricia L. Brantingham
40. **GOVERNING THROUGH COURTS**, edited by Richard A.L. Gambitta, Mary L. May, and James C. Foster
41. **BLACK FAMILIES**, edited by Harriette Pipes McAdoo
42. **EFFECTIVE SCHOOL DESEGREGATION**, edited by Willis D. Hawley
43. **AGING AND RETIREMENT**, edited by Neil G. McCluskey and Edgar F. Borgatta
44. **MODERN INDUSTRIAL CITIES**, edited by Bruce M. Stave

AGING AND RETIREMENT

Prospects, Planning, and Policy

edited by

NEIL G. McCLUSKEY
EDGAR F. BORGATTA

SAGE PUBLICATIONS   Beverly Hills   London

For Elaine and Marie,
Who Have Grown with Us

For information address:

SAGE Publications, Inc.
275 South Beverly Drive
Beverly Hills, California 90212

SAGE Publications Ltd
28 Banner Street
London EC1Y 8QE, England

Printed in the United States of America

Library of Congress Cataloging in Publication Data

Main entry under title:

Aging and retirement.

   (Sage focus editions)
   Bibliography: p.
   1. Retirement--United States--Addresses, essays, lectures. I. McCluskey, Neil Gerard. II. Borgatta, Edgar F., 1924-
HQ1064.U5A6335   305.2'6   81-14415
ISBN 0-8039-1756-2   AACR2
ISBN 0-8039-1757-0 (pbk.)

FIRST PRINTING

CONTENTS

INTRODUCTION

Although sometimes the data have been presented with alarmist and exaggerated overtones, the growth in numbers and proportions of the aged population is an unquestioned contemporary reality. Interest in the field of aging has grown. At some points the growth and use of "buzz" words have led some to believe that much of what was going on was little more than a new fad within the research and service delivery industries. While there may be much useless debris from the current period of research and writing, we sense a clarification and deepening of perspective that should foster progress in the field of aging.

One aspect of the current gerontological enterprise has been a better description and understanding of the facts about aging. A second has been the greater awareness of the interrelatedness of policies and programs of the government, and, it has to be said, how poorly the government has defined what it really wants to do. It is a highly complex situation, and the purpose of this volume is to cover *some* of the areas and issues in one part of this arena of study—aging and retirement. Even this segment is much too large to be treated within the covers of a single book, so we see this as a modest contribution to adding some perspective to the field. The volume has been enriched by the mix of its contributors, who include well-established figures in aging along with talented younger scholars who, we judge, will be joining them.

The facts of aging are not static, and even as this volume goes to press we know that expectations about the demographics will soon be revised. The 1980 Census provided the preliminary finding that projections had underestimated the count by about four million people. It will not be known until 1982 how this reflects the aging of the population, one potentially important aspect to be considered in any analysis of the reasons for an underestimate. The findings may require serious revision of population projections for the future.

Interest in aging not only has had a massive growth, but is now likely to follow a pattern of regularized cyclical stimulation. The White House Conference on Aging held at the end of 1981 is raising the level of the nation's consciousness of aging. The reports, products, and follow-up meetings from the conference are leaving important traces that will continue to influence society into the 1980s, as did the White House Conferences of 1961 and 1971 in their decades. These conferences cover a broad scope of social issues related to the aging group and engender an enormous support basis even if, as always happens, aging advocacy groups feel shortchanged by the difference between their earlier expectations and what the administration delivers. This will be particularly felt during the Reagan Administration.

The White House Conference on Aging follows another event that somehow did not seem to have the impact intended, namely, the presentation of the final report of the President's Commission on Pension Policy. In large part this lack can be attributed to the attitude of one presidential administration saying that it was a commission of a former administration, and thus not to be taken as very important. Moreover, the climate is not conducive to putting credence in the kind of optimistic and generous recommendations that usually come out of commission reports. The Report on Pension Policy presents a reasonable assessment of the facts about aging, and then presents its recommendations. Some recommendations have been generally well-received, others have been rejected out of hand by the current administration, and some are simply in the never-never land of great ideas that have to compete for funds with other equally great ideas.

An early release from the President's Commission reported the demographic basis of the population of the United States. The major points are now well known and can be summarized briefly: (1) the period of high immigration is long past and, except for the post-World War II baby boom, birthrates are low in comparison to past history; (2) death rates have also gone down through the control of communicable disease; and (3) death rates presently are at a relative low. These three facts are associated with a shift from a population with a high proportion of young persons to one that has a progressively increasing proportion of older persons.

Both for its significance in the labor market and its potential impact upon the culture, the 14 to 24 age cohort is the critical factor. This age group has been labeled "the barbarians" by some demographers because they invade society at birth and in time either change it or are themselves changed by it. What roughly determines the outcome is the ratio of invaders to defenders. If the defenders are dominant in numbers, the invaders get absorbed; if the numbers are with the invaders, they tend to take over and overturn the old ways. Between 1890 and 1960 the population grew slowly and steadily with a total gain in the 14-24 age group of 11.3 million. However, in the single decade of the sixties it exploded with an awesome increase of 13.2 million. During the following decade the invader cohort grew by an additional 4.9 million. Now, into the 1980s, it is already declining.

Because this cohort and its immediate predecessor entered the job market, the 1970s saw a vast increase in the total work force, going from 85.9 million in 1970 to 105 million in 1979. (This increase is also due in part to the higher proportion of adults, particularly women, joining the work force.) The baby boom, then, produced productive workers in the current years who are available to contribute to the support of the growing number of older persons. However, there already is in motion a unique demographic factor which will grow more significant as the baby boom cohort itself arrives at older age. Sometime around the year 2010 the proportion of persons in the older age cohorts will have increased to create a situation that could involve serious problems for the management of the economy. The projections used by the Report of the President's Commission suggest a shift from 1980 to 2030 in the range from about 11 percent to 22 percent for those 65 years of age and over. Such a radical increase in the elderly population serves as an important justification for having a President's Commission on Pension Policy and, perhaps even more important, for establishing a permanent Presidential Commission on Aging Policy.

The demographic facts involve some other major items that should be kept in mind. The proportion of *older* old persons is increasing, and these older people will need more services and attention generally. The proportion of females in the older age group is increasing, suggesting that many issues of sex roles, health, and the economics of individual versus family units will be an important part of future studies. For example, labor force participation is associated with earned retirement benefits, but women are still traditionally less deeply involved in the gainfully employed labor force. Shifts are occurring, however, and their consequences are just now beginning to get recognition in the making of broad perspectives of national social policy.

The President's Commission also provided some survey data that confirmed and added to the known facts. For one example, the federal government has a system of pension coverage for its employees that is universal, but in the private sector less than half the employees have coverage. Additionally, many pensions have vesting requirements that turn vesting into a long-time hurdle to be overcome if one is to reap the rewards of many years of work. For instance, if 15 years of uninterrupted work is the vesting requirement, and the employee stops work 6 months short of that length of time, he or she fails to qualify for any portion of the pension.

Additional facts suggest the mixed nature of the economic prospects for retirees in this country. Of those answering a survey, 57.8 percent were expecting social security to be the primary source of retirement income; 21.6 percent employer pension systems; 17.4 percent personal savings, investments, Individual Retirement Accounts (IRA), or Keogh; and the remaining 3.2 percent family, welfare, or disability payments. Women saw themselves dependent on social security as the primary source of income much more often than men.

A later chapter in this volume takes up in more detail some of the major recommendations of the President's Commission, particularly touching on values and policy. Here it can be noted that the several documents making up the full Report of the President's Commission on Pension Policy are important markers that indicate formal recognition of several issues. Among them: (1) economic problems are potentially involved in our demographic shifts; (2) earlier policy on provision of pensions or income maintenance has been erratic; and (3) no carefully thought out plan for managing the retirement years of the American population has yet been devised.

The rhetoric and political platforms and the slogans of advocacy groups have promised or demanded the moon. Even where administrations and people can be credited with good intentions, hard work done collaboratively will still need to go into the study and development of a national retirement policy.

This volume falls into three divisions of unequal length, each of which is introduced by its own brief overview. These divisions are: Part I: AGING AND RETIREMENT PROSPECTS; Part II: AGING AND RETIREMENT PLANNING; and Part III: AGING AND RETIREMENT POLICY.

The reader may find the allocation of material somewhat arbitrary. It is. However, the editors feel that this very element underscores the close interrelatedness existing among prospects, planning, and policy. No attempt has been made to lay down hard and fast definitions of "aging," "the elderly," or "retirement," and the reader may find these terms used by different authors in widely differing senses. At this stage in the life of as youthful a science as gerontology, nothing else should be expected.

In concluding this foreword, the editors wish to record their gratitude and appreciation to the contributing authors, as well as to the staff of Sage Publications for helping us build this book.

Edgar F. Borgatta   *Neil G. McCluskey*
Seattle   New York

PART I
AGING AND RETIREMENT PROSPECTS

Western society is only starting to feel the impact of the increased longevity of its members. A new pattern of life is emerging for the growing numbers of men and women who in full stride have passed the traditional road marker of 65 years. Part I of the present volume takes a prospective view of the retirement years. The introductory chapter focuses briefly on the broad demographic and economic facts that will have to be considered to support citizens as they exit from the labor market in later life.

A following chapter details the significant findings of the Retirement History Study, a ten-year project of the Social Security Administration designed to answer some of the basic questions about retirement and postretirement behavior in the United States. But what then are the career prospects for the post-65 population? The gift of added years becomes a cruel joke if the active and ambitious are denied any continuing productive role in the economic enterprise of society. Chapter 3 discusses the report of the National Committee on Careers for Older Americans, *Older Americans: An Untapped Resource,* as a prime example of how a philosophy can be put to work in the marketplace. Once the reality of the mature, experienced worker is accepted, meaningful options for placing him or her spring up everywhere throughout the workworld. The section closes with a chapter on the aging veteran, presenting data that refutes the old dictum that old soldiers never die but simply fade away. They are not fading away; they are a real presence in the current period. American society is beginning to see the dimensions of the veteran population and its effects upon social structures never designed to cope with such numbers.

1

THE SOCIAL SECURITY ADMINISTRATION'S RETIREMENT HISTORY STUDY

Karen Schwab
Lola M. Irelan

The program of retirement research conducted by the Social Security Administration is the largest and the oldest in the country. Mandated by the Social Security Act and begun in 1940, the research program has focused upon policy studies, investigating the characteristics of beneficiaries and the older population as a whole. The Retirement History Study (RHS), one of the Social Security Administration's recent research projects, provides the best data available on the retirement process and on the effects of retirement. With it a number of policy questions have been addressed, among them: Why do individuals retire before the age of 65? How well does income in retirement replace earnings? What happens to the standard of living after retirement? How do social security and other laws (such as the law delaying compulsory retirement age) affect retirement patterns?

Until RHS was undertaken, answers to those questions were either speculative or based upon responses to retrospective questions. With data

AUTHORS' NOTE: This chapter was written by the authors in their private capacities. No official support or endorsement by the Social Security Administration or the Department of Health and Human Services is intended or should be inferred.

on hand now from RHS's ten-year study of a single sample of older workers, it is possible to begin developing accurate analyses of the factors influencing American workers' retirement and postretirement behavior. It is useful now (about midway through analyses of the study's data) to review its major findings to date. This chapter first briefly describes the study, then discusses in some detail major policy-related findings from the study thus far, and, finally, lists some considerations for future studies.

DESCRIPTION OF THE STUDY

The design of RHS was dictated by the need to serve policy makers concerned with a national program (Social Security) serving all American workers. It was necessary to sample workers in all occupations, in all parts of the country. Consequently, the sample is nationally representative, ranges over all occupations, and, for the first time in a longitudinal aging study, includes large numbers of older women. Blacks are included proportionally to their representation in the population. Women married and living with their husbands at the time of sample selection were not included as primary respondents. Instead the spouses of sample members answered a subset of questions from the questionnaire. The age of primary sample members was 58 through 63 years old as of 1969.

The original sample of 12,549 persons was a multistage area probability sample selected from members of households in 19 retired rotation groups of the Current Population Survey (CPS sample design is detailed in U.S. Bureau of the Census, 1963). In spring of 1969, initial interviews were completed with 11,153 persons. Interviews were conducted biennially through 1979 (when sample members reached 68 through 73 years of age). When a sample member died, the surviving spouse—unless/until remarried— was interviewed using the same instrument as that administered to sample members. This procedure has enabled the development of a separate longitudinal analysis group of over 1,000 widows, for whom extensive prewidowhood data is available. It also has permitted extended analysis of the results (for their widows) of sample members' work and circumstances before death. For both sample members and their spouses, survey data have been supplemented by matching them with individual social security earnings records. These records yield information on the continuity of work history and indicate amounts of benefits to which workers will be entitled.

INITIAL FINDINGS

Analysis began as soon as data were available from the first interviews in 1969. These first reports are found in a Social Security Administration

Research Report (Irelan et al., 1976). In that first year of RHS, 17 percent of the men aged 58 to 63 had already withdrawn from the labor force. Over half of these very early retirees had been without work for three years or longer, most often because of poor health. Level of education, occupational identity, and race were found to make differences in the effect of poor health on work and appeared decisive in premature retirement. Men who retired very early also tended to have lower incomes and fewer assets than their still-working counterparts (Schwab, in Irelan et al., 1976). Among women, health also had a pronounced effect on work life. Some 41 percent were out of the labor force in 1969, with poor health being the most frequently given reason (Sherman, in Irelan et al., 1976).

Not all the workers intended to retire. Most of those who did expected that it would be a pleasant time of life with some manageable financial problems. Many expected retirement income only from social securtiy, although few knew how much they would receive as benefits. Speculating on how they would cope with possible financial problems in retirement, many said they would return to work (Irelan and Bon, 1974).

Data from the first wave of RHS data (in essence, a cross-section view of retirement) has been extended now with data from later waves of interviews. It has been possible with these later waves to look at the actual experience of retirees. Priority has been given to the study of questions of immediate concern to social security policy makers—factors in early retirement, effects of national legislation, women's retirement patterns, and the financial aspects of individual retirement.

The phenomenon of increasing rates of early retirement (before the age of 65) was an important reason for the undertaking of RHS. The percentage of beneficiaries receiving early reduced benefits from social security has grown since it became possible to receive benefits before age 65 (in 1956 for women; 1961 for men). In 1978, 70 percent of persons awarded retirement benefits received an early reduced benefit. The growth in the percentage of social security beneficiaries taking early retirement benefits has concerned many. Early benefits are actuarially reduced, up to a reduction of 20 percent for individuals retiring at age 62, the earliest age at which social security benefits can be received. The concern has been twofold: first, for individuals, who receive permanently reduced retirement income because they retired early; second, for the Social Security trust fund, which can ill afford the reduction in tax receipts occurring with the earlier departure of workers from the labor force.

Several advisory panels have considered delaying the age or ages for receipt of old age benefits. This proposal has been more actively considered recently, as future trust fund problems are better (and more widely) understood. The entrance of the large baby boom cohorts into retirement age, beginning about the year 2010, will cause a decline in the ratio of workers to retirees. The ratio is now 5 to 1. That is, 5 persons of working age (20 to 64 years of age) are available to support each person 65 and older. If ultimate fertility is 2.1, there will be only 3.3 working-age persons to each aged person by the year 2050. Delaying or eliminating early retirement would reduce costs of financing retirement under social security and would therefore reduce the increases in social security taxes projected for the future. Though they have considered such a change in policy, the advisory panels generally have not recommended that such a change be made. Their hesitancy is in part due to lack of information about the effect such a change would have upon future aged workers.

Research analysts have not agreed on the relative importance of health and pension income in early retirement. Though the trend toward early retirement has certainly been associated with the availability of social security benefits at age 62 (and private pension offerings before age 65), research reports have differed as to which workers are taking advantage of the availability of early pension income. Some have suggested that it is workers in poor health who retire early. Other research has suggested that pension income is the primary determinant of early retirement. It is crucial to know which workers take advantage of the opportunity to retire early. Is it those who are relatively affluent? Those in poor health? Those distinguished by other characteristics? If the amount of pension income is the major explanatory factor in early retirement, early retirement might be phased out without causing as much hardship as would be involved if poor health were the major factor.

Research done on this question in the past has generally lacked one or more of the variables considered important to early retirement. Usually studies have not been able to measure the social security income respondents could receive at retirement. In fact, about half of respondents say they do not know (Barfield and Morgan, 1969; Schwab, forthcoming). Most studies have been cross-sectional, comparing retirees with non-retirees, thereby confounding changes occurring after retirement with differences that existed prior to retirement. Few studies have sufficiently large samples of the appropriate age group to look at the factors associated with early retirement in any depth.

The Retirement History Study, on the other hand, has a large sample of persons passing through the early retirement stage, is longitudinal, and has measured most of the key variables, including potential social security income. In an initial longitudinal regression analysis of the Retirement History Study data, Bixby (1976) found health status to be the strongest predictor of retirement, especially early retirement. Preretirement status on attitude toward retirement, occupation, pension coverage, and home ownership were more weakly related to early retirement. Although an earlier, cross-sectional, analysis of the Retirement History Study suggested that the effect of eligibility for pension income fell most heavily upon those with health problems (Quinn, 1977), Bixby did not find this to be true in the longitudinal analysis. If anything, workers *without* health problems seemed more affected by second pension coverage than workers with health problems.

Schwab also examined the effect of preretirement characteristics on early retirement, but with a more extensive longitudinal regression analysis. There were some differences from Bixby's findings, but generally the conclusions were similar. Developing a complex measure of the potential retirement income available to workers from social security and private pensions resulted in a measure more strongly predictive of early retirement than the simpler pension coverage variable. Health status was still found to be the most powerful predictor of early retirement, though not as strong as the measure reported by Bixby (differences may be due to the particular data waves studied or to differences in the time interval selected for analysis). A score on attitudes toward job was correlated with early retirement, but its relative importance dropped when entered into regression equations. Preretirement occupation was also found to be important, as was level of assets. Home ownership was not found to predict early retirement. When separately correlated with early retirement, each appeared to influence early retirement (that is, each correlation was statistically significant). It appeared that four of the variables explained nearly all the variance that could be explained in early retirement: health, pension income, occupation, and attitude toward retirement.

To test for interaction, separate equations were run for men with and men without health problems. Little difference between the two equations could be detected in the strength of the influence of pension income on early retirement. This gives further evidence that pension income and health independently influence early retirement (rather than interactively influencing it). That is, it seems to be the case that a worker may retire early if he is eligible for a good pension or if he is in poor health. If Quinn's (1977) finding of interaction had been replicated in the longitudinal equation, that would have suggested a different interpretation: that workers with good pension income are more likely to retire early, but only if they also have health problems.

EARNINGS TEST AS WORK DETERRENT

It has been suggested that other aspects of the Social Security Act (in addition to its provision of retirement benefits) act to encourage older persons to stay out of the labor force. In particular, the earnings test is frequently labeled a work deterrent. "Earnings test" is a summary phrase referring to the formula which reduces the benefits of beneficiaries earning more than a certain amount in wages. In the 1940s, benefits were suspended for months in which earnings amounted to $15.00 or more. Successive changes liberalized the rule. Until 1973 the test had operated in two steps: First, a beneficiary who earned between $1680 and $2880 annually lost $1.00 in benefits for each $2.00 in earnings over $1680; second, a beneficiary earning over $2880 lost $1.00 in benefits for each $1.00 earned over $2880. Policy makers and many economists have believed that these provisions dissuaded beneficiaries from working. Such evidence as could be had—largely from Social Security Administration earnings records—supported that position. A sample of 1963 records found that slightly more than 60 percent of the 63- to 72-year-old workers kept their earnings at or below the exempt amount (Sander, 1968). In 1973, the 100 percent offset range of earnings was eliminated and a single test level established. Beneficiaries earning above the level now lose one benefit dollar for each two excess earnings dollars. In 1974, the year immediately before the fourth wave of RHS interviews, the test level was $2400 annually.

Motley (forthcoming) has examined the combined association of health and the earnings test level with the level of earnings in 1974 of married male beneficiaries in the RHS. This study group was between 63 and 68 years of age in that year. Of working married male beneficiaries, 68 percent were found to be earning approximately at or below the earnings test level. Among nonbeneficiaries, less than 7 percent had earnings that low. This apparently strong influence of the earnings test regulation is modified by the health status of respondents. For example, it was found that, among men who had since 1969 reported that they had health problems which limited the ability to work, 79 percent of the workers earned at or below that test level. Among working men who reported no such limitations, 17 percent fewer (62) reported their earnings in that category. With two other measures (self-assessed general health and hospitalization history) differences in the same direction, of approximately the same size, were found.

Analysis of RHS data is beginning to clarify the associations between social security policies and retirement behavior. It has also been used in a recent inquiry into the potential impact of another piece of national legislation, the Age Discrimination in Employment Act (ADEA). An amendment of ADEA in 1978 prohibited mandatory retirement, in most occupations, before the age of 70. Questions immediately arose as to the extent to which increased labor force participation of persons between ages 65 and 70 could be expected. Barker and Clark (1980), examining the interplay in RHS among several related influences, predicted a modest increase of around 4.5 percent among 65 year olds.

Mandatory retirement age does not have a simple, direct effect on retirement behavior. Forced exit from a job is not necessarily exit from the labor force. Occupations vary in the extent to which they permit labor market persistence by elderly retirees. They differ, also, in the extent to which workers are covered by pensions—a factor with a strong positive relation to mandatory retirement rules. About 84 percent of the working men in the RHS sample who were subject to mandatory retirement rules were also covered by pension plans. Health, potential earnings from continued work, and total available retirement income will all influence labor force participation after mandatory retirement.

Barker and Clark (1980) focused on sample members who were white males aged 62 and 63 years in 1969, and analyzed their work histories through 1973. All were then over 65, at that time the most prevalent compulsory retirement age. Of these, 40.8 percent were subject to mandatory retirement. Almost half retired before reaching that age, and about two-fifths retired at the mandatory age. About one-tenth reported that the relevant mandatory age was an older one not yet reached. Between 40 percent and 51 percent of working men subject to mandatory retirement age rules will probably retire at that age. Reports from other research indicate that about 40 percent of workers who retire at mandatory ages are both able and willing to remain at work. If this held true for the RHS sample, lifting the mandatory age would mean a 5 percent increase in numbers of workers at age 65. This assumes, however, that a mandatory retirement rule is the only difference between work where it occurs and work where it does not.

In order to allow for other factors that may be associated with both mandatory retirement rules and with withdrawal from the labor force, Barker and Clark (1980) estimated an empirical model of labor force participation, allowing variation in assets, income from assets, pension eligibility, pension wealth, social security wealth, health, and several other variables. An apparent positive relationship was found between compulsory retirement coverage and preretirement earnings, leading to a 5.7 percent increase in labor force participation at that point. Mandatory retirement at age 65 reduces the probability of participation by 16.7 percent. From these estimates, it can be expected that the 1978 ADEA amendments will lead to 4.5 percent higher labor force participation by 65-year-old men.

WOMEN AND RETIREMENT

Women's retirement patterns, as an object of social science research, have had relatively short shrift. However, growing labor force trends have stimulated serious questions, both theoretical and practical, in that area.

As men have been retiring from the country's labor force at increasingly earlier ages, some of the slack has apparently been taken up by growing proportions of women workers. Since 1947 when 28.1 percent of the labor force was female, the proportion increased, by 1979, to 41.9 percent (U.S. Bureau of the Census, 1979: 392). Most recent increases in number of women employed have been accounted for by greater participation of married women. Participation rates of women aged 55 to 65 years, where retirement begins to be a possibility, have been especially interesting. Among single women the rate has changed irregularly from 63.1 percent, in 1948, to as high a rate as 69.1 percent in 1979. The rate for currently married women, over the same period of time, moved fairly steadily up from 16.9 percent to 37.4 percent (U.S. Department of Labor, 1980: 278).

The increasing number of women at work implies their greater participation in private pension plans and in the old age insurance (retired worker) portion of the social security system. With the growing proportion of women working, various proposals have been made to eliminate or to radically restructure the payment of spouse benefits. Now, a retiring worker receives an add-on to his benefit, if his spouse is old enough (62) and has not earned enough under social security to entitle her to her own retired-worker's benefit. Generally, eligible dependent spouses are wives rather than husbands. The size of the spouse benefit depends upon the size of the retiring worker's benefit and upon the spouse's age (the benefit is actuarially reduced if the spouse begins receiving it between age 62 and 64). The recent proposal of changes in the system of social security benefits available to wives of workers has made it particularly desirable for policy makers to know more about influences on working women's retirement—particularly, working wives' retirement.

Research extant in the early 1970s was already reporting some of the determinants of women's relation to the labor force. Education, age, and previous work experience are repeatedly found to be associated with labor force participation (Sweet, 1973; Jaffe and Ridley, 1976). A probably reciprocal influence exists between married women's work patterns and the natural life cycle of the family. They are more likely to work before and after the primary childbearing ages than during those years (Kreps and Clark, 1976). Of their patterns of withdrawal from work, next to nothing is known. Currently, the RHS is probably the best available source of data for analyses of women's retirement patterns. Reports have already been published from two such projects.

Between 1969 and 1973 the nonmarried women sample members aged from 58 to 63 years and from 62 to 67 years, a period of transition to retirement for most working Americans. Henretta and O'Rand (1980b), examining data on those with meaningful periods of work, found their retirement during 1969-1973 affected by the same factors that influence men's retirement: poor health and coverage by a private pension. Women who reported health problems that limited ability to work were 14.4 percent more likely than others to have stopped work by 1971. Those covered by private pension plans were 13.4 percent likelier to have retired by 1971 than those without coverage. There appear to be no differences between black and white women.

The same investigators analyzed the retirement of working wives, that is, of the women who, not included in the sample themselves, were married to sample men and contributed a limited set of data on their own work, economic, and family characteristics. Since they were interviewed regardless of age, a number of them were younger than 58, making possible some comparison of influences upon younger and older working wives of retirement-age men. Henretta and O'Rand (1980a), examining only the workers among the wives, found distinct differences between the two categories. Age makes a difference. Each additional year of age past 58 years was found to reduce the probability that a wife would be found working in 1971 or later. For the younger wives, coverage by a private pension was not related to retirement. Their older counterparts were strongly influenced: Those covered in 1969 were 16.2 percent more likely than the noncovered to retire by 1971. Among the 1971 workers, coverage meant that they were 23.2 percent more likely to retire within two years. For those older wives, their husbands' health was a considerable influence. If the husband reported a work-limiting health condition in 1969, his wife was more likely than not to continue working.

Another family type consideration emerged as definitely important. Current support given a child or parent seemed to delay a wife's retirement. However, Clark and his colleagues (1980), analyzing data from the same RHS years on both husbands and wives, found this effect not quite so straightforward. There is some suggestion that when data on both spouses are considered, husbands are found more likely to be working, and wives less so, when there are dependents in the household. These researchers, however, were considering the work patterns of all married couples. Henretta and O'Rand (1980a) limited their focus to wives with noticeable work histories. Future analysis should probably look separately at the effects of dependents' presence on wives with different types of work histories.

Looking at all the couples in the study, the Clark et al. analysis investigated the effect on each partner's retirement of the other's work characteristics. Working spouses appear to contribute each to the other's likelihood of working. However, the likelihood of remaining at work in preference to retirement, while positively related to an individual's own wage, is negatively related to the spouse's level of earning. Wealth and asset income also reduce the likelihood of remaining at work.

In a separate report to the Social Security Administration Clark and Johnson (1980) discuss the long-term implications of their findings for the rate of early retirement among men. Long-term rises in women's wages, currently declining numbers of children per couple, improved household technology—all encourage young wives to enter and remain in the labor force. As older working wives they will be earning higher wages, be more likely to be eligible for private pensions, and be more likely to have their own records of social security contributions—factors which this analysis shows to be related to a husband's earlier retirement. If this process has been contributing to the already remarked nationwide decline in retirement age of men, that decline could be expected to slow as the movement of wives into the labor force stabilizes.

RHS data has been a source for more detailed study of the financial aspects of individual retirement than has hitherto been possible. Its timing over the decade of the 1970s make this a particularly valuable capability to social insurance policy makers. The mature social security program has proved a more expensive package than its inventors probably envisioned. Until the early 1970s, every amendment to the program was expansionary and liberalizing. In 1972 future benefit levels were tied to changes in the cost of living, so benefit levels would automatically keep up with inflation. Congress also created a number of special programs to aid the elderly in the 1960s and 1970s—Medicare, Meals-on-Wheels, and Foster Grandparents are a sampling of these. Some state and local governments legislated special tax breaks for the elderly, such as lower property taxes. Now, in the less opulent beginning of the 1980s, the priority of programs for the aged is being seriously questioned. Proposals are being made for changes in the social security law which would make it a measurably less generous source of income for the aged. It has been pointed out, for example, that the theoretical ratio of benefits after retirement to earnings before retirement (the replacement rate) is very high and that it is possible for retirees to receive from Social Security alone more than they earned while working.

COMPARISON OF PRERETIREMENT AND POSTRETIREMENT INCOMES

Until the longitudinal data from RHS was available, no empirical analyses of replacement rates could be made. It has provided material for several examinations of the financial positions of retirees compared with their own situations while still working. The panel design of the study has proved especially valuable in these analyses. It has been possible to compare postretirement with preretirement incomes, to examine retirement-related changes in assets, to compare pre- and postretirement expenditure patterns, and to measure the impact of the 1974 recession on private pensions and social security benefits.

The replacement rate has received special attention recently. By comparing the incomes individuals have after retiring with earnings they had before retiring, it focuses directly on the effect of retirement upon individual income. Most attempts to measure replacement rates have used aggregated data and theoretical extrapolations. Some of these have suggested that the typical retiree would have nearly as much income in retirement as he or she had while working. Using social security record data to estimate the three highest of the last ten years of earnings, and its information on social security benefits received by retirees, Fox (1979) constructed actual replacement rates for married couples. He found that in 1973-1974 social security benefits replaced a median of 45 percent of a couple's preretirement earnings; 3 percent of the couples had replacement of 80 percent or higher. Adding the private pension income reported by respondents in their interviews increased the median replacement rate to 55 percent.

These replacement rates are lower than replacement rates found when aggregated date is used. Fox (1979) explains these differences as a result of incorrect assumptions frequently made in the literature of retirement income. It has often been assumed in the calculation of replacement rates that most workers retire at age 65 (which would entitle them to full, rather than reduced, social security benefits), and that wives, also age 65, qualify for dependents' benefits (that is, 50 percent of their husbands' retirement benefits). In fact, most workers were found to have started collecting retirement benefits before age 65, wives tended to be two years or so younger than their husbands, and many wives were found to have recent earnings. All these characteristics of retiring couples depress replacement rates from the levels they would have reached if the hypothetical conditions were typical.

Few retirees have assets that would noticeably supplement their lowered incomes. It had been expected, in some quarters, that social security benefits would be only a part of Americans' retirement income, and that they would be supplemented by both private pensions and income from assets. Friedman and Sjogren's (1981) recent analysis of 1969-1975 RHS data makes it clear that private savings do not serve that purpose. They found that in 1969 the median value of assets held, including home equity, was $17,350 for married men, $6,000 for nonmarried men, $4,500 for nonmarried women. The frailty of such amounts as sources of potential income is self-evident. Friedman and Sjogren found no association between amount of assets held and tendency to retire. Nor did they find consistent evidence of asset dissolution. In short, few retirees were found to have assets sufficiently large to supplement retirement benefits. And, at this early stage in retirement, few appeared to be dispersing them.

The question of adequacy of retirement income is an important one for policy discussions of the future of social security and private pension programs. If current levels of retirement income allow retirees to live better in retirement than they did while working, that would suggest that retirement benefits and pensions could be lowered. On the other hand, if retirees are having to cut back, that would give pause to advocates of social security retirement.

Knowing replacement rates and typical asset holdings of retirees gives clues to adequacy of retirement income, but it is necessary to look at what retirees are able to do with their incomes. One investigation of food expenditures before and after retirement found that retirees spent about the same amount for food after retirement as they had before retirement. Prices of food had increased by about 30 percent over the period studied, the same increase in money spent on food by sample members whether retired or not (Murray, 1978).

A recurring problem for social insurance policy makers is that of preserving, in the face of inflation, the real value of retirement benefits. A now debated solution was arrived at in 1972, when legislation was passed tying future benefit levels to changes in the cost of living. The picture of private pension benefits is still a mixed one. Some plans were amended in the early 1970s to allow some adjustment for inflation. Thompson's (1978) analysis of RHS data is the first analysis of private pension and social security benefit levels in a time of inflation. Her analysis focused on data for completely retired persons receiving private pension income in both 1972 and 1974, and on trend data for 1970, 1972, and 1974 for all completely retired recipients. She found that while benefits from private pensions did increase slightly in the first half of the 1970s, their purchasing power deteriorated markedly because of the rate of inflation. At the same time, social security benefits rose more than the cost of living. Thus, for most retirees, total retirement benefits came close to maintaining their purchasing power.

It has been impossible, within the scope of this chapter, to refer to all findings from the RHS. What have been reported here are completed analyses most closely related to questions of social insurance policy. Significant work with other foci is being carried on, primarily by academic analysts. And more work remains for social security researchers—the 1979 wave of data not yet (March 1981) available for analysis. Analyses thus far completed have been valuable contributions to the national discussion of retirement policy. They have served as accurate testimony to the nature of retirement patterns under current policy changes. They have refined and extended already available knowledge about retirement, set right some "commonsense" lore on the subject, and, a few times, brought new facts to light.

CONSIDERATIONS FOR FUTURE RESEARCH

The project itself has served as one of two large national applications of longitudinal methodology in policy research. To date neither the National Longitudinal Studies of Labor Market Experience nor the RHS has been systematically evaluated. Even without such evaluation, however, it is possible to list some considerations which should be included in the planning of future retirement research:

(1) Narrower, more focused questions should be studied. Large surveys, including RHS, have produced broad findings about relations among categories of events and characteristics. It seems timely now, rather than continuing that tradition, which is actually one of hypothesis generation, to pursue the hypotheses. For example, the two analyses that have been done using data on working couples in RHS show clearly that spouses work/retirement patterns interact with each other. More intensive research examining how, why, and the patterns in which that interaction takes place would be a valuable contribution to both social gerontology and retirement policy knowledge.

(2) For the sake of rational, economic choices of research techniques in the future, longitudinal methods need careful evaluation. In particular, two technical matters should be studied in detail:

  (a) What kinds of questions, in what areas, can profitably be asked retrospectively rather than longitudinally? For example, given an older person's relatively high interest in health, is it possible that he or she would give as accurate an account from memory of the five-year development of a disability as that which an interviewer would get in three interviews over the five-year period?

  (b) When a longitudinal study is done, what considerations should affect the decision on interview frequency? When RHS was designed, a two-year interval was selected because of planners' need for as frequent, accurate reports as possible on changes in income from all sources. Annual interviews were precluded by their cost, and, indeed, it was not felt that they would be otherwise justified since changes in other areas under study would not be so hard to report accurately.

(3) Any retirement study, particularly in the near future, must be done with an alert eye on cohort effects. The RHS sample comprised persons born between 1905 and 1911—one of the first cohorts of a postagricultural economy and the first to have spent most of their working lives under the guaranty of social security retirement benefits. How far this has influenced the retirement process for them is not known. National concern with both manpower and the welfare of the aged ensures that future retirees will be affected by different legislation. As yet unmeasured, there are probably already some effects of the changed level of permissible mandatory retirement. Volatile national economics, in conjunction with policy changes, make it certain that older workers will have to cope with different socioeconomic conditions from those influencing the RHS sample. Provision in future retirement studies for comparability with both RHS and the National Longitudinal Studies will be a means for some control of cohort effects.

REFERENCES

BARFIELD, R. and J. MORGAN (1969) Early Retirement, the Decision and the Experience. Ann Arbor: University of Michigan.

BARKER, D. J. and R. L. CLARK (1980) "Mandatory retirement and labor-force participation of respondents in the Retirement History Study." Social Security Bulletin 43 (November): 20-29.

BIXBY, L. E. (1976) "Retirement patterns in the United States: research and policy interaction." Social Security Bulletin 39 (August): 3-19.

CAMPBELL, C. D. and R. G. CAMPBELL (1976) "Conflicting views on the effect of old-age and survivors' insurance on retirement." Economic Inquiry 14 (September): 369-388.

CLARK, R. L. and T. JOHNSON (1980) "Retirement in the dual career family." Final report, Social Security Administration Grant 10-P-90543-4-02 .

——— and A. A. McDERMED (1980) "Allocation of time and resources by married couples approaching retirement." Social Security Bulletin 43 (April): 3-15.

FOX, A. (1979) "Earnings replacement rates of retired couples: findings from the Retirement History Study." Social Security Bulletin 42 (January): 2-24.

FRIEDMAN, J. and J. SJOGREN (1981) "Assets of the elderly as they retire." Social Security Bulletin 44 (January): 16-31.

HENRETTA, J. C. and A. M. O'RAND (1980a) "Labor force participation of older married women." Social Security Bulletin 43 (August): 10-16.

——— (1980b) "Family economic status and the labor force participation of older women." Final report, Social Security Administration Grant 10-P-97004-4-02.

IRELAN, L. and K. BOND (1974) "Retirees of the 1970's," pp. 42-63 in C. C. Osterbind (ed.) Migration, Mobility and Aging. Gainesville: University Presses of Florida.

IRELAN, L., D. K. MOTLEY, K. SCHWAB, S. R. SHERMAN, J. H. MURRAY, and
   K. BOND (1976) Almost 65: Baseline Data from the Retirement History Study.
   HEW Publication No. (SSA) 76-11806. Washington, DC: Government Printing
   Office.
JAFFE, A. J. and J. C. RIDLEY (1976) "The extent of lifetime employment of
   women in the U.S." Industrial Gerontology 3 (Winter): 25-35.
KREPS, J. and R. CLARK (1976) Sex, Age and Work: The Changing Composition of
   the Labor Force. Baltimore: Johns Hopkins University Press.
MOTLEY, D. K. (forthcoming) "Health and the earnings of social security benefi-
   ciaries." Social Security Bulletin.
MURRAY, J. H. (1978) "Changes in food expenditures, 1969-73: findings from the
   Retirement History Study." Social Security Bulletin 41 (July): 3-11.
QUINN, J. F. (1977) "The early retirement decision: evidence from the 1969
   Retirement History Study. U.S. Department of Health, Education, and Welfare,
   Social Security Administration, Office of Research and Statistics, Staff Paper No.
   29.
SANDER, K. G. (1968) "The retirement test: its effect on older workers' earnings."
   Social Security Bulletin 31 (June): 3-6.
SCHWAB, K. A. (forthcoming) "Longitudinal analysis of factors in early retirement."
   Social Security Bulletin.
STREIB, G. F. and C. J. SCHNEIDER (1971) Retirement in American Society:
   Impact and Process. Ithaca, NY: Cornell University Press.
SWEET, J. A. (1973) Women in the Labor Force. New York: Seminar.
THOMPSON, G. B. (1978) "Impact of inflation on private pensions of retirees,
   1970-74: findings from the Retirement History Study." Social Security Bulletin
   41 (November): 1-10.
U.S. Bureau of the Census (1979) Statistical Abstract of the United States. Washing-
   ton, DC: Government Printing Office.
——— (1975) Historical Statistics of the United States. Washington, DC: Government
   Printing Office.
——— (1963) The Current Population Survey—A Report on Methodology. Technical
   Paper No. 7. Washington, DC: Government Printing Office.
U.S. Department of Labor (1980) Employment and Training Report of the President.
   Washington, DC: Government Printing Office.

2

CAREERS FOR OLDER AMERICANS

Neil G. McCluskey

For the next 20 years and more, the American population will continue to *gray*. At one end of the scale, older people are living longer and, at the other, the declining birthrate is reducing the number of young people. The impact of this changing demographic scene is discussed from different points of view throughout this volume, but this chapter will present some of the responses to the pressures this social change is placing upon traditional career patterns. New career concepts are being developed and new approaches are being tested to make it possible for older men and women to remain in or to reenter the economy, thereby contributing in important ways to the productive life of society as well as permitting this growing segment of the population to continue growth as persons. It is heartening, moreover, to learn that some organizations, corporations, and institutions are beginning to put these ideas into practice. Some examples will be described.

For generations American society has striven successfully to eliminate health hazards, improve health care and diet, and broaden educational opportunity. The result has been the evolution of perhaps the largest, healthiest, best educated, and longest-lived population recorded in history. However, the supreme irony is that, just at the point when we should be capitalizing on the valuable asset represented by this group in the population, society continues to follow public and private policies designed to shunt it aside. A chronological guillotine is sprung to separate senior men and women from the work force just when many of them are in their prime. Little thought is given to continuing them in useful capacities, either in their original jobs or in some related area of employment, as paid, self-employed, or volunteer workers. The fact that such great attention is given to the occasional public figure in government, business, or labor, who, at 70 or 80, is still fully active in a leadership role or has launched another successful career, underscores how exceptional these people are to the general rule. For there are millions of trained and experienced older men and women who form a vast untapped pool of workers—paid, self-employed, or volunteer. They are truly victims of agism. For differing reasons, few of which are any longer valid, many of these talented people past 65 succumb to the expectation that they withdraw from life. Layoff or involuntary retirement, or simply the absence of invitations, bring a halt to their productive lives with devastating effects upon their personal lives.

NATIONAL COMMITTEE ON
CAREERS FOR OLDER AMERICANS

Foremost among the new initiatives to influence national policy by increasing the productive value of older people in the economy is the National Committee on Careers for Older Americans. Formed in 1978 under the leadership of Merrell M. Clark, Executive Vice President of the Academy for Educational Development, and Arthur S. Flemming, former Secretary of the Department of Health, Education, and Welfare and former Commissioner of the U.S. Administration on Aging, this distinguished group of concerned citizens took as its first order of business the preparation of a report. The document, *Older Americans: An Untapped Resource,*[1] is a compendium explaining why this resource must be tapped as well as a thoughtful detailing of how this can be done. The report has brought together the pertinent facts that govern the issue and has developed specific recommendations for action. To implement the report on a local level, the National Committee on Careers for Older Americans has established organizing committees across the country. The local groups of 12-17 members typically have representation from the chamber of commerce, the Labor Council, local universities with aging expertise, the Urban League, the United Way, the Junior League, human resource departments of several corporate employers, Senior Corps of Retired Executives (SCORE), the area Agency on Aging, and a senior employment agency. The organizing committees review the national study design and adapt it to best suit the distinctive needs of the local community. They then invite individuals to serve on the area steering committee who are able to provide different points of view and experienced leadership in undertaking action programs. By the close of 1980, organizing committees were functioning in San Diego, Los Angeles, San Francisco, the San Francisco Bay Peninsula, Portland, Seattle, Flint, Detroit, Cleveland, Boston, New York, and Philadelphia. Other areas are gradually being added to the list.

The report, initially supported by funds from the Edna McConnell Clark Foundation, is the blueprint behind the movement. It examines the factors behind our failure to make positive use of "the resource represented by older people from all walks of life—both those who have occupied positions of leadership and those who have not." Through it the committee calls for a reversal of attitudes and practices relative to providing paid, self-employed, and volunteer work opportunities for America's elderly. It asks for the continued or increased involvement of the elderly in both the social and economic life of the community. It lays down specifics for removing or reducing impediments to this involvement. The report is also sensitive to the issue of competition for employment between older people and those of other age groups.

QUESTIONS TO BE ANSWERED

There are forces at work which, it can be hoped, will reverse what up until now has been a trend toward early retirement, and will place new emphasis on keeping people in the work force, or, in many cases, giving them reentry to it. The NCCOA report offers questions to employers, and, in some cases, labor unions, that they will need to answer as they adapt personnel policies to match the set of contemporary facts of life newly emerging:

(1) What ways can be devised to continue using the skills and experience of older workers to best advantage?

(2) How and at what points can more individualized judgments be made on a basis other than age as to who shall continue to be considered for promotion, training, and development?

(3) What arrangements can be made to avoid discouraging the employment and advancement of younger workers as older workers stay at work longer and remain fully eligible for promotions, training, and development?

(4) How will fringe benefit packages be modified to reflect the greater longevity of older people, the longer spans of work age that such greater longevity will permit, and the income and insurance needs of people living and working longer?

Because the ravages of inflation will force many who have retired to reenter the work force, additional questions are posed by the report that will have to be answered:

(1) By what means can the private and public sectors provide adequate full-time and part-time paid jobs for increasing numbers of men and women 55 years of age and older?

(2) In what ways will employer policies and union agreements have to be modified to provide additional flexibility and work options for older workers?

(3) Can additional employment of older workers be accomplished without arresting or at least slowing current tendencies in industry and government toward job reduction through use of labor-saving technologies and processes?

(4) How can fringe benefits be structured usefully and cost effectively to meet the needs of older people who work part-time?

(5) What steps can be taken to encourage older persons to develop skills that could be helpful in enabling them to earn income in self-employed capacities?

DESIRE TO WORK AND COMPETITION

For anyone who may doubt that older people are interested in some kind of role in the work force, and, indeed, are doing something about it, the report cites the findings of the Harris Surveys of 1974 and 1979. The first Harris Study (1974) found out that of 21 million Americans aged 65 and over at that time:

• 9 million were 75 years and older;

• 2.8 million of those 65 years and older (including 1 million who were 70 years and older) were working;

• 4 million people 65 years and older (3 out of 10 in this age group) who were not working said they wanted to work;

• 4.5 million people 65 years and older were working as volunteers; and

• another 2.1 people 65 years and older who were not working said they were interested in volunteer service.

Moreover, the 1979 Harris Study found:

• 88 percent of current employees and 67 percent of the business executives surveyed felt that nobody should be forced to retire because of age;

- 51 percent of the employees surveyed wanted to continue working in some capacity rather than retire;

- 48 percent in the age group 50-64 wished to continue working after age 65;

- 46 percent of those already retired would have preferred to be working; and

- 53 percent of those retired wish they had never quit.

The NCCOA report (p. 10) draws the following conclusion:

The answer to whether older people would really respond to work opportunities depends on whether meaningful work options are absent or very limited for older people. If they are denied meaningful roles and fair treatment on training, development, and promotion, they will likely view the whole subject with disinterest or frustration. If on the other hand, productive roles—paid, self-employed, or volunteer—are available to them, the whole picture will change.

Realistically, the opportunities for further careers for older people in full-time employment must be balanced against the present job needs of youth and the 25-54 age group. However, as the report points out, there are full-time positions, such as in training and in the work of community service organizations, that require the kind of unique contributions that only experienced older people can make. Moreover, the demographic tide has been inexorably receding so that, barring the intervention of some new factor, the youth-elder competition for paid employment may quietly disappear. Why is this predictable?

Between 1970 and 1976, the 65-plus population increased by 3 million, or 14.8 percent, while during the same years the number of children under 14 dropped by 5.5 million, or -0.3 percent. Between 1960 and 1977, the under-20 population fell from 40 percent to 35 percent of the total, and the number of high-school-age youngsters began to decline. In 1977, the total of 15-19 year olds was 21.2 million, but it is projected to diminish each year until 1992, when it will bottom out at 16 million. The impact of these shifts upon the size of the next age cohort, the 20-24-year-old group, is strikingly revealed in the following figures, developed from U.S. Census Bureau data.

Numbers in Ages 20-24	*Birth Years*
In 1970—17.1 million	1946-1950
In 1977—20.1 million	1953-1957

In 1985—20.5 million   1961-1965
In 1990—17.9 million   1966-1970
In 2000—16.9 million   1976-1980

In 1985 the 20-24 age population will have peaked, reflecting the high birthrates of the 1950s and early 1960s, but then the decline will begin, reflecting the sharp drop in the birthrate that started late in the 1960s.

PART-TIME, SELF-EMPLOYMENT, AND VOLUNTEER OPPORTUNITIES

For many older workers, part-time work seems to be a promising source of employment. Actually, many older men and women prefer to work according to a less demanding and more flexible schedule. Since many have other sources of income, the reduced salary level would not cause for them the same economic hardships as for younger workers. In any event, more and more older workers are discovering new careers through paid part-time work. In 1967, 3.49 million persons 55 years of age and above worked in part-time jobs. In 1977, this figure had risen to 4.25 million. One could argue that more people are in part-time employment because they cannot find full-time positions, but it is the age 65-and-over group which shows the greatest increase in part-time work experience during the years measured. The wider the door of opportunity, the more our elder citizens can move through it; part-time employment is a natural way of deploying this much underutilized resource. The report urges the need to build bridges between these opportunities and the 4 million people over 65 who would like to begin new careers by working and being paid for it, and quotes Louis Harris saying that, once the bridges are built, retirees "will fly across, not just walk."

As has been noted, today's collectivity of older Americans possess a range of skills and talents unheralded in history. Additionally, through hobbies and other leisure interests, more older Americans than ever before have developed skills beyond those used during their work careers. Moreover, older people have enrolled in educational or other training institutions at record-breaking levels. Some have in mind to prepare for new or higher paying jobs, while others are pursuing knowledge and skills without specific job objectives in mind. Still others are simply using their free time to satisfy old interests or to pursue new ones for personal pleasure. In any event, as a result of these efforts a reservoir of skills that is a considerable national asset has been expanding year by year.

That there is a market for these products and services seems clear from the remarkable increase in the number of people during the last decade who are earning money through the sales of their arts and crafts. Many others, working from home or office bases, are offering services on a fee basis, from accounting to tutoring to report writing. Those who work in this way as self-employed avoid the risks inherent in starting a small business because they can begin with relatively modest investments in tools, materials, equipment, space, and staff help. For those of traditional retirement age there is the further advantage of preserving flexibility of hours and of keeping long-term obligations, such as loans and leases, to a bare minimum or avoiding them altogether.

The National Committee on Careers for Older Americans, through its local committees, attempts to augment cooperatively the work of local chambers of commerce, trade associations, training institutions, and other local groups in identifying business and public service needs in the community that are not effectively being met but that could be provided by self-employed older persons. NCCOA urges counseling and training programs through which older persons and others desiring self-employment could be assisted in learning the skills required to enter these areas.

Many older people are in the fortunate situation of having achieved basic economic security. They can live adequately on the income available to them from social security, private or public pensions, investments, and other sources. Actually, they do not feel the need for full-time or part-time paid employment. However, they do feel the need to participate on a regular basis as volunteers in activities whose goals they share, thereby making meaningful contributions to the social, political, or economic life of the community. According to the Harris survey (1974), there are 4.5 million or more of them over age 65 currently working as volunteers, to say nothing of an additional 2 million older people who have expressed the desire to start new careers as volunteers but have not yet been plugged in.

HOW DO WE GO ABOUT IT?

The committee document lists six steps that need to be taken in order for the resources offered by older people to be tapped effectively. These are:

(1) Counseling, training, and placement services must be provided.
(2) Employers need to reexamine personnel policies and practices relating to further careers for older people.
(3) Community, trade, education, and other organizations need to encourage persons interested in self-employment.
(4) Organizations that recruit volunteers need to reexamine their policies and practices.
(5) Major attention needs to be given to the transportation problems of older people.

(6) There needs to be a better understanding of the Social Security Retirement Test.

Let us examine this list point by point.

Provide Counseling. It is a fact that millions of older workers *desire* careers as paid, self-employed, or volunteer workers, but, alas, many do not *know* what has to be done to realize their desires. So far, society has been slow to extend them a helping hand. The preparation for first careers in our society is elaborate, sophisticated, and heavily subsidized. We must be prepared to make significant investments in parallel preparation for older people desirous of new careers.

The need for ready access to community centers, where information on job possibilities as paid or volunteer workers and on the ways of qualifying for such positions may be made available, is obvious. Counseling and supplementary training should be a standard part of the process. Who should be responsible for these steps? The report calls this responsibility one that must be shared by both public and private employment agencies, and calls for a reversal of the "all too prevalent attitude of ignoring or assigning a very low priority to the needs of older people for such services."

Reexamine Personnel Policies and Practices. In general, current personnel policies and practices militate against the utilization of older people in the work force. With a view toward helping public and private administrators to strengthen their organizations by tapping this pool, the committee asks them to review the following items:

(1) flexibility in hours of work, part-time versus full-time opportunities, job structures, skill and performance requirements;
(2) salary and bonuses, physical working arrangements, including atmosphere, access to job locations and security condition;
(3) counseling regarding job requirements, career paths, training opportunities, development, and promotion;
(4) fringe benefits, particularly in the area of disability insurance (most important to part-time workers and those not covered by social security disability benefits), group insurance coverage for nonreimbursable health care needs, and long-term help for catastrophic illnesses;
(5) linkages with employment services and educational institutions so as to
    (a) facilitate a better understanding of older employee needs;
    (b) create opportunities for orientation visits, career and job counseling and placement, trial internships, and training; and

(c) refine training resources and activities to meet the knowledge and skill requirements for broader job opportunities.

Encourage Self-Employment. Public and private community organizations and local chambers of commerce can assist older persons interested in self-employment by surveying areas of unmet service, needed products, or other requirements of business, government agencies, private service organizations, cultural groups, and the public. Trade and industry associations, educational institutions, and other organizations are urged to find the resources to furnish counseling and training for older people seeking to qualify and function on a self-employed basis.

Reexamine Volunteer Policies and Practices. School and community service organizations are highly vulnerable to inflation and budget cutbacks even as demands for their services soar. Some alleviation of this problem is offered by the voluntary sector. However, existing policies and practices do not seem designed to make the best use of older people now working as volunteers, to say nothing of another two million older people who are interested in going into volunteer work. The report calls for a special review of policies affecting these particulars:

(1) opportunities for growth and development by volunteers on the job and through participation in training programs
(2) full integration of volunteer help into their regular operations
(3) provision of adequate full-time staff for support of volunteer activities
(4) recognition, on a systematic and well-publicized basis, of the dollar value represented by volunteer services
(5) provision for payment of "out of pocket" expenses
(6) physical working arrangements and atmosphere, transportation accessibility, and security conditions
(7) liability insurance coverage
(8) linkages with placement services, educational institutions, and other organizations to assure that needs for volunteer services of older people and job requirements are well understood and met

Attend to Transportation Problems of Older People. The lack of adequate transportation to ease the search for work or to commute to a job is a problem for every worker but a special problem for many older men and women. Inflation generally and the price of gasoline in particular have made driving a car more and more expensive. For this reason, some elderly are forced to abandon the use of a private car. For reasons of frailty others are compelled to seek alternate means of transportation. Older people are among the heaviest users of mass transit, but often available service does not correspond to job location. Elderly job seekers who reside in central metropolitan areas increasingly find that the available jobs are in outlying areas. Older men and women residing in suburbs find that they are forced to travel long distances with interruptions, transfers, and delays if they are going to try to find or hold paid, self-employed, or volunteer jobs.

Public transit services in most communities have been unable to keep up with dispersed living and working patterns. In fact, rising operating costs have curtailed service in many cities and towns. The words of the committee report, in summing up the situation, barely hint at the anguish it brings to so many lives: "Therefore, longer distances to and from bus stops and transit stations must be negotiated. Many areas do not have service. Even where service exists it is often unreliable or slow. For these reasons, many older people are literally marooned, or they cannot find day-to-day dependable service." The travel to work needs of our elderly are but one aspect of the mismatch between transportation requirements and resources available in most of our urban communities.

Understand the Social Security Retirement Test. The Social Security Retirement Test determines the amount of money that may be earned by social security retirees without losing all or a portion of their retirement benefits. Specifically, for every two dollars a retiree earns over an amount determined by law (in 1981, $5500), he or she forfeits one dollar in retirement benefits. The so-called unearned income from stocks, bonds, savings, private pensions, and annuities is not counted in determining the amount of social security benefits that must be forfeited.

More and more older people look upon the Social Security Retirement Test as a disincentive to returning to paid employment, for it is effectively a 50 percent tax on wage earnings. As the report points out, the reasons for the test, the arguments for and against it, and the continuing trend toward its liberalization are not widely understood. Accordingly, the report offers a brief summary to assist in understanding the Social Security Retirement Test. Since a more detailed discussion and analysis of the issues surrounding social security may be found in several chapters of the present volume, we shall add nothing more here.

HOW IT CAN BE DONE

Perhaps the most practical section of the National Committee on Careers for Older Americans report is Chapter 7, "Moving Forward: Action Programs and Ideas for Utilizing Services of Older People," which we will here synopsize and highlight. The chapter aims (1) to identify some of the organizations that have had encouraging results in their efforts to tap the skills of the nation's reservoir of older people; (2) to identify some of the programs, particularly in the area of community service, wherein older people have a special capability for service; and (3) to discuss bridge building between older people and those in need of their services.

INVOLVEMENT OF ORGANIZATIONS

Especially in recent years, national organizations, both public and private, have initiated projects aimed at demonstrating that older men and women have both the desire and the capacity for involvement "in new or further careers of productive value in the economic and social life of the nation."

The report cites exemplary programs under the sponsorship of such national organizations in the private sector as the American Association of Retired Persons/National Retired Teachers Association, the National Association of Retired Federal Employees, the National Association for the Spanish Speaking Elderly, the National Center on the Black Aged, Inc., the National Council of Senior Citizens, the National Farmers Union, and the National Indian Council on Aging. With some assistance from the Department of Labor, operating under the Older Americans Act, programs under the sponsorship of these organizations have made use of the skills and experiences of older men and women as paid workers or volunteers in projects involving a wide variety of community services.

The International Executive Service Corps, in collaboration with the U.S. Agency for International Development and private groups, has long been recruiting retired or soon-to-be-retired business executives to assist in the solution of financial, procurement, and management problems in developing countries. A parallel arrangement has been made through the National Executive Service Corps to bring the services of retired business executives to help strengthen operations and management of domestic nonprofit institutions.

Among the federal agencies, ACTION has supported paid and volunteer programs such as the Retired Senior Volunteer Program (RSVP), Foster Grandparents, and Senior Companions—programs designed to help young and old in school, home, and community services. The Senior Corps of Retired Executives (SCORE) has been funded by the Small Business Administration to match retired executive talent with the operating problems of small businesses. The U.S. Forest Service has a program that employs older people in conservation projects. In collaboration with the network of State and Area Agencies on Aging, the U.S. Administration on Aging has underwritten projects to help place older people as paid workers and volunteers. It must be noted here, however, that the future of some of these programs has become highly questionable because of changing priorities in the national budget. Nonetheless, even their brief history has established the validity of these programs, and it can be predicted that in one or other modified form most of them will continue.

Important initiatives have also come from the private sector. In 1978, the Committee for Economic Development published a report identifying specific techniques in successful use among private businesses for meeting the employment needs of the hard-to-employ, including older workers. The committee likewise recommended ideas that seemed promising for wider application (Committee for Economic Development, 1978). That same year saw a significant publication by the Conference Board (1978) which drew attention to corporate retirement practices as well as to the retirement activities of middle to top managers formerly employed by large corporations.

Other initiatives to test or promote ideas for increasing work options for older workers have been developed in different localities. In the remainder of Chapter 7 of the NCCOA report, some of these programs are discussed and areas of still unmet needs are identified. A basic premise of this part of the report is that society is paying a steadily increasing price for our inadequate efforts to cope effectively with crime, delinquency, alcoholism, drug abuse, discrimination, unemployment and underemployment, substandard housing, inadequate transportation, alienation, and isolation. The committee report makes an often overlooked point, that "our public budget and bookkeeping systems rarely are able to relate specific dollar investments in staff and services which have to be included in current budgets to the tangible and intangible longer term savings that accrue from the prevention, resolution, or mitigation of these problems." The report continues:

> Our failure to deal adequately with these problems has lowered the quality of life, blighted the prospects of many young people and turned old age in some communities into a nightmare of economic insecurity, fear and isolation. It also has led to losses in productivity and low quality work in the economy, both of which have added to business costs and charges to consumers. Inadequate remedial efforts have led to tolerated neglects which have culminated in greater dependency for growing numbers of people, and consequently, to larger welfare rolls and higher tax burdens [p. 30].

The obvious answer lies in strengthening community services. This remains true despite the occasional failure of such programs in the past. Year follows year, the needs are still not being met, and the financial drain on society steadily increases. The challenge is to come up with better ways for improving the delivery of services so that community needs can be better met. Older people could here play a central role. Who understand better than they what these community services mean in ensuring quality of life in a neighborhood? Who suffers more when these services are neglected or shabbily managed? The committee suggests that, once such people have received training, they can become involved as paid workers or volunteers.

The chapter closes with a sample listing of the kinds of services older people can provide the community (see Figure 2.1). In schools they could be trained to give remedial help to children with reading or learning disorders, such as dyslexia. They could serve as tutors in the area of functional illiteracy—a national shame most of us prefer to believe could not possibly exist in contemporary America. It is still hard for us to comprehend that at least 23 million Americans are classed as functional illiterates. Many of these people, who are unable to read or perform simple arithmetic, are less than 40 years of age. Very often they are of average or above-average intelligence and are still educable. The system currently cannot take care of them, so they remain a burden to themselves and to society, or, at best, make a minimal contribution.

During the past decade the Edna McConnell Clark Foundation took the lead in helping to test ways of using older men and women as volunteers to assist school teachers and administrators by easing their teaching, counseling, supervising, and administrative burdens. Foundation funds were used to employ coordinators to assist in recruiting and scheduling thousands of older volunteers for work in the schools. The foundation likewise supported efforts of colleges and universities, especially community colleges, to enlarge the pool of trained older volunteers for tutoring hard-to-employ people and to expand community literacy programs.

Many of our urban areas are facing the mounting problem of a permanent subclass of unemployable youth. Many of these youngsters belong to families in which unemployment has been the rule for two or more generations. They are bereft of skills and, to compound their unemployability, are complete strangers to work discipline and standards of work quality. The experience and care qualities of older persons make them uniquely capable of helping young people in this category.

In a number of communities there are programs using older volunteers to follow up on the conditions of discharged hospital patients. The deinstitutionalization of mental health patients has created new burdens on the existing community outpatient resources of many communities. Discharged patients often now are no longer subject to systematic care and institutional observation. The situation damages not just the people involved, but it weakens the effectiveness of existing outpatient facilities and resources, jeopardizes the operation of other service programs, and destroys public confidence in this kind of mental health treatment. In

TRANSPORTATION
- station information aides
- bus drivers
- van drivers
- pool arrangers
- improved route sign advisors
- service assistance locators

CULTURAL ACTIVITIES
- performers and artists
- programmers
- trainers
- sales and promotion workers
- facilities maintenance workers
- fund raising counselors and assistants
- audience development specialists
- arts conservators and technicians
- resource and information assistants

EMPLOYMENT
- job finders
- trainers
- job developers
- career and job counselors

NON-PROFIT ACTIVITIES
- fund raising/membership counselors
- bookkeepers and accountants
- government regulations and compliance counselors
- coordinators of volunteers
- incorporation advisors

ENVIRONMENT
- counselors on pesticides and safety
- extended sanitation and special clean-up workers
- monitors
- materials recycling aides
- environmental impact analysts

EMPLOYEE RELATIONS
- mediation, arbitration, and counciliation specialists (both employee/management and employee/employee relations)

NEIGHBORHOOD
- guards and monitors
- clean-up aides
- repair workers for substandard housing
- energy conservation advisors and workers
- mediators, conciliators, and arbitrators
- fire and safety inspectors
- pest control workers
- translators and communicators

HEALTH
- hospital technicians and aides
- home health care providers and aides
- rehabilitation technicians and aides
- medical equipment operators

EDUCATION
- discipline aides
- tutors and resource specialists
- class administration aides
- library workers
- career and other counselors
- special populatic education programmers and advisors
- fund raisers
- special skill enrichment advisors and aides
- financial aid advisors

SPECIAL SERVICES TO DEPENDENT PERSONS
- companions
- nutrition advisors
- form fillers
- eligibility & assistance advisors
- readers & communicators
- recreation advisors and workers
- meal providers and/or feeding helpers
- day care providers
- home health care aides
- rehabilitation technicians & helpers
- representative payees & guardians
- homemakers
- shopping assistance helpers

MANAGERIAL ROLES
For all of the activity areas on this chart —
- project managers and sub-unit directors
- legal, financial, and planning advisors

Figure 2.1 Job Options for Older People in Meeting Community Needs

SOURCE: Reprinted with permission from: **Older Americans: An Untapped Resource**, the National Committee on Careers for Older Americans, copyright 1979 by the Academy for Educational Development.

paid, self-employed, or volunteer roles, older people can help in program management, provide direct services to patients, or work with professionals in rendering these services.

The report also lists other areas of potential service by elders to the community: community mediation and conciliation services, paralegal services, homemaker-home health aid service, home repair services, and the roles of surrogate parents and service facilitators.

OPPORTUNITIES IN SMALL BUSINESS

In an age dominated by corporate giants, small business tends to be overlooked. There are, the report points out, approximately 10.7 million non-farm small businesses in the United States, constituting 98 percent of the nation's commercial establishment. Between 1969 and 1976, small businesses created some 6 million of the 9 million new jobs established during those years. Small businesses make extensive use of part-time and seasonal help. There are many experienced older men and women who possess the skills to help organize new small businesses or strengthen those in operation. Some older people who may not care for the entrepreneur or management sides of business could still serve as consultants here. They could supply advice and practical assistance in such matters as development, product design, production requirements and flow, market analysis, procurement, merchandising, inventory control, sales promotion, advertising, accounting, cash flow management, financial control, and tax and legal matters. It is even conceivable that profit or nonprofit organizations staffed by older people could be developed to provide these services on a minimum- or no-charge basis. The key to much of the above lies in effective counseling and training programs, but this should not present any insurmountable problem. Already every year society is making a major financial investment in a national network of public employment offices financed by the federal government and operated by the individual states. These offices have not yet well served older workers, and probably will not until private and public employers communicate to them their own interest and commitment to full use of the untapped resource of the older worker.

ROLE OF EDUCATIONAL AND CULTURAL INSTITUTIONS

Agism, according to the National Committee on Careers for Older Americans, has played an insidious role in many educational and other cultural institutions. Too often, says their report, if any attention has been paid to opportunities for serving older people, it has been an afterthought. Very few institutions have put near the top of their lists of priorities objectives relative to older people such as the following:

- to challenge them to participate in educational programs that will keep them in touch with society and will point up opportunities for their involvement in economic, social, and cultural activities;
- to provide counseling services designed to match their skills and abilities with available and evolving opportunities for further careers;

- to help prepare them for such careers; and
- to provide placement services that will help them get started in the career areas for which they have prepared.

If these priorities are honored, continuing education for older Americans will no longer be the stepchild it is now; it will become an integral part of the American educational edifice, and endow it with new strength and beauty. Do we not have the right to expect that one of our greatest national resources, our educational system, will lead the way in turning around the current social policy which is wasting one of our greatest unused human resources—the nation's older people?

The National Committee on Careers for Older Americans has put the entire country in its debt with the clear call for action voiced in *Older Americans: An Untapped Resource.* The document deserves wide and careful study. The editors of the present volume are grateful to the committee for providing the opportunity to make it better known.

NOTE

1. Copies of the report are available at $8.50 from the Academy for Educational Development, 680 Fifth Avenue, New York, NY 10019. The author wishes to express his appreciation to the committee for permission to use material from the report, a license which he has used liberally.

REFERENCES

Committee for Economic Development (1978) Jobs for the Hard-to-Employ: New Directions for a Public-Private Partnership for Economic Development. New York: Author.

Conference Board, Inc. (1978) Older Workers and Retirement. New York: Author.

Louis Harris and Associates (1979) Study of American Attitudes Toward Pensions and Retirement: A Nationwide Survey of Employees, Retirees, and Business Leaders. Commissioned by Johnson & Higgins, conducted by Louis Harris and Associates, Inc., February.

——— (1974) The Myth and Reality of Aging in America: A Study for the National Council on the Aging, Inc., conducted by Louis Harris and Associates, Inc.

3

THE AGING VETERANS

Wyatt C. Jones

Veterans of military service in the United States occupy an anomalous status: They are citizens, and therefore eligible for all civilian services provided by the nation; they are also survivors of its wars, and, as such, are eligible for a variety of additional services. With almost half of the male population classified as veterans, the impact of this special status on retirees is of particular interest to planners, researchers, and policy makers.

In 1980, the veteran population reached more than 30 million. However, veterans in civilian life account for only one-third of all the people potentially eligible for benefits and services. Although very few of their 24 million spouses, 24 million dependent children, and 11 million other family members will receive direct services, benefits paid to veterans will indirectly affect the health and welfare of more than 90 million people, or approximately 40 percent of the entire U. S. population.

Older veterans, those 65 years of age and older, now total almost 3 million (nearly 1 out of every 10 living veterans). These numbers will rise dramatically during the next 10 years—reaching 7 million in 1990 (1 out of 4) and 8 million by 1995 (Figure 3.1 and Table 3.1). By 1990 more than half of the U. S. males over 65 years of age will be veterans and by 1995 veterans will exceed 60 percent of the total male population (Figures 3.2 and 3.3). The episodic pattern of American wars has produced increased numbers of veterans, relatively close in age, at roughly generational intervals. Most of the surviving World War I veterans are now 85

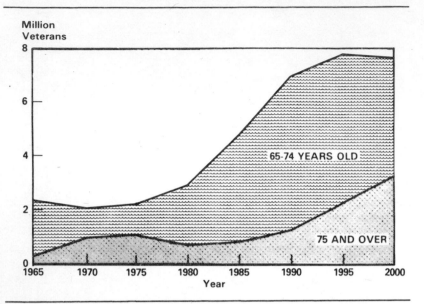

Figure 3.1 Number of Veterans 65 Years of Age or Older, 1965-2000 (in millions)

TABLE 3.1   Number of Veterans 65 Years of Age or Older, 1965-
             2000 (in millions)

Ages	1965	1970	1975	1980	1985	1990	1995	2000
65-74	1.95	1.07	1.15	2.22	4.10	5.88	5.68	4.43
75-84	0.34	0.91	0.95	0.49	0.63	1.19	2.19	3.09
85+	0.02	0.02	0.11	0.26	0.23	0.12	0.18	0.30
Total								
65+	2.31	2.00	2.21	2.97	4.96	7.19	8.05	7.82

years of age or older. The majority of World War II veterans, now 55 to 65 years old, and Korean veterans, now 45 to 55 years old, will reach retirement ages during the next 2 decades. The vast majority of these veterans are male; only 2.3 percent (679,000) are female, with an average age of 45 years. While less than 65,000 female veterans are now over 65 years of age, some 200,000 will reach 65 during the next 10 years. Since current surveys do not sample female veterans, they are not considered in the data presented here.

The Veterans Administration (VA), which, by federal statute, has primary responsibility for national oversight of veteran affairs, maintains

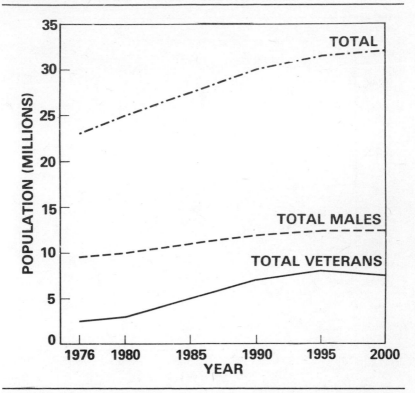

Figure 3.2 Total Number of Individuals Over the Age of 65 Years, 1976-2000

extensive statistics on its services and programs. However, recent comparative data on veterans and nonveterans and the socioeconomic characteristics of eligible recipients are available only from a mail survey conducted
in 1977 of a sample of males drawn from the Current Population Survey
(CPS) who had indicated that they had been in the armed services (see VA,
1980a, 1980b). An earlier report (VA, 1977) that assessed the present and
future medical needs of aging veterans has no data on nonveterans. For the
future, the National Medical Care Expenditure Survey, also conducted in
1977, will provide more comparative health care information (Lawson,
1981) and the long form of the 1980 Census will, for the first time, have
extensive data on veterans and nonveterans.

Among the congressionally mandated VA services, a number of programs apply only or largely to younger veterans or their beneficiaries—
educational benefits (GI Bill), housing assistance, life insurance, and employment assistance. Income maintenance, health care, and the national
cemetery system are of particular importance to aging veterans. Each of

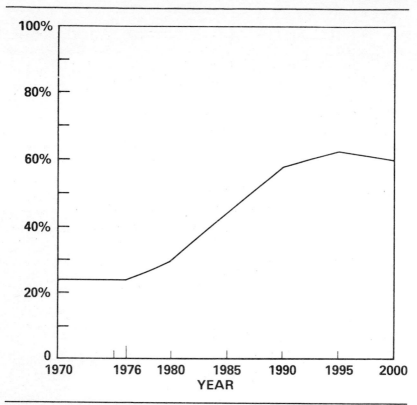

Figure 3.3   Veterans Over 65 Years as Percentage of All Males Over 65 Years, 1970-2000

these programs has a special eligibility requirement that places a limitation on the kind or amount of entitlement. For veterans of any age whose disabilities result from military service (so-called service-connected), the VA provides not only monthly compensation payments based on the percentage of disability but also comprehensive medical care, rehabilitation therapy, and prosthetic devices, in addition to nursing home, domiciliary, or board-and-care home care where indicated. For elderly and needy veterans with non-service-connected disabilities, the VA provides income-tested pensions for those who served in wartime and medical care in VA medical centers on a space-available basis for those suffering from conditions not resulting from military service. For eligible survivors and dependents of veterans, the VA provides monthly compensation, education and training, and income-test pensions for needy survivors of disabled wartime veterans.

Maintenance of this service network requires vast resources: the VA is larger than any other part of the government except the Defense Department (200,000 employees), has an annual budget that is larger than most Cabinet departments ($25 billion), and operates the largest hospital system in the Western world (172 medical centers). The VA appears to have survived the early budget cuts of the Reagan Administration with its programs largely intact. (The numbers of veterans and the influence of their service organizations constitute perhaps the single most effective lobby in Washington today.) Over the years, critics of the VA have maintained that veterans' payments bear little relationship to their military experience, that the payments are more generous than those available to other poor people, and that they are not subjected to the same scrutiny as other income-maintenance or disability programs. Such criticism, whether accurate or not, has not weighed very heavily with Congress or with any administration, regardless of political party.

COMPENSATION AND PENSIONS

In 1979, the income-maintenance program of the VA cost $10.5 billion. These funds were distributed to almost 2.3 million service-connected disability compensation recipients, more than half of whom are World War II veterans, and to almost 1 million non-service-connected disability pension recipients, of whom 20 percent are World War I and 70 percent are World War II veterans. Annual rates of service-connected compensation range from $528 for 10 percent disability to $9,708 for 100 percent disability. Allowances for dependents and for aid and attendance are also available for those whose disabilities are rated at 30 percent or more. In addition, compensation up to $27,696 per year is paid for specific severe disabilities, determined on an individual basis. The maximum annual pension for non-service-connected disability for a veteran alone is $3,902, with $1,210 added for one dependent, $2,341 for aid and attendance, or $868 if housebound. These rates are scaled by the percentage of disability suffered by the recipient. Payment for surviving spouse and dependents is about two-thirds of that awarded to the veteran. These rates are indexed to social security cost-of-living increases, so that no pensioner's benefits are reduced solely as a result of rises in social security payments.

In theory, veterans with no service-connected disability are entitled to pensions only if they are disabled and totally destitute. In practice, wartime veterans over 65 years of age are considered "permanently and totally disabled" under VA rules without physical examination and are declared impoverished if they make this claim. There is an annual questionnaire for people receiving non-service-connected pensions. If the questionnaire is not completed, the funds are terminated. It is estimated that 22.6 percent of all veterans over 65 years of age receive such pensions (Lindsay, 1975).

HEALTH CARE

The VA is a comprehensive health service resource provided as a prepaid benefit and available to all veterans discharged under conditions other than dishonorable as eligibility is achieved. The VA medical system, with an annual budget of $5.5 billion, includes 144 general medical and surgical (GM&S) hospitals (60 with extended hospital care beds); 28 psychiatric hospitals (60 percent of the psychiatric beds are in GM&S hospitals); 49 independent clinics; 92 VA nursing home units: and 15 VA domiciliary care homes (plus support of 40 state veteran homes). Since a large majority of elderly patients in VA long-term care facilities have no real homes of their own, a number of extended-care programs have been created as alternatives to institutionalization. Personal care (or foster) homes, originally devised to provide a basic level of social support in a family setting for discharged psychiatric patients, are now being used for GM&S patients and for older veterans without families. Hospital-based home care (HBHC) at 30 hospitals provides the patient and his family with necessary supervision and support to maintain him at home. Congregate housing, geriatric day care, and senior centers are other options in various stages of development. These resources can be expanded as alternatives for veterans seeking hospitalization due to inability to maintain themselves in the community without support, for discharged patients unable to return to independent living, or for some veterans applying for hospitalization or other institutional care (VA, 1977). Some comparative analyses of outcomes and costs of these alternatives have been undertaken and further study is indicated. The recent authorization to expand its ambulatory (or outpatient) care services has enabled the VA to treat more patients for more conditions, thereby preventing hospitalization and reducing the length of hospital stay. Patients over the age of 65 years make up 15 percent of this caseload.

Under the priority system of the VA, approximately 2 out of 5 veterans are eligible to receive care in or through its facilities (VA, 1980a). For wartime veterans over 65 years of age, bed capacity rather than eligibility becomes the operative limitation on their use of VA facilities. The numbers served by the 172 VA medical centers are impressive. At the last available survey (September 1979), more than one-quarter of all VA hospital patients were 65 years of age or older. These included 10,313 with general medical and surgical conditions, 3,278 with psychosis, 2,501

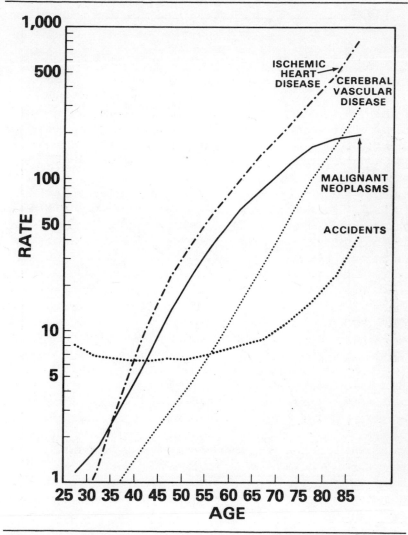

Figure 3.4 Age-Specific Mortality Rate per 10,000 Male Population, U.S., 1974

with other psychiatric problems, 2,244 with neurological diseases, and 130 with tuberculosis. During 1979, among 2.8 million veterans 65 or older, some 212,000 hospital patients (76.8 per thousand) were discharged from VA facilities or contract nursing homes (VA, 1980b).[1]

The experience of the VA shows that with increasing age from 65 to 85 years there is a rapid rise in morbidity from heart disease, cancer, respiratory disease, diabetes, arthritis, and accidents (Figure 3.4). Surgical proce-

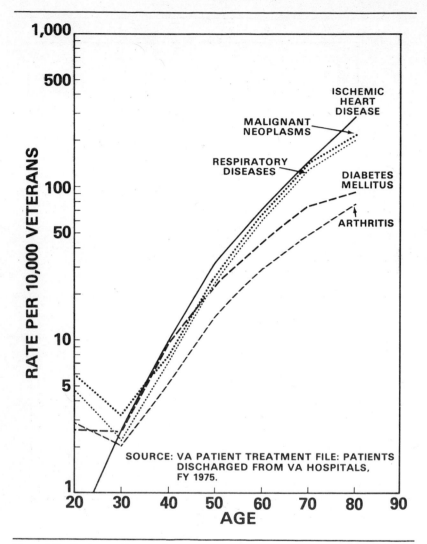

Figure 3.5a Common Disease Classes: Discharges from VA Hospitals per 10,000 Veterans, by Age, 1975

dures for cataracts, prostate, and hip fractures show comparable increases. For psychiatric conditions, there is a precipitous decline in alcoholism (from 50 to 15 per 10,000), a disappearance of drug dependency, a slight decline in schizophrenia, and a dramatic rise in senile psychosis (Figures 3.5a-3.5d).

Since veterans will constitute the major portion of the aged male population for the remainder of the century (in the decade 1990-2000 more

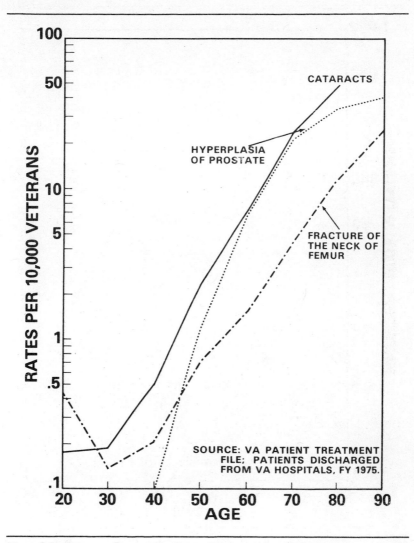

Figure 3.5b Common Surgical Problems: Discharges from VA Hospitals per 10,000
        Veterans, by Age, 1975

than 60 percent of all males over 65 years of age will be veterans), their general characteristics will lie close to the means for all males of the same age. Therefore, whatever health resources exist or are planned for the aged will also be accessible to veterans. This has not been the case in recent years. While complete data are not available, for a great many veterans the VA has been the first choice for health services, and it represents a

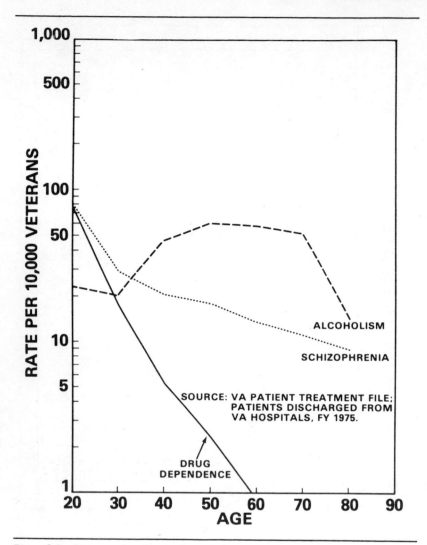

Figure 3.5c Common Psychiatric Conditions: Incidence of Disease for Discharged
Veterans, by Age, 1975

catastrophic or last-resort resource of care for all veterans who do not use
it routinely. The 1977 survey showed that 94.4 percent of veterans over
65 years of age have insurance coverage (8.4 percent have private insurance; 81.1 percent have Medicare; 4.9 percent have Medicaid or other
public insurance; only 5.6 percent have no insurance). These percentages
are roughly the same for nonveterans (Lawson, 1981). None of the
insurance benefits can be used by patients in VA facilities. As an example,

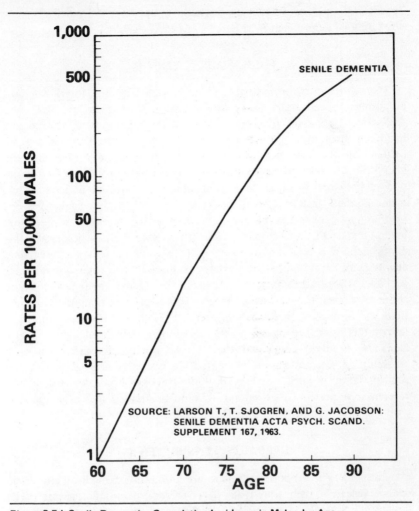

Figure 3.5d Senile Dementia: Cumulative Incidence in Males, by Age

the current End State Renal Disease (ESRD) program, wholly financed by Medicare, makes the VA's kidney dialysis and transplant units largely redundant. In most of these instances, scarce VA resources are used for patients who otherwise are covered by third-party payers or are eligible for other public programs. A three-year study by the National Research Council (1977) of the National Academy of Sciences concluded that this nationwide system of veterans' hospitals, clinics, and nursing homes is wasteful and should be integrated with military health facilities and regular public and private hospitals. The VA has taken the position that the "portion of the total veteran need which should be met by the VA must ultimately be determined by others" (VA, 1977: 85).

POLICY IMPLICATIONS

There is no question but that the VA is a "good thing" for all veterans, an absolute necessity for many who are poor or disabled, and possibly a "soft touch" for some freeloaders. Considering the dire predictions of the imminent insolvency of the Social Secuurity system, the slim chances of a national health insurance program in the foreseeable future, and the uncoordinated state of social services for the elderly in the general population, at least half of the male population may be fortunate indeed to have their veterans' benefits to fall back on. Issues of equity aside—and the predominance of males in the veteran population and the increasing predominance of females in the elderly population as a whole make this discrimination a very serious issue—the economics of a separate income maintenance and health care system exclusively for veterans and their dependents is surely debatable. As costs of the VA system expand to equal and even exceed those of other governmental services, the policy implications will have to be faced. As long ago as 1956, a blue-ribbon commission (appointed by President Dwight D. Eisenhower and headed by General Omar N. Bradley) concluded that a time ought to come when fully rehabilitated veterans should be treated like everyone else. A quarter of a century later, it might be argued that everyone should be treated like veterans. Or possibly that veterans should be treated like other people, with a new concept of what people should expect in our society.

RESEARCH POSSIBILITIES

While the VA supports an elaborate program of medical and basic science research, its research on the social and economic aspects of its mission is minimal. Its university affiliations are largely limited to medical schools, and clinical investigators dominate the research program. While outside researchers are welcomed, the financial resources are allocated by merit review to researchers with VA appointments. The problems of using VA data for secondary analysis, as noted earlier, are complicated by the fact that the unit of analysis as recorded is not the individual veteran, and it is prohibitively expensive to perform any meaningful record linkages. Despite these difficulties, the VA, its staff and clients, represent important research opportunities for field investigations. For example, most of the problems associated with the introduction of Medicare and Medicaid could have been predicted from the utilization of VA resources by veterans.

Further, the public response to a national health insurance scheme could be simulated from VA experience. Researchers interested in the prospects, planning, and policy of retirement would be well advised to consider this national resource as a fertile field for research, particularly since veterans potentially represent such a large segment of the aged population.

NOTE

1. The VA's annual statistics are based on "discharges" or "episodes of service," and cannot be directly translated into numbers of individual patients served. One patient may have several admissions and discharges to more than one VA unit during the year. This recording convention, required by congressional allocation of funds, seriously impairs the usefulness of these data in comparative or longitudinal studies.

REFERENCES

LAWSON, W., Jr. (1981) Health Insurance Coverage of Veterans. Data Preview 4. Hyattsville, MD: National Center for Health Services Research, Publications and Information Branch.

LINDSAY, C. M. (1975) Veterans Administration Hospitals: An Economic Analysis of a Government Enterprise. Washington, DC: Institute for Public Policy Research.

National Research Council (1977) Report on the Study of the Veterans Administration. Washington, DC: National Academy of Sciences.

Veterans Administration [VA] (1980a) National Survey of Veterans. Washington, DC: Government Printing Office.

——— (1980b) 1979 Annual Report. Washington, DC: Government Printing Office.

——— (1977) The Aging Veteran: Present and Future Medical Needs. Washington, DC: Government Printing Office. (Also available as House Committee on Veterans' Affairs Print No. 77, January 5, 1978.)

PART II
AGING AND RETIREMENT PLANNING

An 80-year-old person today could perhaps look back to a birth in a typical American small town of, say, 1000 inhabitants. According to the 1900 Census, the town's population would be distributed like this: 238 children below the age of 10; 204 children and adolescents above that age; 94 people above 55 years; and some 21 beyond the age 65. The latest available figures (1976) show a startling reversal of the way the population is distributed—a change that took place within a single life span. In that same typical small town, we would now find only 152 children under 10; 190 older children and adolescents; 200 persons at 55-plus years; and 108 beyond 64 years of age. How is the nation planning for its growing graying population? Part II examines some of the psychological and social tasks of retirement living. "Preparing for the Transfer Point" suggests new terminology and offers a positive approach to living out life's mature years. There are myths and stereotyped expectations about retirement which this opening chapter attempts to put in perspective. The following chapter reviews developments during the preceding decade, when retirement planning became a major concern for the industrial community and certain other agencies. What was their involvement? How extensive was it? How successful? What can be expected in the 1980s? The concept of quality of life is central to the succeeding essay, an idea that has grown in popularity with the growth of environmental concerns and the development of social indicators. How do these enter into the framework of retirement planning? The next chapter looks at the housing options for the retirement-age population and probes the future of retirement communities and housing. Perhaps nowhere are the characteristics of a new retirement culture more evident than in the area of housing. Although people often help to mold an environment, rarely does this happen in advance of a demand. Contemporary changes in housing patterns are a response to new needs of the elderly population.

Health care, disabilities, and psychological well-being are each taken up in separate chapters. Health is a ubiquitous variable in considering the status and activities of persons as they grow older. We are forced to anticipate changes in health status, but what must be passively accepted and what can be actively controlled? Though disabilities are also mostly associated with the elderly, new research findings are helping the health care community to adopt new approaches to the care and cure of the disabled older person. Current social and scientific interest is profoundly altering the conception that psychotherapy is wasted upon older people. The many consequences of this new awareness in the field of mental health are explored in the chapter entitled "Psychological Well-Being in Retirement." The section concludes with an essay on the role of the family in retirement. The author contends that we have romanticized the concept of the extended family while underestimating and downgrading the nuclear family. But will the nuclear family be able in future years to support its elderly retired given new variables such as the increased divorce rate and the sharp decrease in the birthrate? As our knowledge base widens and deepens, so our social planning should become more effective.

4

PREPARING FOR THE TRANSFER POINT

Neil G. McCluskey

INTRODUCTION: TRANSFER POINT

Other chapters in this volume discuss some of the startling changes in the nation's demographic pattern that have opened up for most people the prospect of a longer, more active, and potentially richer span of life than was dreamed of by their forebears. But the United States is only slowly adjusting to this new demographic phenomenon. As regularly happens in history, social structures and social attitudes lag far behind social realities. Science and medicine have lengthened the human life span, but society is only beginning to adjust to the implications of a longer life—as if mankind could not believe such a good thing were truly taking place. Older people have become a more potent presence in the total population, and, as has been indicated elsewhere, their absolute and relative numbers will continue to increase for the remainder of this century and into the next.

Yet most Americans still consider the years past 60 as the worst part of adult life—a drab period of loneliness, inactivity, and poor health. Beyond doubt the principal reason for this situation is the lack of proper preparation for the retirement period or, in Stevenson's (1979) happy phrase, "the late adult years."[1] Despite its narrow and largely negative meaning, we continue to use "retirement" synonymously with the late adult years.

It is too late to banish the word from the language, but at least here an attempt will be made to give it a truer and more positive meaning.

Since the advent of retirement planning, the emphasis has been on retirement as a *terminal* event after a lifetime of work. Sometimes it was welcomed as a surcease from toil or accepted as an earned reward. Where persons facing retirement experienced fear or dread, it was usually because of a social conditioning that connects retirement with such stereotypes as being "at the end of the line," "on the shelf," "over the hill," and "put out to pasture." In the future, more and more Americans will benefit from a longer life, and retirement is now more accurately viewed as a normal span of mature life or a process for which one must prepare in order for this second part of adulthood to be meaningful and rewarding. No longer should a man or women be regarded as occupying a box labeled "retired" or "not retired." What should be emphasized is continuity—the life span nature of the process—not a retirement *from* but a retirement *to* something new and normal.

In response to this new understanding, new conceptual models have been advanced in recent years to explain the sequence of events in a mature person's life that calls for plans and decisions. In the literature we now find such terms as *stages, passages, seasons,* and *transitions* (Levinson, 1978; Sheehy, 1976; and others). Perhaps the most accurate concept of retirement is as a "transfer point" in a person's life—*point* for the event and *transfer* for the implication of dynamic change. Transfer point is where an adult person changes from one vehicle or track to another, where he or she transfers skills and talents from one set of tasks to another, where he or she can shift priorities and change the tempo of activity. Likewise, the retirement event itself can be construed as the document of transfer which admits a person to a new vehicle or track. Transfer applies to the area of finance in the choice of pension options or new income-generating investments. Transfer also is involved in the realignment of medical and hospital support through enrollment in group plans or special insurance. Transfer can be applicable to decisions regarding change of residence and lifestyle. Transfer covers the development of new activities, interests, and goals. The transfer, in sum, is a transition into a new phase of mature adult life with its own special expectancies, tasks, and challenges. From childhood we have been conditioned to view the later years of life as a deficit period, which it may once have been for most people. This attitude has powerfully influenced many of our social institutions and structures, which are still largely designed without reference to men and women beyond 65 years of age.

PREPARATION FOR RETIREMENT AND AGING

Preparation for retirement and preparation for aging are very often considered the same thing, and, as a matter of fact, most in-depth programs are more preparation for aging than for retirement. This combination seems eminently practical for several reasons. The two concepts are so inextricably entwined in real life that one cannot be treated without reference to the other. Retirement for many people not formally in the labor market means simply retiring from middle age. This is more true of this generation of older women, the majority of whom have not held career jobs outside the home. They will continue, pretty much, to do what they have always done as homemakers and housewives. Retirement planning can open up new paths of meaningful activity for them, but an even greater need is preparation for the personal adjustments called for by a new phase of life. For this reason, preretirement planning programs that leave wives out are far less effective than those which include them.

The large majority of the nearly 13 million women 65 and over constitutes a rich untapped resource. The talents and experience of these women could be of immense benefit to society in many ways. Moreover, preparing older women to engage in contributory roles would greatly reduce the numbers of premature dependents and early victims of senility. In one way, aging can be regarded as a women's problem: Women outlive men by nearly 8 years. In 1976 there were 13.9 million women and 9.5 million men past 65. The census projects that by the year 2035 America will have 34 million older women and 23 million older men.

Another reason it is common sense to combine preparation for retirement with preparation for aging is that, as far as full-time employment goes, only a relatively small number of those past 65 have remained in the work force—either voluntarily or involuntarily. Where in 1900 about one-third of this population was retired, today more than 75 percent is outside the work force. These proportions may change somewhat as a result of recent legislation (discussed elsewhere in this volume), so that at present we can only speculate as to how many men and women will elect to exercise their prerogative of remaining in full-time employment past age 65.

A final reason for the mixture of retirement and aging preparation is to prepare people for leaving the full-time occupational role. Many older people, most often the affluent, do adjust rapidly and comfortably to a life of leisure. Most others, however, find that their self-views are closely tied to their occupational roles, and, as Peterson and Bolton (1980) have said, "When that is removed, they have difficulty maintaining their self-image, self-esteem, and self-motivation." This calls for the kind of help offered through preretirement counseling.

Midcareer counseling is usually an amalgam of personal and career counseling. Personal counseling involves support processes that allow an individual to understand the nature of the personal or economic changes he or she is undergoing through one-on-one counseling, self-awareness sessions, or crisis intervention workshops. As an outcome, the counselor may suggest referral to an analyst or mental health agency for therapy or other psychological support.

On the other hand, career counseling, according to Entine (1977), includes processes that identify appropriate career and work options that match an individual's aptitudes, interests, skills, experience, and limitations. The techniques used here usually include aptitude testing, individual or group workshops, and the identification of appropriate educational and training programs. The career counseling process may lead the client to an employment service for help in job placement. Entine (1977) proposes for the postretirement period *activity counseling* as a substitute for career counseling. By activity counseling he means "individual and group sessions which can identify appropriate work (full-time or part-time) and training sessions, and may lead to referrals to voluntary employment agencies, senior citizens' recreation centers, and retirement communities."

It can be argued that activity counseling should also go hand in hand with career counseling as a normal part of preretirement education. Many people, both men and women, with higher educational achievements, higher levels within the occupational structure, and higher income levels, are likely to remain longer in the work force than those of a lesser socioeconomic status (Streib and Schneider, 1971). Accordingly, most of them are not planning new full-time careers in the job market, but are seeking a variety of new or enlarged activities to fill their retirement years.

Some writers feel that at times too much stress is laid on measures of social adjustment and psychological well-being at the expense of what Monk (1979) calls "activity behavioral sets." If the preparation is related to the close of one's paid employment status, he urges that consideration be given to new career interests and occupational retraining and especially to "the increasing demand for new career escalators, even to the notion of leisure careers." The point is well taken, and certainly a preretirement education program that slighted the preparation of concrete steps for an active retirement life would be deficient.

The retirement period—whatever its precise meaning, whenever it begins, whatever its length—is becoming more and more a situation to be faced and a challenge to be met. It is a milestone, a transfer point, that lies ahead, and more and more people are beginning to think about it. Studies show that preretirees, even those at midcareer point, are increasingly interested in making plans for retirement, but they are looking for guidance and attractive plans.

OBJECTIVES OF PRERETIREMENT EDUCATION

The basis of preretirement education in the broad sense is understanding and coping with maturing human development. It is simply coming to terms with the changes and trade-offs of aging. Upon this foundation a man or woman then needs to understand better the community from which they draw support and to acquire information and skills for handling the problems and challenges of daily living. As one early planner in the field of aging has stated it, "The overall objective of retirement education is . . . to help the individual clarify the situations he is likely to confront in retirement and to encourage him to initiate attitudes and behavior which will enhance his ability to live satisfactorily during the retirement years" (Hunter, 1978).

The best preretirement education combines the cognitive and the affective, the theoretical and the practical. That is, we learn about it, feel something should be done about it, and then, ideally, do it. However, since it is the starting point, the most important step is that of acquiring an attitude toward retirement that sees it as a transfer point and the commencement of an important new phase in one's life. Preretirement planning entails arming oneself with accurate information, reviewing one's present status, exchanging ideas and plans with others, reducing anxieties, and selecting retirement actions. Hunter (1978) offers a list of concrete action steps among which a person can choose during the preparatory phase: changing one's diet, getting a physical checkup, evaluating one's financial situation, learning a craft or hobby, seeking new friendships and relationships, exploring possible new living sites, budgeting one's income, making major household expenditures or repairs while still employed, enrolling in adult education courses, studying living options in the community, and investigating volunteer work.

WHO IS RESPONSIBLE?

There is much confusion in contemporary society over who has the responsibility for preretirement planning; a moment's reflection tells why. Each person divides his or her life among a variety of subgroups in the larger society to which he or she belongs. The length and depth of involvement or commitment vary widely with each individual, but everyone is defined in some way by family, marriage, clubs, church, school, professional groups, and business or corporation. Each group has some interest in seeing its members prepared for living in their mature years, but none of these subsocieties is totally responsible for preretirement planning, any more than any single one of them is totally to blame for the unhealthy socialization of aging of which we are all victims.

A long tradition points to the family as the chief support system for its older members as they approach retirement or are already retired. The employer has an obligation to help all employees plan for the years after retirement in fair return for the investment of time that they have made in his or her enterprise over the years. The union or professional association has more and more in recent years been pressured to assume responsibility for the preretirement planning of its members with measures such as sponsoring courses and programs, and bargaining for specific retirement-related benefits, such as cost-of-living increases in the pension and health insurance, and so on. Religious or fraternal organizations bring people together for common purposes connected with the quality of living, so that pre- and postretirement activities should have a natural place within them. The very raison d'être of aging organizations is the well-being of their members during their later years, and these organizations are logical sites for intensive planning and programming for retirement. At all levels, government has become the main purveyor of social services and health benefits to the nation, so that it is fitting that government continue, directly and indirectly, to concern itself with the preparation of its citizens for the wide-ranging changes of later life. Finally, there is public education. As the central agency already assuming primary responsibility for continuing education, a strong case could be made for public education's leading role in preretirement preparation. Moreover, the public school is in the best position to command broad public support in fulfilling this role, and it provides a unique community base that presumably transcends class and privilege.

However, when all is said and done, whatever each of the foregoing agencies can contribute, the primary responsibility for preretirement planning remains with the individual. He or she should make use of whatever support is available from every possible source but the ensuing mix will be different in every case. The mistake of the seventies, we are beginning to discover, was that in our preretirement planning we attempted to do the identical thing for everybody at the same time in exactly the same way. Somehow preretirement planning programs then pushed too specific an ideal of the "good life" to be pursued after retirement. Retirement "salvation" was seen as centered in the image of the smiling grandmother bustling about her dozen charities or the tanned grandfather buoyantly riding his golf cart down the eighteenth fairway. For many, retirement living turned into a fad, cultivated with the same assiduity with which people had earlier taken up suburban living. Priorities for future options differ greatly. Much of the information and knowledge needed must be geared to specific needs. The kind and extent of professional advice or training to be sought before making critical decisions hinges on individual needs. But the pivot around which all preretirement planning must move is *one's own personal satisfaction*—nothing is more subjective.

Government- and foundation-sponsored research are beginning to provide solid new data relating to the ways people view retirement and aging and themselves in the transition process. A 1978 General Accounting Office study summed up existing studies in adjustment to retirement, stating that there is a clear correlation between an individual's adaptability to retirement living and the degree to which he or she planned for retirement. Or, stated negatively, "the less the preplanning for retirement, the poorer the post-retirement adjustment." An early start on planning is likewise highly important because it lengthens the time span over which people can develop and test options.

In studying the variables that contribute to successful adjustment to retirement and aging, Manion and his associates (1969) at the University of Oregon found that attitudes and beliefs along with plans were the key factors. Other research has confirmed these findings. Education for any phase of a person's life entails a formative aspect. Knowledge and skills are important, but at least equally necessary is the inculcation of attitudes that will govern the use of knowledge and skills. Preretirement education can be successful only to the extent that it includes preparation for aging. But for what are we preparing? Human aging is unique in our universe. It is a profound and intimate experience that transcends any other developmental phenomenon in nature. Aging has a supreme value that is inseparable from the way it is defined. The answer to the question of what aging is must include some kind of answer to what aging is all about.

THE AMBIGUITIES OF AGING

In the human experience nothing is more ambiguous than aging. For the young, growing old seems no better than death; for the already old, aging is as precious as once was youth; for the in-between, old age is something that happens to those 15 years older than they are. Our thoughts about aging are deeply colored by this ambiguity. We are not sure, as one author has put it, whether aging is "a phase of living that is both healthy and normal, or unhealthy but still normal, or whether it is unhealthy and abnormal" (Berg and Gadow, 1978). If aging is a disease, when does it begin? At the hour each of us is born? Then in measuring our development are we compelled to side either with the pessimist who reports that the bottle is half empty or with the optimist who rejoices that the bottle is still half full? Should we try to prevent, slow down, or cure aging? Should we curse it, bear it, or revere it?

With few exceptions, men and women have a fear of aging. The degree of fear varies widely but almost no one is free from at least the occasional cold clutch of tiny fingers deep down reminding us that our bodies are undergoing changes, that we are ripening, that we are getting on. In large part this attitude arises from two related factors in the socialization process—both negative. The first is the static understanding of what is essentially a developmental process. The other is three related myths based upon misunderstandings of the changes that take place as human beings grow old. It is important that we honestly examine these factors in order to understand the source of our negative attitudes and try to replace them by gaining a true understanding that can be conducive to behavioral modification.

STATIC CONCEPTION OF AGING

A highly negative influence on our attitude toward aging is the static manner in which it has been generally conceived. Somehow we have tended to view the years past 60 or 65 as nothing more than a holding pattern, as a clinging to what remains of life, as a slowdown of life's march, as an exchange of a brisk climb for a dull shuffling along a plateau whose edge might appear at any time. "Old age" is something uninvited, unexpected, and unplanned for. It simply happens with grim inevitability.

The attitude that life past 65 must be static is a mind set no longer valid. Given the continued lengthening of life expectancy for Americans, it is outmoded, unreal, and harmful. Recall that in 1900 the average life span was 49 and in 1940 it was 63. In 1977, the average life expectancy at birth was 70 years for males and 77 years for females. However, those men and women who by now have reached age 65 can expect an even greater span of years. A 65-year-old woman can look forward to an average of 16 or 17 additional years and her male counterpart can expect another 13 or 14 years. Why? Simply because their death-prone contemporaries have already dropped out of the statistical tables. So, life expectancy for the nation's elderly elite is now around 85 years and, if you came into this world in the mid-1920s or even earlier, the chances of your becoming a member of that group is steadily improving. It is highly significant that now the mean age for *admission* to intermediate-care facilities is approximately 82 years, and for skilled-care facilities about 78 years. Some actuarial projections put the average life expectancy in the next century *beyond*

120 years. However, other authorities are quick to question the validity of these projections unless some radical changes alter the basic course of aging (Eisdorfer, 1971). Those who argue that the normal life span will continue on and on base their claim, as Stevenson (1979) explains, on "observations that 60-year-olds of today resemble 40- or 50-year-olds of a century ago in terms of the aging process as evidenced by muscular agility and strength, skin turgor, and other indices of youthfulness *versus* senescence."

The average American man or woman at 65 is vigorous, alert, and independent. He or she pursues an active, productive, and meaningful life, a living refutation of the negative stereotypes of old age that seem to cling so stubbornly to some minds. It is a fact that 95 percent of the total 65-and-over population are a regular part of the everyday world, and only 5 percent are confined to nursing homes. Some 91 percent of the 75-and-over population remain active in the day-to-day world and 9 percent of them are in nursing homes. Figures for white single women who are 85 years and over show that 73 percent are still in the mainstream world, while the other 27 percent reside in nursing homes. It is clear that no longer can life past 65 be accurately depicted as a period of torpor or stagnation. It is not a state of suspended animation or the final limbo of life. The vast majority of Americans over 65 are active, independent, and able. In increasing numbers they belong to the mainstream of our society. Our population has changed, but our mind sets and social institutions have yet to conform to this new reality.

It is true that, year by year after age 75, the chances increase that an older person will need extra health vigilance and additional support for physical disabilities. But this number, or at least the proportion among this number, continues to diminish and the need for extraordinary support lessens because the new cohorts continually reaching age 75 have been the beneficiaries of the amazing improvements in health care, nutrition, and medical care which were not available to the elderly they replace. Each new cohort of 75 year olds is physically younger and better educated than its predecessor. They are living longer and healthier lives. The changes that have come over the pattern of living within two or three generations and that have transformed life for the elderly are awesome. Indeed, why should the process not continue for an increasing number of people into the ninth and perhaps tenth decade of life? Who is to predict the limits of change in the future? Helander (1978) asks the relevant question, "Suppose we could raise from the dead someone who was 70 at the turn of the century and tell him what it is like being 70 today—would he believe us?" So many features in the life of the older person that were accepted in 1900 as inevitable we would find intolerable today. Many of the negative stereotypes which now color our ideas about aging and the aged were, no doubt, occasioned by memories of grandparents and elderly uncles, aunts, or friends who represented for us what being "old" meant. The image of 50- and 60-year-old men and women with bent backs, gnarled limbs, heavy gaits, shrunken frames, wrinkled skins, and wheezing voices is perhaps the chief source of the fear most people have of aging.

MYTH I: THE WORN-OUT BODY

Despite the significant growth in our knowledge and understanding of the aging process over the past 25 years, our ignorance remains enormous and frustrating. Finch (1979) has stated it honestly: "Since most *mechanisms* underlying aging changes remain obscure, it may be said that we don't know what we don't know." Eisdorfer and Cohen (1980: 49) have added: "Our current knowledge does not allow us to tell with a high degree of accuracy what biological and psychological deficits occur as a function of aging." One major complicating factor is that in death-risk research in the biomedical laboratory we are obviously restricted to experiments involving lower species, such as flies, rodents, rabbits, and so on. Another limiting factor is that when we study older persons we are looking not merely at the effects of a process but at age plus a combination of many other factors, the occurrences of which rise in direct proportion to the length of life. In other words, more things have happened to the 60 year old than to the 30 year old. Many changes take place in the human body as it grows, but they are not all age-related, nor necessarily deficits. A child's blond hair darkens and a soprano voice deepens to tenor. These are changes, not deficits. Even the profound changes in bodily functions at menopause are more properly developmental changes than biological deficits; they are not like the loss of eyesight or use of a limb, but are normal development changes.

Is aging the same thing as growth or development? In the sense of *chronological* aging, yes. A six-month old infant has actually *aged* six months by the clock. However, the majority of biologists and gerontologists distinguish growth or maturation from senescence or *biological* aging. Normal growth is an increase in size or number of cells permitting progressively higher functional levels through increased efficiency or differentiation of function. Many members of the biomedical fraternity also clearly define a middle category of development, *maturity,* which they describe as the slowing down of the progressive increases of growth and the leveling off of functional capacity at a fixed peak level. *Senescence* is true biological aging. It begins at some point in time when a progressive decline in the level or efficiency of functioning is observable, that eventually leads to an increased susceptibility to disease and death. Used as a description, then, the word *aging* applies to a long sequence of changes across a lifetime and covers every living cohort from infancy to those in their final years.

None of this is intended to overlook the fact that, in general, older people visit doctors more, take more medication, and spend more time in hospitals than do young people. Nor can it be overlooked that the general measure of bodily vigor and sharpness of the senses is tilted in favor of the young. In general, older people are more prone to diseases. Yet, with the major exceptions of atherosclerosis and high blood pressure, from a biological point of view almost no diseases would qualify as aging changes. Of the 65-plus group, three-quarters suffer at least one chronic disease and nearly one-half have some limitation upon daily activities. The point, however, is that many of the changes in later life are not directly related to age. In fact, much of the malfunctioning in the bodily systems of the elderly can be traced to either hereditary weakness, environmental harm, or self-inflicted damage. We still do not know completely how or why many changes occur, so that our ignorance should prevent us from jumping to the facile conclusion that all bodily changes are age-related. The increasing number of vigorous 80 year olds provides living added testimony to this reality.

MYTH II: DECLINE IN COGNITIVE CAPACITY

A second myth deals with the steady decline in mental ability. A young adult brain contains about 12 billion neurons (the cells which transmit nerve impulses through the brain system), and each day the adult brain shrinks from the loss of 100,000 neurons (see review, Brody and Vijayashankar, 1977). After decades the shrinkage of these irreplaceable cells adds up to ounces in weight, and the conclusion used to be that this loss paced a steady decline in the function of the human mind. But, as Eisdorfer and Cohen (1980) have pointed out, there has not been a scientific determination of the relationships existing between this loss and performance. They write, "The simplisitc notion of a 1:1 correspondence between anatomic loss and ability has led to the assumption that brain size predicts the level of intelligence. We know that this is false, yet we have believed that computerized axial tomograph (CAT) scans of the cranial cavity could predict the extent of dementia. Only now do we have evidence that this may not be true and that behavioral indices are important for the diagnosis of dementing illness (Nathan, 1978)." There are obvious modifications over the life span in the way a person learns. Some early research, based on cross-sectional analyses of intellectual testing (that is, IQ tests) seemed to show a peak in most cognitive abilities between the late teens and the mid 20s, and from that point on a steady movement downward (Wechsler, 1944).[2] Today these conclusions are challenged by new data which suggest no clear peaking of cognitive abilities during the 21-30 decade (Jarvik et al., 1973; Eisdorfer, 1978a). Honzik and MacFarlane (1973) reported stability between 6 and 40 years. Other findings stress the conclusion that, barring illness or abuse, cognitive stability remains the norm even through the ninth decade (Jarvik et al., 1973; Savage et al., 1975).

Schaie (1970) gives this summary: "From the evidence now accumulating, it appears that the earlier notion of an irreversible decrement model for intelligence can no longer be upheld. Indeed, there is reason to believe that, given a suitably favorable environment, there may be gain in certain intellectual functions into very old age." A consensus is emerging among psychologists that the more accurate statement of cognitive abilities over the life span is that human intelligence is composed of several "intelligences," of which some show a decline with aging and others do not. For example, verbal ability shows little or no lessening with years, but psychomotor-related cognition declines appreciably. In timed IQ tests that reward speed of performance, a 20 year old normally will outpace a 60 year old because he or she has a quicker eye and a quicker hand. Retrieval of information from the recall memory may also be superior in the young mind, but a more mature mind generally has a more finely tuned recognition memory.

In test situations, older persons respond from distinct motives which lead to a common but false interpretation of their cognitive functioning. As Eisdorfer and Cohen (1980: 60) have pointed out, "Cautiousness, fear of failure, and withholding responses are among the characteristics observed in the older adult which may be incorrectly interpreted as 'deficit' behaviors." These same characteristics, they point out, can also be interpreted as part of an "adaptive response repertoire" reflecting different motivation or experience in older persons. They conclude:

> Development is more than adding new skills and subtracting them incrementally, but also involves the organization of abilities. Therefore, it may be unreasonable to assume that changes with aging should be analyzed as simple increases of losses or even as curvilinear change. It is also not appropriate to assume that older persons will exhibit deteriorating cognitive and personality functioning as part of normal aging (during which numerous biological changes occur) [Eisdorfer and Cohen, 1980: 61].

MYTH III: INEVITABLE SENILITY

The fear of becoming senile is the single greatest dread most people have about growing old. It would help ensure a more tranquil approach to the late adult years if common sense were brought to focus on the facts surrounding this subject. To begin with, senility is not an inevitable result of the aging process, nor is it even a disease. *Senility* has become a catchall word to describe diverse conditions arising from different causes, a large number of which are susceptible to successful treatment.

What symptoms characterize what is called, so often incorrectly, *senility*? They include serious forgetfulness, mental confusion, disorientation, and speech difficulties, as well as certain other medical and emotional disturbances in behavior. In our "labeling-prone" culture, old people are sometimes the victims of too-hasty diagnoses which result in their being labeled as senile, with horrible consequences for the duration of their lives. "Thus," as the Public Health Service of the National Institute of Health (1979) warns, "it is imperative that a complete, careful investigation of the source of these symptoms be made so that proper treatment can be initiated." The report goes on:

> Some 100 reversible conditions may mimic a few irreversible brain disorders (such as cerebral arteriosclerosis, senile dementia, and Alzheimer's disease). A minor head injury, a high fever, improper nutrition, or adverse drug reactions, for example, can temporarily interfere with the supply of blood and oxygen to the brain and thus inhibit the normal functioning of extremely sensitive brain cells. If left untreated, such medical emergencies can result in irreparable damage to the brain, and possibly even death.

The true senile population of the United States is relatively small. Estimates are that 15 percent of those 65 to 75 years old and 25 percent of those 75 years and older are senile, an approximate total of four million, or 1 out of 6, of the complete elderly population. According to National Institute of Health statistics, about 60 percent of the just under one million nursing home patients past 65 are senile.

Medical science does not know the cause of senility. Medical researchers have found it difficult to pinpoint the precise nature of the anatomical changes in the brain and almost impossible to correlate these changes with the patient's symptoms and behavior. While we wait for further advances in our knowledge of senility and its causes, we can take satisfaction in what has been accomplished up to now. For instance, only in the past few years has research established that hardening of the arteries (arteriosclerosis) has far less to do with senility than had been believed and that deeper lying causes for it must still be found.

CONCLUSION: THE MEANING OF LONGEVITY

Those who are most successful in planning for the transfer to the late adult years have come to terms with aging itself. They continue to grow but worry not about growing older. Or they may be growing older, but without growing old. Their energy is not wasted in trying to do a rerun of earlier decades. They do not judge successful aging by its resemblance to youth or middle age. They have established a basis for self-worth that does not depend on some earlier peak of economic productivity or social role. They do not pretend that aging is something other than it really is. They do not attempt to disguise the negative realities of aging with some kind of painted mask. While they have left some things behind, they know their years have purchased other things of equal or greater value. They look to the future, not the past. They have bested the temptation to linger on in time as aging playboys and playgirls. Their eyes are ahead upon new goals and new challenges. They have heard what Carl Jung spoke nearly 50 years ago: "A human being would certainly not grow to be 70 or 80 years old if this longevity had no meaning for the species to which he belongs. The afternoon of life must also have a significance of its own and cannot merely be a pitiful appendage to life's morning. . . . Whoever carries over into the afternoon the law of the morning—that is, the aims of nature— must pay for so doing with damage to his soul just as surely as a growing youth who tries to salvage his childish egoism must pay for this mistake with social failure" (Jung, 1933).

Distinctive new tasks lie waiting to be accomplished, especially designed for the afternoon of life. To identify and to prepare for them, while activating the inner resources needed to carry them out, is how mature men and women go about preparing for the transfer and making it effectively.

NOTES

1. The *late adult years* begin at 70. Stevenson (1979) has coined a delightful word to describe two preceding age spans: Middlescence I—30-50; and Middlescence II—50-70 or 75.

2. Commenting on this subject, Kunze has a little fun: "Authorities in the field of the age-intellect relationship appear to be improving with age. Their early studies (a decade or more ago) suggested that the cognitive growth process reversed itself around age 30 and kept dropping slowly from that point on. Not expecting to sharpen their wits with age, they sharpened their pencils, came up with some more sound research designs, and ultimately with better findings—at least for those over 30" (in *Finding a Job: A Resource Book for the Middle-Aged and Retired,* by N. Sprague and H. F. Kuatz, Adelphi University Press, 1978).

REFERENCES

BERG, G. and S. GADOW (1978) "Towards more human meanings of aging," in S. F. Spicker et al. (eds.) Aging and the Elderly: Humanistic Perspectives in Geron- tology. Atlantic Highlands, NJ: Humanities.

BORGATTA, E. and N. G. McCLUSKEY [eds.] (1980) Aging and Society: Current Research and Policy Perspectives. Beverly Hills, CA: Sage.

BRODY, H. and N. VIJAYASHANKAR (1977) "Anatomical changes in the nervous system," in C. Finey and L. Hayflick (eds.) Handbook of the Biology of Aging. New York: Litton.

EICHORN, D. H. (1973) "The Institute of Human Development Studies, Berkeley and Oakland," in L. F. Jarvik et al. (eds.) Intellectual Functioning in Adults. New York: Springer.

EISDORFER, C. (1978a) "Psychophysiologic and cognitive studies in the aged," in G. Usdin and C. K. Hofling (eds.) Aging: The Process and the People. New York: Brunner/Mazel.

――― (1978b) "Societal responses to aging: some possible consequences," in L. F. Jarvik (ed.) Aging into the Twenty-First Century. New York: Gardner.

――― (1971) "Background and theories of aging," in G. Maddox (ed.) The Future of Aging and the Aged. Atlanta: SPNA Foundation Seminar Books.

――― and D. COHEN (1980) "The issue of biological and psychological deficits," in E. F. Borgatta and N. G. McCluskey (eds.) Aging and Society: Current Research and Policy Perspectives. Beverly Hills, CA: Sage.

ENTINE, A. (1977) "Counseling for mid-life and beyond." Presented at the Conference on Mid-Life Planning, CASE Center for Gerontological Studies, City University of New York, December.

FINCH, C. E. (1979) "Perspectives in biomedical research on aging." Contribution No. 44 from the Neurobiology Laboratory of the Andrus Gerontology Center, excerpted in Columbia Journalism Monograph No. 3.

HELANDER, J. (1978) "The richness and poorness of being old in Sweden." Presented at the seminars on Facing an Aging Society: USA and Canada, New York, October.

HICKEY, T., A. KRIESBERG, B. FATULA, and D. HAMEISTER (1975) Retirement Planning: Selected References. University Park, PA: Pennsylvania State University College of Human Development.

HONZIK, M. P. and J. W. McFARLANE (1973) "Personality development and intellectual functioning from 21 months to 40 years," in L. F. Jarvik et al. (eds.) Intellectual Functioning in Adults. New York: Springer.

HUNTER, W. (1978) Preretirement Education Leader's Manual. Ann Arbor: University of Michigan Institute of Gerontology.

JARVIK, L. F., J. E. BLUM, and C. EISDORFER [eds.] (1973) Intellectual Functioning in Adults. New York: Springer.

JUNG, C. (1933) Modern Man in Search of a Soul. New York: Harcourt Brace Jovanovich.

LEVINSON, D. (1978) The Seasons of a Man's Life. New York: Knopf.

MANION, U. V., M. GREENE, H. PYRON, and H. WINKLEVOSS (1969) Preretirement Counseling, Retirement Adjustment and the Older Employee. Eugene: University of Oregon.

MONK, A. [ed.] (1979) The Age of Aging: A Reader in Social Gerontology. Buffalo, NY: Prometheus.

NATHAN, R. J. (1980) "Cerebral atrophy and independence in the elderly." Presented at the meeting of the American Psychiatric Association, Atlanta, Georgia, May.

National Institute of Health (1979) Special Report on Aging: 1979. Washington, DC: Government Printing Office.

PETERSON, D. and C. BOLTON (1980) Gerontology Instruction in Higher Education. New York: Springer.

SAVAGE, R. D., P. G. BRITTON, N. BOLTON, and E. H. HALL (1975) Intellectual Functioning in the Aged. New York: Harper & Row.

SCHAIE, K. W. (1970) "A reinterpretation of age-related changes in cognitive structure and functioning," in L. R. Goulet and P. B. Baltes (eds.) Lifespan Developmental Psychology: Research and Theory. New York: Academic.

SHEEHY, G. (1976) Passages: Predictable Crises of Adult Life. New York: Dutton.

STEVENSON, J. (1979) Issues and Crises During Middlescence. Englewood Cliffs, NJ: Prentice-Hall.

STREIB, G. and C. SCHNEIDER (1971) Retirement in American Society. New York: Cornell University Press.

WECHSLER, D. (1944) The Measurement of Adult Intelligence. Baltimore, MD: Williams and Wilkens.

5

WHAT HAPPENED TO
RETIREMENT PLANNING IN THE 1970s?

Robert C. Atchley

Retirement planning is concerned with easing the transition to retirement and with putting retirement on a sound footing with respect to finances, health, and lifestyle. The transition to retirement is affected by employers' retirement policies, how the individual comes to be retired, and the extent to which he or she can approach retirement with confidence. Successful retirement depends on having met the financial, physical, and psychological prerequisites.

Though various approaches to retirement planning have emerged over the past decade, it is important to be open to a reexamination of several issues that have arisen from our experience with retirement planning. The first issue is just how much is known about the prevalence of retirement planning, who offers programs, what formats they take, who participates, and the several categories of people who are underserved. Another issue is what prevails now in terms of program features, approaches, and assumptions. A third issue is what employees want from retirement planning, and, finally, this chapter will take a look at where we need to go.

WHAT DO WE REALLY KNOW?

Despite the growing number of retirement planning programs offered by industry, government, educational institutions, and other organizations, it appears that only 5 percent to 10 percent of the population approaching retirement participates, and that this proportion has not increased much over the past 20 years (see Addendum). Although the proportion may have increased markedly among large industrial and government employers, any gains have been offset by a decline in industrial employment as a proportion of the total and by the fact that the fastest growing sectors of the economy—service and local government—are far behind in terms of providing retirement planning programs. Estimates of prevalence based on recent surveys of companies (O'Meara, 1977; Research and Forecasts, Inc., 1979) range from 23 percent to 37 percent and estimates of the percentage that offers more than pension and health insurance information range from 6 to 29 percent. One difficulty with these estimates is that response rates for the surveys have generally been below 40 percent. And the higher the response rate, the lower the estimate of prevalence. Common sense suggests that employers who do not respond to surveys on retirement planning are more likely to be those who offer no programs.

It is noteworthy that neither Parnes National Longitudinal Studies nor the Social Security Retirement History Survey have included questions on the prevalence of retirement planning. This is unfortunate since it would be useful to be able to examine the long-term effects of planning for retirement. A random community sample of adults age 50 or over was asked if they had either participated or had access to a retirement planning program. Only 4 percent responded affirmatively.

PROGRAM FEATURES, APPROACHES, AND ASSUMPTIONS

The overwhelming majority of retirement planning programs are offered by employers who provide private pensions and retirement fringe benefits to their employees. The Retirement History Survey found that in the private sector only 49 percent of men and 21 percent of women approaching retirement age were covered by private pensions. By contrast, about 80 percent of government employees are covered by job-related pensions. Even among large corporations retirement planning programs are uneven. The reason for this is that retirement planning is seen as a *local* labor relations or personnel matter, largely optional with local management. Government programs are also quite variable. Thus, in both the private and public sectors, retirement planning is seen as a "middle management" issue that does not require a centralized, coordinated effort. This is a good indicator of the low priority attached to retirement planning by even the best employers.

Retirement planning programs offered by local colleges and universities by senior centers, and other organizations serving the entire community are much less prevalent than employer-operated programs. Yet these programs have the potential, most of it still to be realized, of serving several categories of people who are not being served at all by employer programs.

To a sizable proportion of employers, providing information on social security, Medicare, pension benefits and options, and supplemental medical benefits on a one-to-one basis is all that is necessary. This type of approach assumes that the employer's responsibility ends with informing employees as to what benefits they will receive. Planning for retirement is seen as an individual responsibility. Other employers assume that employees want and need assistance in planning for retirement. These employers usually offer comprehensive programs that cover a variety of issues. Over 90 percent of employers surveyed by the Research and Forecasts Study (1979) agreed that employers had at least a moderate degree of responsibility to assist employees in preparing for retirement. Over 90 percent of *employees* in a recent survey (Atchley et al., 1978) felt that employers should provide assistance and over 90 percent felt that not enough assistance was currently available to them. Thus, it would appear that comprehensive programs are more in line with what both employers and employees see as the need. Yet right now limited approaches outnumber comprehensive approaches by about two to one.

WHAT THE EMPLOYEE WANTS

About half of retirement planning is handled by in-house staff on a one-to-one counseling basis. Yet Kasschau (1974) concluded that group programs oriented around providing information and developing skills were more in tune with what employees needed and wanted. Among employers that do group programs, about half use in-house staff and in-house programs and the other half use outside resources. Programs developed most recently are especially likely to utilize materials prepared by professionals and purchased by the employer. There are at least a dozen prepackaged programs available and there is considerable overlap in the topics covered and approach to each topic.

Those who currently participate in retirement planning programs are very often those who are already oriented around planning for the future. Many have already taken concrete steps to plan for retirement. They tend to be relatively well-off in terms of anticipated retirement income, health, and number of activities. One paradox is that those who are approaching retirement with little prospect for adequate retirement income are those who need to plan for retirement the most and are the least likely to do it. Likewise, those for whom retirement is health-related are less likely to plan. Women, people who have had unsteady employment, those who arrive at retirement after long-term unemployment, and people who work in small businesses are also not likely to have had opportunities to participate in retirement planning programs. Another paradox is that while 70 percent of industrial employees see a need for retirement planning and express an interest, only 10 percent follow through.

The picture that emerges thus far is that: (1) retirement planning is not very available; (2) when it is available it is often limited in scope; (3) comprehensive information-oriented programs that utilize prepackaged materials are on the increase; (4) information models fit employees' wants and needs better than counseling models do; and (5) programs have not been very successful in reaching those categories of people who need retirement planning the most.

The difficulties with the current level of effort can be traced to shortsighted and isolated retirement policies of employers. The problem of low rates of participation may be largely due to several faulty perspectives that underlie current programs, even those that are comprehensive.

If employers saw retirement planning programs as a useful tool for implementing their retirement policies, most would offer them. However, right now most employers do not have retirement policies apart from a pension program and sometimes a mandatory retirement age. Most employers do not see retirement policies as a way of *managing* their labor force. They see them mainly as a way of getting rid of undesirable employees. Incentives for early, normal, or late retirement, and partial retirement options are but two examples of retirement policies that can be used to influence the skill and experience mix of the labor force and to influence the pressure on pensions as sources of retirement income.

For example, an aircraft company was faced with the loss of one-third of its most skilled engineers over a ten-year period because its greatest labor force growth had occurred just after World War II. Partial employment allowed the company to retain skilled people who otherwise would have retired fully. Pension incentives for delayed retirement also helped. Likewise, partial employment, with its capacity to grow with inflation, reduces the demand for pension income, which in turn affects employer investment in retirement benefits. In order to be most effective, such policies must be actively promoted among employees, and retirement planning programs are a good place for that promotion.

WHERE WE NEED TO GO

Most retirement programs, even the comprehensive ones, are in a rut. They assume that retirement will be as early as possible and will be total. Seldom is any effort made to examine the value of staying on the job, either for the employer or the employee. Pension and benefit information is generally provided too late to be of value in long-range planning and long-range planning is the only way to secure adequate retirement income. Most programs, especially those that use one-to-one interviews, support a passive stance toward the employment/retirement decision. It is simply assumed that retirement is for the best and will occur. There is no focused dialogue between the employee and those with whom he or she works most closely. Most employers are entirely too permissive in letting employees delay confronting the issue. They should require their employees to at least be *aware* of the major decisions to be made about the timing of retirement and the financing of it. The appeal used to attract employees to retirement planning programs still too often stresses avoiding problems of social adjustment rather than the hard facts about economic issues. This is self-defeating, because most employees do not anticipate social adjustment problems in retirement. They do anticipate financial problems.

Without question, financial planning is the number one priority among workers. More than two-thirds see a need for planning in this area (Fitzpatrick, 1978). Retirement planning programs will attract hard-to-get people only to the extent that they offer genuinely helpful information and skills in this area.

Effective retirement financial planning requires a threefold approach. First, in most cases the planner must recognize that income will probably drop considerably no matter what steps are taken. This means that planning has to center around getting along with less money. Fortunately, most retirees find that they are able to do this. Second, the planner needs accurate, *unbiased* information on alternative ways to generate retirement income. Finally, the planner needs to consider ways to minimize demand on retirement income. Carrying less cash to discourage impulse buying and eliminating shopping as a leisure pursuit are examples of steps that could be considered.

Programs sometimes turn off participants by confusing retirement with aging. Most people retire long before physical aging becomes a serious limitation. Thus, most of the information on health, finances, and lifestyle should be that which would be useful to any middle-aged adult.

The information and skills that people find useful in planning for retirement are neither complicated nor mysterious. They all revolve around "how to" questions:

- how to get the best return on their assets
- how to get the most from their consumer dollars
- how to locate employment opportunities

- how to maintain good health
- how to identify new opportunities to participate
- how to handle legal issues, such as liquidating assets to provide income, transferring property, or making a will
- how to decide where to live in retirement

Because most of these "how to's" involve a lot of individual decision making, the best approach is usually to provide general background information on the issue and relatively structured concrete tasks that will lead people through the information-gathering and decision-making processes. This most important process element is too often left to the participant's imagination in current programs. An example of a program that employs a process approach is the recently developed NCOA-Industry Consortium Retirement Planning Program (Fitzpatrick, 1979). This program was developed around the idea of performance objectives such as inventorying financial papers, developing an estimate of retirement income compared to expenses, or learning to use basic measures to evaluate savings or investment alternatives.

Finally, retirement planning programs rise and fall depending on the *people* who run them. Effective trainers themselves must be well trained. A weekend workshop won't do.

Retirement planning is a low priority among most employers. One advantage of presenting retirement planning programs as a personnel management tool as well as a service to employees is that employers may be more willing to support adequate training of people to do the job. It is also important that the training be sound. In the past several years, training workshops have become a big business. And retirement planning is one of the areas where too many workshops are being given by people who have spent too little time learning about retirement in the broad sense. To offer sound retirement planning programs requires a thorough understanding of what retirement is and is not, how it affects employers' operations, how it affects people's lives, what employees' concerns are, and what employees need to know. Of course, it is possible to learn these things by experience, but there is literature available that can help accelerate the process and well-trained trainers should be familiar with it. Right now they usually are not.

Well-trained trainers also need to be sensitive to the human issues involved. That is, they need to be sensitive, warm people who can operate on a model of assisting the capable rather than a model of helping the helpless. In short, they need a respect and positive regard for the people they will be training.

Where do we go from here? First, we need to be more aggressive in prodding workers to think about long-range financial planning. For example, a checklist of important retirement planning steps could be distributed to all employees. This could be done by employers, unions, or even the Social Security Administration. And it could be done at an early enough age to possibly do some good. The point is to *sensitize* people to the issues. Because employers may be reluctant to do this for fear of increasing pension demands, some sort of public approach may be needed. Just getting the point across about the impact of inflation on nonindexed pensions could have a substantial effect. For example, when one realizes that 18 percent inflation would cut a nonindexed pension in *half* in just five years, that has to have a real impact!

Second, we need widespread availability of partial retirement options in the future. Otherwise there will not be much in the way of resources to plan with. Partial retirement will increase the flow of cash to support social security and at the same time moderate the demand for pension income. We are going to have to handle the population explosion of older adults. We need to think about discussing these issues in retirement planning programs.

Third, we need to do better evaluations of programs in order to be able to demonstrate their results. This is another virtue of the performance objectives approach—industry consortia such as the NCOA program referred to earlier. It is a lot easier to demonstrate that someone learned how to do a retirement income profile than it is to show that his or her morale or productivity went up. This is an important tool in being able to sell retirement planning to employers.

Fourth, we need to pay more attention to what is keeping people away. We all have our hunches about why participation rates are low. But until someone starts trying to find out why systematically and starts experimenting with new approaches, we are going to continue aiming in the dark.

ADDENDUM

As Professor Atchley points out in the preceding pages, the response rates for surveys made of corporate retirement preparation programs have generally been below 40 percent. The editors include here for the record some detailed information on the extent of these programs, acknowledging the limitations of the data.

PREVALENCE OF RETIREMENT PLANNING PROGRAMS

In 1959, the California Institute of Technology studied what 756 companies were doing to aid employees during the transition to retirement. Some 161 (39 percent) of the 415 responding firms indicated some type of program, with 136 of them offering a comprehensive program which was defined by the researchers as one combining the social, psychological, and financial aspects of preparation. The findings of this survey, however, differ from later surveys in that no other study found so many comprehensive programs.

The Conference Board has made several studies on a nationwide basis. Their 1955 survey showed 212 (65 percent) of 327 companies involved in preretirement activity, but only 34 would qualify as formal or well-organized programs. A study in 1964 by the same group found that 633 (65 percent) of the 974 respondent companies gave some kind of retirement assistance, but over one-half, or 344, indicated that the program was limited to an explanation of company benefits and social security. In 1975 the University of Michigan and Wayne State University studied what *Fortune*'s 500 largest corporations were doing in preretirement programming. Only 172 companies collaborated, but the findings were consistent with those of earlier surveys: Only 43 (25 percent) had anything like a formal program in operation. A 1976 survey by the American Association of Personnel Administrators (AAPA) and Prentice-Hall indicated that three-quarters of the 269 responding companies had some kind of retirement preparation programs in operation, but the latest survey conducted by the Conference Board, in 1974, best tells the story of the somber state of preretirement planning in the corporate world. The survey of 800 companies indicates that, as far as preretirement assistance goes:

(1) 96 (12 percent) offer none at all;
(2) 371 (53 percent) give no more than bare-boned financial data—the amount of income retiring employees will receive from the company and from social security and the payment options open to them;
(3) 170 (24 percent) add basic health information—Medicare coverage and any further medical benefits available from the company;
(4) 60 (8 percent) add written counseling—special handbooks or subscriptions to publications prepared by outside professionals; and
(5) 103 (15 percent) add personal counseling—individual or group advice in one or more of 7 possible retirement problem areas: financial planning, health, housing, lifestyle adjustments, legal matters, second careers, or use of leisure (O'Meara, 1977).

Do America's citadels of learning and repositories of wisdom have any better record in offering preretirement planning for their own people? The Educational Research Division of the Teachers Insurance and Annuity Association (TIAA), sponsors of the nation's largest retirement and annuity program for university and college personnel, set out to find an answer. They found that "just four percent (96) of the 2,210 responding institutions had a formal program to help employees prepare for retirement" (Mulanaphy, 1978). Of the institutions surveyed, 7 had been in the business for over 10 years, 66 had operated programs for less than 5 years, and 44 for less than 2 years.

Two decades of surveys establish that at least interest has grown among corporations and institutions of higher learning, but that their preretirement programs remain generally superficial and markedly uneven in quality. Relatively few go beyond an explanation of the company pension plan and accompanying health benefits. In fairness to the corporate world and the university world, however, it should be admitted that the question of who is responsible for preretirement planning remains very much an unresolved problem in the United States.

—The Editors

REFERENCES

ATCHLEY, R. C. (1980) The Social Forces in Later Life. Belmont, CA: Wadsworth.
——— (1978) "Retirement preparation for women," pp. 126-139 in Women in Midlife—Security and Fulfillment. Washington, DC: House Select Committee on Aging.
FITZPATRICK, E. W. (1980) "An introduction to NCOA's retirement planning program." Aging and Work 3, 1: 20-26.
——— (1979) "Evaluating a new retirement planning program—results with hourly workers." Aging and Work 2, 2: 87-94.
——— (1978) "An industry consortium approach to retirement planning—a new program." Aging and Work 1, 3: 181-188.
KASSCHAU, P. L. (1974) "Reevaluating the need for retirement preparation programs." Industrial Gerontology 1: 42-59.
MULANAPHY, J. M. (1978) Retirement Preparation in Higher Education. New York: TIAA-CREF.
O'MEARA, J. R. (1977) Retirement: Reward or Rejection? New York: Conference Board.
REICH, M. H. (1977) "Group preretirement education programs: whither the proliferation?" Industrial Gerontology 4: 29-43.
Research and Forecasts, Inc. (1979) Retirement Preparation: Growing Corporate Involvement. New York: Author.

6

A QUALITY OF LIFE FRAMEWORK

Abraham Monk

PRERETIREMENT PROGRAMS AT A CROSSROAD

Studies testing the effectiveness of early preretirement preparation programs rendered moderately favorable conclusions. Those programs apparently succeeded in easing the transition from work to retirement, which is generally assumed to be painful or even traumatic. Significant relationships were thus statistically established between participation in programs and successful retirement variables—favorable attitudes and acceptance of retirement, sound financial plans, lifestyle changes, development of leisure habits, and so on.

It is important, however, to consider the possibility of selective bias in those research findings of the 60s and 70s. As Kasschau (1974), Heidbreder (1972), and others have suggested, those who are most likely to experience problems with the impending reality of retirement may be the least likely to plan for it, while those who do participate in planning may already be mindful and accepting of this new stage in life.

Comparative program evaluations are beginning to shed light on the debate surrounding the relative effectiveness of various program modalities. Kasschau (1974) has classified programs in terms of a "planning" or a "counseling-adjustment approach"; Monk (1979), in turn, identified 5 prevailing conceptual models. Bolton (1976) assessed a humanistic-affective perspective; Glamser and DeJong (1975) compared a group discussion model to an individual instruction model using an experimental-control design; and Boyack and Tiberi (1975) contrasted 3 approaches—a group counseling model, a lecture discussion model, and an information media model. Research to date on program content and delivery techniques implies that a variety of methods are effective on different outcome measures related to the major goals of preretirement planning. Programs must be comprehensive in scope, individualized, and possibly reinforced through multiple program activities. A new focus is beginning to emerge on the retirement needs of special populations, defined in terms of socioeconomic levels, educational attainment, ethnic background, environmental conditions, and occupational identification. A new field of inquiry in this sense is related to recent changes in the patterns of labor force participation of women. Contrary to popular belief, recent research has shown that women find adjustment to retirement as difficult as men do (Streib and Schneider, 1971; Atchley, 1976).

Preretirement preparation programs are at a historical crossroad. The demands for greater attention to the individual and to a universe of different subgroups seem to add to the impatience for evidence of successful outcomes. Furthermore, preretirement preparation programs are also expected to pay more attention to a broader spectrum of life events, stretched over more years of the human life span rather than limited to the confines of the retirement stage. New sets of educational and counseling resources will have to be tested as potential methodologies for a new "generation" of preretirement preparation programs. Examined in this chapter are four such resources: the concepts of (1) lifelong learning, (2) andragogy, (3) quality of life, and (4) intergenerational exchange.

LIFELONG LEARNING

Lifelong learning is postulated as a necessary prescription for survival in a society characterized by critical shifts in national and community priorities, the sudden emergence of new social problems and conditions, and the exponential growth of knowledge.

People can no longer anticipate living their lives in the same world into which they were born. The imbalance between social conditions, mores, and technological advances requires repeated adaptations throughout an individual's lifetime. The premises that formal education is reserved for the young only and that education received early in life is enough to carry one through a lifetime are perilous misconceptions for which people may pay dearly in later years. However, "lifelong learning," is a catchall label that has not yet been properly defined. It usually includes:

(1) a form of continuous self-learning, without formal structures, curricular prerequisites, or conventional faculties, which, consequently, represents a shift away from educational institutions toward informal learning in the community;
(2) a search of life options adequate to the new life conditions;
(3) a cooperative process between instructor or counselor and students where the instructor acts more as a resource person;
(4) an orientation toward life skills as linked to the changing environments and a collaboration between factory or business setting and community; and
(5) the learning of new work patterns in later life that attend to needs of part-time work, second careers, changing work styles, and increased leisure time.

Preretirement programs would then lose their distinctiveness as specialized forms of anticipatory socialization if subsumed under "lifelong learning." They would become part of a "learning society," one where learning will become an ultimate objective, in its own right, and as an ingrained lifestyle modality.

ANDRAGOGY

Andragogy is the second new method under consideration. It has emerged in recent years as a new educational method for adults. It is usually defined as the art and science of leading adult learning. While it is often confounded with "lifelong learning," and the two overlap to a large degree, they are different in scope. Andragogy is a specific methodology, a guided process within the broader spectrum of "lifelong learning." The andragogical method is based on interpersonal group work, in a self-directing, adult learning environment. The life experiences of all participants are valued as resources for learning, and mutual helping relationships are encouraged in an atmosphere of acceptance. Learning tasks are defined with a "here and now" orientation, as an internal process of ego involvement in self-directed inquiry. One of the major liabilities of current preretirement programs is that they constitute "one shot" operations. An andragogical approach provides instead the opportunity of continuous, ongoing review and updating of personal plans.

Individual participants go through the following sequence: *needs assessment* or identification of personal lags and life problems that require resolution; *competency model building* or analytic inventories of the individual's potential capabilities in different aspects of life. Participants start finding out what they can do, what they would like to do, what the gap is between the two, and what it may take to overcome such a gap. It is assumed that the awareness of a gap between "that which I *can* do and that I *would like* to do" acts as a formidable motivator for individual reeducation and development. As in a management by objectives design, participants ask themselves some basic analytic questions:

- Where am I?
- How did I get here?
- What do I need?
- What do I want?
- What is my state of affairs?
- What am I capable of doing?
- What are my weaknesses?
- What are my strengths?
- What are my opportunities?
- Where do I want to go?
- How can I get there?

A validation procedure tests the confidence of the participants in attaining their objectives. Risks, assumptions, and constraints may be discussed either in the group situation or in the counseling relationship. A "dry run" may simulate the effects of errors, contingencies, and risks. The "dry run" is particularly applicable in the successive reexaminations of the individual's plans or objectives, with the counselor retaining a motivating, stimulating, and coaching role.

QUALITY OF LIFE AND COMMUNITY ORIENTATION

Most preretirement programs are implicitly concerned with the quality of life (QOL). Shorter programs deal with financial and health matters, whereas more comprehensive programs may include changing roles, use of leisure time, and psychological attitudes and adaptions. None, however, has been deliberately designed with an explicit QOL perspective, that is, based on those dimensions of life through which people experience levels of happiness or unhappiness, fulfillment or frustration of value aspirations. QOL concepts entail a normative definition of the "good life," or the better life to which people strive. Toffler (1970) viewed QOL as something that a person achieves when he or she has learned to cope with change.

Having "copability" would prevent future shock and obsolescence. Atkinson and Robinson (1969) write in terms of "amenities," a cluster of variables or meanings the importance of which increases as more and more people populate dense urban regions.

It must be borne in mind that the quality of life concept is basically a subjective one, and it is determined by what people feel they need, value, or believe (NVB). It is this NVB triptych or paradigm that reflects a person's outlook or philosophy as well as his or her life aspirations. Graves et al. (1965) suggested that an NVB change requires three conditions:

(1) a sense of dissatisfaction with present life;
(2) the mobilization of energies to initiate a restructuring of life circumstances; and
(3) the insight and awareness to know where and how to induce that change.

To the extent that preretirement planning programs enable a person to reach that insight and subsequently encourage a personal change process, they are not only enhancing a person's quality of life, but are also facilitators of personal growth.

The QOL concept has been initially influenced by ecological variables, as it tended to include environmental qualitative characteristics such as pleasant surroundings, clean air, good transportation, shelter, open spaces, and so on. A comprehensive category listing of a complex QOL system is the Environmental Evaluation System (EES), developed by the Battelle-Columbus research team (Whitman, 1971), that included ecological, environmental pollution, esthetic, and human interest factors. These categories encompass in turn 17 environmental components and 66 measurable parameters. The environmental pollution category, for instance, comprises the following components: water, air, land, and noise. They are disaggregated into these parameters:

(1) *water pollution:* alga blooms, dissolved oxygen, evaporation, fecal coliforms, nutrients, pesticides, herbicides, Ph, river characteristics, sediment load, stream flow, temperature, dissolved solids, toxic substances, and turbidity
(2) *air pollution:* carbon monoxide, hydrocarbons, particulate matter, photochemicals, and sulfur oxides
(3) *land pollution:* land use and misuse, soil erosion, and soil pollution
(4) *noise pollution:* noise

It is not the purpose here to present the whole EES classification category. The components and parameters outlined above are, however, valid examples of its thoroughness and detail. It is essential to keep in mind that some parameters are more easily quantifiable than others and that it is easier to express objective value levels for environmental pollution than for the human interest category. Furthermore, the recorded experience of application of the EES is limited. This instrument may well constitute a preliminary attempt in the design of a measurable and practical system of environmental indicators. It is most unlikely that a person contemplating his or her impending retirement will inquire about sulfur oxides or alga blooms, but people are becoming increasingly more aware of some of these parameters when considering the best potential environment for their retirement years. It is conceivable that, as the preretirement counselors of the future will foster a greater awareness, they will also provide quality of life information about the objective risks and assets of specific environments.

The Community Analysis Bureau (CAB) of Los Angeles operates upon similar concepts. In the early 70s, they developed a computer technique for evaluating the quality of urban living. It rates each of the city's 65 community areas along the following 20 indicators, which are divided into 4 categories as shown:

(1) *public safety:* malicious false alarms per 100 population, felonies per 100 population, engine companies per 1000 acres, police costs per acre, structural fires per 100 acres;

(2) *education:* dropout rates, percentage of minority enrollment, percentage of voter participation, classroom instruction costs per average daily attendance, mean tenth-grade reading achievement scores;

(3) *housing and neighborhood:* percentage of renter occupancy, high school transiency rate, percentage of public housing, median household rent, percentage of sound housing;

(4) *income production:* percentage of white-collar employment, percentage of families with two breadwinners, percentage of discrimination of income, unemployment rate, median household income.

A subsequent step consisted of the development of a Scientific Urban Matrix (SUM) aimed at describing and assessing the urban blight and its interrelationships for the Los Angeles 65 community areas (Joyce, 1972). Again, it would be too cumbersome to describe how the system operates. It may suffice to mention that it handles over 8 million records in order to give some idea of its real magnitude. Its purpose is to describe the actual condition of each area and to provide a determination of the possible courses of remedial action. Essentially conceived as a program for city survival, it is also a model of data base organization and planning for all urban areas, large or small. Preretirement programs cannot guide individual planning in an environmental vacuum. They simply cannot assume that the environment remains constant and unchanged. Counselors need to find out whether urban analysis methods such as the CAB are in place and what information they are apt to provide to preretirees concerning the quality of their immediate environments.

A QOL orientation thus aims to increase the person's capability to assess the level and quality of those "supports" and "resources." It involves:

(1) an inventory and evaluation of existing services and resources;
(2) determination of patterns of utilization of those resources and satisfaction among the adult retired population;
(3) determination of conceptual designs for filling gaps and deficiencies in existing services and resources;
(4) selection of promising courses of action for implementing those conceptual designs;
(5) establishing action-oriented programs for locality development;
(6) updating the resource file and information and referral service for supports and resources;
(7) monitoring performance of new services;
(8) evaluating impact and suggesting corrective action;
(9) assessing impending threats to the community's QOL; and
(10) determining requirements to meet the threat.

Preretirement programs usually ignore the fact that most trainees will continue residing after retirement in their present communities. They have both an emotional and economic investment in their homes and neighborhoods. Their roots are with the friends and relatives in the area. A few may entertain the idea of relocating, but the majority cannot afford it or dread the thought of being forced to move because of adverse circumstances, such as high crime rates, lack of public transportation, pollution, higher taxes, urban blight, and so on.

However, most preretirement programs seldom venture into environmental, QOL, or community topics beyond a discussion on living arrangements or housing. The latter usually consists of a consideration of upkeep, maintenance, mortgages, condominium versus apartment living, costs of eventual relocation, heating and insulation, energy efficiency, and the like. These are indeed timely and essential issues but they are dealt with on an individual, self-contained level. The broader, systemic relationships to the community and the concerted action for improving communities are largely ignored at present.

INTERGENERATIONAL EXCHANGES

Traditional societies are known to underscore the continuity of generations. They are age-heterogeneous because members of all groups share common interests and provide mutual support. In technologically advanced societies such as ours, the opposite is more likely to occur. Generations are cut off from each other with little or no opportunity to relate beyond superficial exchange. Individuals often find more reliance in their peer (age-homogeneous) groups than in their family groups. Their cleavage is basically one of communication and interaction, although at times it may also carry ideological connotations of value confrontation. Middle-aged people, those approaching retirement, often get caught in the bind of multiple obligations to their own children and to an increasing number of elderly family members. They must begin reconciling dependent relationships, not with just an occasional widowed parent, but possibly with two sets of parents. People in their fifties may therefore soon be faced with the responsibility of taking care of as many as four parents, several grandparents, and their own nonemancipated offspring.

Their preparation for retirement may, therefore, consist of attending to the impending impairments not only of their own aging, but possibly those of two older generations and one younger generation. This is a yeoman's task and it can boggle the mind. It definitely transcends the resources of a single generation and calls for wider community awareness and participation.

Why not test retirement planning programs that bring representatives of community and voluntary agencies, as well as younger people, to participate in community and quality of life workshops? Younger workers and younger community residents may then familiarize themselves with the concerns and needs of the older and middle age groups. By contributing to the enhancement of the group's quality of life, they may learn to shape their own subsequent roles and to prepare a better old age for themselves.

FUTURE CONCERNS FOR PRERETIREMENT PLANNERS

Preretirement programs will indeed reflect the impact of changes in the actual retirement age. The current thrust toward early retirement will not be suddenly stopped by the 1977 amendments to the Age Discrimination in Employment Act (ADEA), which allow for the optional postponement of the mandatory retirement age to 70 years. Yet the early retirement option does not presuppose a workless culture. Many retirees may be engaged in seasonal, part-time, or full-time unreported work. This "clandestine" work by retirees is blamed by some economists for the higher unemployment rates in other segments of the population. It may be on the increase because of the precarious situation of pension plans due to persistent inflation, or to the public concern about social security financing, higher life expectancy, and simply, the rising expectations regarding income adequacy.

Preretirement planners will be confronted with issues such as:

- the relationship between inflationary projections and the performance of pension plans;

- the relative costs of supporting large cohorts of retirees;

- the possible reversal of the early retirement trend and the preference to remain indefinitely in the labor force if given the opportunity;

- variations in the optimal retirement age by occupational groups;

- the degree to which automation, energy costs, and labor-intensive production may impinge upon the age composition of the labor force and consequently affect the retention of older workers;

- the future of Social Security financing; and

- the experimentation with cyclical, rather than the current linear, life plans (education-work-retirement).

In essence, are older workers going to remain longer in the work force, and are work patterns due to change? How will retirement be financed? What models are people projecting for their retirement? When confronting these issues, preretirement programs will be expected to provide guidelines for an enriched life experience. Present kits for basic survival will not suffice.

REFERENCES

ATCHLEY, R. C. (1976) The Sociology of Retirement. Cambridge, MA: Schenkman.

ATKINSON, A. A. and I. M. ROBINSON (1969) "The concept of amenity resources," in H. S. Perlof (ed.) The Quality of the Urban Environment. Washington, DC: Resources for the Future.

BOLTON, C. R. (1976) "Humanistic instruction strategies and retirement education programming." Gerontologist 16, 6: 550-555.

BOYACK, V. L. and D. M. TIBERI (1975) "A study of pre-retirement education." Presented at the Twenty-Eighth Annual Meeting of the Gerontological Society, Louisville, Kentucky, October.

GLAMSER, F. D. and G. F. DeJONG (1975) "The efficacy of pre-retirement preparation programs for industrial workers." Journal of Gerontology 30, 5: 595-600.

GRAVES, C. W., W. I. HUNTLEY, and D. W. LaBIER (1965) "Personality structure and perceptual readiness: an investigation of their relationship to hypothesized levels of human existence." (mimeo)

HEIDBREDER, E. M. (1972) "Factors in retirement adjustment, white collar/blue collar experience." Industrial Gerontology 12: 69-74.

JOYCE, R. (1972) "Systematic measurement of the quality of urban life pre-requisite to management." (mimeo)

KASSCHAU, P. L. (1974) "Re-evaluating the need for retirement preparation pro-grams." Industrial Gerontology 1: 42-59.

MONK, A. (1979) "Pre-retirement planning models: social models for pre-retirement planning," in A. Monk (ed.) The Age of Aging. Buffalo, NY: Prometheus.

STREIB, G. F. and C. J. SCHNEIDER (1971) Retirement in American Society. Ithaca, NY: Cornell University Press.

TOFFLER, A. (1970) Future Shock. New York: Bantam.

WHITMAN, I. L. and staff (1971) "Design of an environmental evaluation system." Batelle Columbus Laboratories, June.

7

RETIREMENT COMMUNITIES

Sheree West
Edgar F. Borgatta

The housing situation of American elderly and those approaching retirement is part of and reflects the national housing situation. The age
structure of the country and steep inflationary pressures in the housing
market are creating acute difficulties in housing for many elderly, but also
offer positive opportunities for others. This chapter will discuss some
general issues in housing policy, but will focus on the location and
relocation decisions of the mature population and current research, policy,
and planning regarding retirement housing.

The demographic situation is combining with a sustained popular desire
for home ownership to create a demand for owner-occupied housing that
is likely to continue through the 1980s and into the 1990s. The baby
boom cohort created a peak in annual net household formation in the
early 70s. At the same time, the proportion of older households has been
growing, with a notable jump in the years 1970-1975 in home ownership
and households headed by single older women (Struyk and Soldo, 1980).

The first year that the percentage of U.S. households aged 65 or over
was greater than the percentage of households under age 30 was
1979/1980. Through the 1980s the number of households aged 65 or over
will grow about 50 percent faster than the number of households aged 30
or less. By 1990, households whose heads are 65 or over will be 26 percent

of the national total, and the proportion will continue rising to 2000 and beyond (Spink, 1980).

As the demand for family-size, single-family houses continues in the 1980s, market forces may make a trade-down in housing attractive to people of retirement age who are living in too-large, family-sized houses (Baer, 1980) and who find their ownership an increasing burden. However, attractive alternative housing must be available in order for this to occur. Financial, tax, and housing supply policies that encourage this turnover of housing from one generation to another would be helpful to both older and younger persons during this expected period of high housing demand (Noto, 1980).

Because of the diversity in economic status and living situation among the elderly, as all classes age, it is important to avoid stereotypes in thinking about retirement housing for the maturing population. Among housing programs and policies in the last decade, HUD-assisted rental housing for the elderly has been very popular and successful for urban apartment dwellers. Approximately 4 percent of those 65 and over live in housing designed for the elderly, with roughly 800,000, or 3 percent, in HUD-assisted public housing or Section 202 projects. However, much of the newly maturing population spent its adult, family-raising years in the suburbs, and that is where they are likely to remain. Their pattern of lifestyles, social contacts, and housing preferences is anchored in suburban patterns. For many people approaching retirement in the 1980s and 1990s, there is little accessible attractive alternative housing. A larger supply of appropriately designed housing within local communities would provide a useful alternative to the frequently too-large empty nest and would add a "pull" to the existing "push" situation.

The location and relocation of older people have begun to be the focus of several large-scale surveys and census data studies. For some time central cities have been recognized as having a high proportion of elderly. In 1975, 32 percent of the elderly lived in central cities. However, due to a dramatic (26.5 percent) increase in the elderly population of suburbs from 1970 to 1975, an equal proportion (32 percent) also lived there. The remaining 36 percent lived in nonmetropolitan areas (Golant, 1977). In 1975, 8 percent of the suburban population was age 65 or more, due primarily to the aging-in-place of the families in the suburbs. The implications of the coming rapid increase in suburban older populations for service planning, local housing and zoning policies, and macrodesign have been little explored, but will need attention (Spink, 1980).

Ownership as a form of tenure continues to be as highly valued by retirees as by other age groups. Of those aged 65 or more, 73 percent are homeowners, compared to 65 percent of the rest of the population. About

78 percent of household heads age 55 to 64 are homeowners (U.S. Bureau of the Census, 1978). Home ownership is maintained by a high proportion even beyond age 75, when approximately 31 percent live alone (Moore and Publicover, 1979). The housing of most older homeowners is not necessarily very valuable. It tends to be modest, to have been built before 1940, and, in urban areas, is often situated in older, declining neighborhoods. An estimated 30 percent of all elderly live in substandard dwellings (Soldo, 1980).

The two most vulnerable elderly groups from the standpoint of housing are low-income urban renters and rural residents. Many homeowners, particularly widows living alone, also experience severe housing pressures. Maintenance, taxes, heating and utility bills, and heavy yard/housekeeping chores make continued living in their own homes difficult.

Older people are often characterized as being reluctant to move. Indeed, compared to other age groups their mobility is relatively low, with estimates of 6 to 9 percent of people over age 65 moving in one year (U.S. Bureau of the Census, 1977; Federal National Mortgage Association, 1979), compared to 19 percent for the population as a whole. The likelihood that people will move gradually decreases after age 45. This aging-in-place contributes more to changing proportions of retirees in an area than does net migration. Nevertheless, the mobility of those of retirement age is not insignificant, and there are clues that it is probably increasing. Even small net changes in local proportions of older residents can have significant service planning implications (Biggar et al., 1980). During one 5-year period (1965-1970), over one-quarter, 28 percent, of Americans age 64 or more moved at least once (Flynn et al., 1979; Golant, 1977). Long and Hansen (1979) found, in their sample of all people who moved between 1973 and 1976, that only 3 percent gave retirement as a reason for moving, but fully 20 percent of households of all ages moving between states were receiving some form of pension income! This suggests that "retirement" is not so much a reason as an *occasion* for relocation, and that many see it as a time for transition to other lifestyles or new careers (Long and Hansen, 1979). Also, becoming eligible for a pension and activating it while intending to be gainfully employed simply may not be retirement but a matter of strategic (imaginative) economic planning.

Most elderly residential moves are local, with only 14 to 16 percent of moves being interstate (Golant, 1977; Longino, 1979; Wiseman, 1980). Interstate older migrants, compared with nonmovers, are more likely to be relatively younger couples, with higher incomes and education, and in better health. Possibly this reflects a concept of more economically secure persons moving to their retirement homes from their occupationally oriented households. As the popular media portrays, Florida and California are the primary receiving states. New York and the Midwestern states are the main sending states (Flynn, 1980). The two periods with relatively higher likelihood of moving appear to reflect two different types of moves in life circumstance and motivation. One small peak associated with retirement is during the period from age 60 to 69, and is more likely to be a longer distance move toward destinations offering climatic, recreational, and scenic amenities (Wiseman, 1980; Barsby and Cox, 1975; Flynn, 1980). The other noticeable mobility period occurs after age 75. Most of these moves are local, and are probably health or assistance related (Golant, 1977; Lawton et al., 1973; Newman, 1976).

The older people most likely to move live in central cities. The suburbs are their preferred destination, although a substantial percentage also go to nonmetropolitan areas (Golant, 1979). Far more elderly movers are renters than homeowners. In the 5 years prior to 1970, only 17 percent of individuals who owned their homes moved, while 51 percent of elderly renters did so (Soldo, 1978). The mobility of owners rises with age, while that of renters falls after age 75 (Golant, 1979), both probably adaptations to declining energy and resources.

WHY PEOPLE MOVE

The few attempts to understand motives and reasons for moving and not moving, as well as for where movers choose to relocate, have revealed the complexity of the psychosocial and economic considerations that are weighed, and the difficulty of making predictions about who will move. Residential moves are usually occasioned by life events and health changes, some of which can be anticipated, even though their timing remains unpredictable. Decline in health is by far the chief reason given for seeking a new residence (Newman, 1976). For example, Newman found in Detroit that 51 percent of respondents considered moving due to a serious disability, and 93 percent of those actually moved, while only 13 percent considered a move at death of a spouse, and 12 percent at retirement.

Lawton et al. (1973) found that even though residents of a badly deteriorated urban neighborhood were highly dissatisfied and wanted to move, actual moving behavior could not be predicted by their attitudes or personal characteristics, except that those with the least economic, social, or psychological resources were least active in seeking new residences. Smith and Hiltner (1975) found that less than 40 percent of the variation in urban location of older people could be accounted for by the social area variables of median value of the housing, distance from urban center, decade of construction, or multiple-family dwelling. In the Long and Hansen (1979) study previously mentioned, the most frequently given reason for moving by people over age 55 was to be closer to family, followed closely by retirement, and then climate. The study did not differentiate between reasons for moving and reasons for choice of destination. Maintenance difficulties and desires for smaller, more convenient residences are strong factors in motivating changes of residence or attracting older movers to different housing (Federal National Mortgage Association, 1979; Sherman, 1971; Urban Systems Research and Engineering, 1976). Many middle-income retirees still prefer single-family houses that they can own, and say that availability of suitable alternative housing is the single largest factor influencing whether they would move (Federal National Mortgage Association, 1979).

Elderly are much more likely to report being satisfied with both dwelling and neighborhood than nonelderly, even when objective indicators of quality are low. Carp (1976) has discussed several reasons that this may be, focusing principally on cognitive dissonance in the face of no available alternatives. Possible reasons for not moving, even when circumstances may make a move seem logical to an external observer, have been suggested by a few researchers, and would be a fruitful avenue for future research. "Preference for the familiar," "nostalgia," "place as identity" (Lawton et al., 1973; Rowles, 1980), and "immobilization effect" (Brody, 1978) have been suggested as possible psychological reasons for not moving; these suggestions should be further explored. A familiar neighborhood is a physical matrix that supports daily routines, social relationships, and identity, and becomes more difficult to leave when physical stamina and other resources may be limited. We do not mean to imply that moving for the sake of moving is desirable and should be expected of most persons. Predictability and stability are more characteristic of humans than change, so possibly the appropriate research emphasis should be on the factors associated with various types of change when they occur.

Many decisions not to move appear to be at least partially rational economics, even if the current home is inappropriately large or difficult to maintain. For example, Blonsky (1975) found that nonmovers into neighborhood senior housing considered the sacrifice of private space in moving into efficiency apartments not worth the potential gains in newness, convenience, and so on. The low cash cost of living "rent free," and federal, state, and local tax policies provide incentives for keeping one's long-time residence (Noto, 1980; Struyk and Soldo, 1980), even if maintenance and repair are not possible.

Given the multifaceted nature of housing and neighborhood satisfaction and what we are realizing about the evolving dynamics of people changing (functional capacity, financial resources) in changing environments (Lawton et al., 1980), considerable careful thought and research will be necessary to understand the complex trade-offs and compromises involved in housing and locational choice for people whose resources are not unlimited. We need to know much more about the timing and the process, the emotional and economic considerations and their weighting, for different groups of older people, as they make location/relocation decisions. The simple typology of amenity, assistance, and return moves (Wiseman, 1980) will probably be considerably elaborated.

Focused studies of less aggregated populations and specific groups in their contexts may help develop our understanding more than some large-scale census data/surveys. For example, Rowles (1980) explored in depth the memories and emotions that anchored long-time residents of a small rural town to familiar places. Henig (1981) focused on the population changes in particular neighborhoods in eleven American cities, and found that net outmigration of retiree households occurred simultaneously with net inmigration of younger professionals. Gentrification was more likely in census tracts with high proportions of retired households, particularly near the business districts. A comparison of the housing considerations and plans of elderly in gentrifying versus declining urban neighborhoods would provide very helpful information.

ALTERNATIVES IN HOUSING

During the 70s a growing awareness of the great diversity of situations of older people accented a need for a much greater diversity of living options, so that people might better choose suitable living arrangements for their needs. The theme of "alternatives to institutionalization" was prevalent in the 70s, and led to exploration and development on a limited scale of several options in the gap between completely independent living and institutional living. This concern and research focused primarily on the needs of the fastest growing segment of the older population, the frail elderly, who often are vulnerable and liable to institutionalization. Possibly this is the group most in need of new living options (Donahue, 1977; Federal Council on Aging, 1978; General Accounting Office, 1979).

Much environmental research at the beginning of the 1970s focused on the effects of larger-scale new rental housing for the elderly. The early research clarified the role of the environmental context—the fabric of housing design and accessible neighborhood services, transportation, and personal social networks—in supporting the independent functioning and well-being of older community residents. Continued integration into informal social networks is an important contributor to morale and well-being (Cantor, 1975; Rosow, 1967). Much of daily life and social involvement is grounded in the physical matrix and perception of a familiar local neighborhood. Persons making plans and choices about housing in retirement may consider that housing design and location can facilitate continued self-reliance and involvement with friends, family, and community activities if resources of health, money, and mobility decline.

For the elderly, housing consists of more than "bricks and mortar." The traditional programmatic separation of shelter provision and service provision is not cost-effective and meets their needs poorly. Minimal support services integrated with housing, whether it is owned homes or special housing for elderly, can effectively allow older individuals to continue reasonably independent living in the community (Carp, 1966, 1975; Donahue, 1977; Gutowski, 1978; General Accounting Office, 1979). On a government agency level, attempts have been made (with varying success) to coordinate the elderly-related programs of HUD, traditionally involved only with housing stock supply, and AoA, which is oriented to provision of services to the elderly. This awareness of the interrelatedness of shelter and service needs for elderly has led in two directions in the last decade—senior citizens' apartments and community-based services.

SENIOR CITIZENS' APARTMENTS

The most widely familiar living alternative for the elderly, which integrates some services, is the larger-scale HUD-assisted housing for elderly. These are newly constructed apartments, plus varying degrees of support services and common spaces, for the relatively well elderly who can live more or less on their own. Typically mid- and high-rise buildings in urban areas, they are either public housing for low-income elderly, or housing for low- to moderate-income elderly, built by nonprofit sponsors. Nonprofit groups, such as churches, unions, and fraternal orders, use Section 202 direct loan financing from HUD at reduced interest rates. All or part of the units are now linked to Section 8 rent subsidies, assuring that at least 20 percent of the residents will be low income, but also allowing an economic mix.

All Section 202 projects are required to provide access to some services, but funding for services is not included in the program. In the view of some observers, this proves to be a major problem. Those projects providing at least group dining facilities, and usually additional services, are called "congregate housing." In a distinctly new development, HUD is sponsoring a demonstration congregate services program in several public housing and Section 202 projects for elderly, where most residents moved in at approximately the same time, functioning independently, but have aged together and, as a group, need somewhat more support services than when they moved in. An awareness of the evolution of changing populations in changing situations is now appearing in discussions of management strategy and service planning (Lawton et al., 1980). It applies to privately built retirement communities as well as to publicly assisted housing for elderly.

Congregate housing attempts to build in, architecturally and programmatically, supports for easy access to others, ease of mobility, support for involvement and activities, and access to services. Congregate housing is also, by its very nature, age-segregated. The projects are a programmatic attempt to create conditions that contribute to positive morale and life satisfaction, in addition to the basic goal of providing decent, affordable housing. Research and evaluations indicate that for the residents these environments appear to contribute to higher morale, activity, social involvement, and even to better health and longevity (Carp, 1966, 1975; Sherwood and Greer, 1973; Lawton and Cohen, 1974; Hochschild, 1978; Lawton et al., 1978; Urban Systems Research and Engineering, 1976).

Apartments for the elderly and congregate housing have been enormously popular, and often have been judged successful. The availability of this package of independence, support, and security seems to tap and reveal a large latent demand, demonstrating a surprising willingness of some elderly to move when the alternatives are attractive and appropriate. Waiting lists for these projects often equal or exceed their total capacity. It has been observed that even an excess of severe unmet housing needs will not necessarily translate into market demand unless the package delivered supports the lifestyles and values of the intended users (Bokser, 1979; Blonsky, 1975). The large number of "overeligible" cases discovered when home care programs have been instituted (Taber et al., 1980) attest to older individuals' determination to stay in their own homes regardless of the hardship when the alternatives seem to be institutions of unknown benevolence.

For what, exactly, is this popularity expressing a demand? Key elements of this success seem to be the low cost (through subsidy) and the essentially residential nature of the package, which allows continuation of independence and involvements with friends and community activities, minimization of maintenance and heavy chore requirements, and—for many a prime concern—security, both from crime and in the simple availability of others nearby. It supports continuity of identity, lifestyle, and independence, and unobtrusively accommodates to developing social, physical, and economic changes.

Recent discussions, however, raise concerns for the long-term costs and equity of Section 8 rental subsidies (General Accounting Office, 1980; Olsen and Rasmussen, 1979). New construction is a costly way to provide housing needs, and many times does not serve the most needy eligible. The reservoir of unmet needs cannot be met entirely with relatively high cost

new construction/rent subsidy programs, and, strategically, building to
meet potential needs could lead to other later problems of dislocation of
resources. Coupled with this has been a new awareness of the needs of
low-income elderly homeowners and a stated desire to preserve their
housing stock and neighborhoods.

The enormous popularity of the senior housing and services package
may stimulate private market suppliers to rise to the middle-income
demand if the interest rate/construction climate experienced in 1980-1981
improves. The private sector already is responding to some of this demand
by building retirement communities for upper-middle-income households
in nonmetropolitan areas featuring climatic and recreational amenities.
Attention to this market in local communities might also prove profitable,
but the situation is not likely to develop new housing unless the economic
realities become attractive to developers. In general, developers respond to
demand, sometimes real and sometimes imagined. The market that is least
likely to be convincing as an attraction is that for persons just well enough
off to be disqualified for subsidies and not well enough off to be able to
purchase—particularly in a market in which inflation has made new construction look exhorbitant in comparison to older concepts of the value of
the dollar. Possibly, for a broad band of persons between the poor and the
well-to-do, modest retirement housing may not be accessible as an alternative.

COMMUNITY-BASED SERVICES

Programs of services to community-dwelling older adults have also been
developed, including Meals-on-Wheels, friendly visitors, chore and home-
maker/home health aides, transportation, shopping services. These programs attempt to utilize but not strain natural family supports and existing
social networks. These are, however, still sparsely and unsystematically
available (General Accounting Office, 1979), in spite of attempts to
develop "comprehensive, coordinated community-based systems."

As the research on independently dwelling older people and their
natural social networks has debunked the myth of family abandonment,
increasing attention is turning to ways of supporting the often heroic
efforts that families do make to support their older relatives in the
community. Support and occasional relief for family caretakers, many of
retirement age themselves, are becoming the focus of some research and a
few demonstration programs.

Support for a policy of deploying community-based services to the
elderly has been spurred by the steeply rising costs of institutional medical
care, by findings on the social and psychological benefits for older people
of continued tenure in the community, and by increasing recognition of

demographic trends that will produce a greatly increased older population in the future (Federal Council on Aging, 1978; Soldo, 1978). Such policy has been reflected only partially in the long-term care orientation, but results from several demonstration programs are now coming in (Applebaum et al., 1980; Eggert et al., 1980; Hodgson and Quinn, 1980). They suggest that community-based single-entry service delivery can be structured so that good quality, minimal support services are provided, improving clients' morale, maintaining ability to live and function in the community, reducing hospital and nursing home use, and using personal and family resources without burnout, and at favorable costs compared to more conventional, fragmented, institution-centered health services. Principal concerns recently have been with the appropriate mix and most needed services, and with appropriate delivery mechanisms for the tremendous variety of situations in which elderly Americans live. These impressions fit common sense, but will surely be examined in more detailed research in the immediate future.

EVOLVING DIRECTIONS

Policy discussion in the areas of health and long-term care, services, and housing generally have such common goals as: to allow older adults to preserve maximum independence and autonomy, and to live in their own homes in the community as long as feasible. Additional goals are directed to providing the services needed to support continued self-reliant functioning without creating unnecessary dependency; to ease the financial burden of rising living costs; and to support maintenance of integration into existing social networks.

Recent discussions emphasize development of social, in addition to medical, supports for frail elderly who may have difficulty living on their own due to chronic health problems, low incomes, reduced mobility, social isolation, or fear of crime. Programs to strengthen family and informal social support of the elderly, and to develop coordinated, preventive, community-based services are receiving more attention and have been worked into more demonstrations. Larger-scale housing for elderly is designed, through location, architecture, and programming, to support needs for easy access to other people, shopping, and services, and needs for activity and involvement.

However, very few people live either in retirement communities or housing for elderly. They already live in communities, and usually express a desire to stay there. What policy and program directions are evolving that may support those wishes? Planning and policy efforts in housing and services appear to be moving toward finer grained, local, smaller-scale efforts to support the environmental/social fabric of older people, and to support their own efforts to create a suitable housing situation.

Given the high costs of new construction and the clear wish of older people to remain in their own homes, attention is turning to potential means of serving older people where they live, in the community. Ways of integrating minimal support services with this in-place housing, and of creating affordable housing units out of existing structures in local communities are being explored. Several interesting new ideas or programs which would provide additional living options in the community where people live without relying on new construction, are being tried in different localities. Some of these are outlined below.

(1) Home Maintenance and Repair Assistance. A constellation of findings prompt Struyk and Soldo (1980) and others to suggest a program of HUD-assisted home maintenance and repair for low-income older homeowners, particularly aimed at neighborhoods with high concentrations of low-income elderly in older housing stock. Although 73 percent of the elderly are homeowners, until recently no HUD assistance programs were for homeowners. Many elderly homeowners live in older, central-city urban neighborhoods which are vulnerable to deterioration, or in small rural towns where housing is likely to be substandard (Atchley and Miller, 1979). Although, as a group, older homeowners have substantially higher incomes than renters, this in no way suggests that they are all in good condition economically. More than half live in homes built before 1940, as we noted earlier. Pressed by steeply rising costs for food, fuel, and medical expenses, many homeowners with low incomes find it necessary to defer maintenance, and thus the housing deteriorates. Since older urban neighborhoods have high percentages of old homeowners, this can have the cumulative consequence of a neighborhood decline. Maintenance is a burden, both physically and financially. Demonstrations are now under way in 7 U.S. cities of different ways to deliver a home repair program. Some operate on the basis of cash grants or low-interest loans and technical assistance. This is a relatively low-cost type of program, which spreads resources over a number of households. It is one of the few housing programs which specifically tries to improve the neighborhoods of the elderly and attempts to be responsive to their desire to stay in their own homes. It may also help prevent displacement of elderly in urban neighborhoods in which gentrification is occurring.

This raises the question of whether it is reasonable to provide further incentives for older people to remain in their own homes even when they are largely overhoused, their tax and fuel bills are high, and they may have difficult access to others and to services. However, the programs we just described are not really incentives, since older homeowners have already demonstrated that, for the most part, they are committed to staying in their own residences.

We must look very closely at the financial, emotional, and physical elements that contribute to the oft-cited desire of elderly to remain in their own homes. Is it possible that for many a large component of that wish is a reflection of a very constricted set of acceptable alternatives? Certainly capacity to manage one's own home is a cultural symbol of autonomy and independence (Lee, 1959), both for youthful and older Americans. But is a commitment to maintaining that independence necessarily a commitment to the same residence? For some, no doubt, it is. But there is much we do not know about what is involved in this orientation. In the presence of other alternatives that particular commitment might to some extent disappear.

(2) Senior Home Conversions. Some homeowners in large older houses have created apartments in them, sometimes with the aid of low- or no-interest loans and technical assistance from a local housing authority (Fox, 1979). These apartments give an income resource, potential companionship and security, with adequate privacy, and create additional dwelling units of useful size out of existing housing stock. Such conversions, as well as the informal taking-in of boarders, have occurred for some time as homeowners have tried to cope with rising operating expenses and continue to maintain their homes (Tri-State Regional Planning Commission, 1981). An estimated 300,000 rental units annually have been created within single-family homes in the last 5 years (Hughes, 1981).

Local communities now wrestle with zoning and regulatory tangles, finding that attempts to be too stringent simply result in homeowners not reporting their conversions. These conversions supply additional rental housing for smaller households in local communities, usually for moderate-income or low-income rentals. Resistance to such conversions stems from a concern for preserving the single-family character of a neighborhood, and from concern that conversions may not conform to city building codes, not provide for parking, and so on. An example of changing attitudes to such conversions is reported in a Seattle *Times* editorial (July 13, 1981). Seattle is considering a proposal for standards and a code to cover these conversions. Interestingly, in that area the conversions are known as "mother-in-law" apartments, pointing to the fact that the conversions serve the senior tenants as well as the landlords, who may be young or seniors. The principle is general, however, that is being explored. With more small family units, many of which are older persons living alone or in couples, more small rental units at modest cost are required. Conversion of oversized older housing is one potential source.

(3) Shared Housing. Some people are rethinking the meanings of privacy and social participation, and more actively planning to include both in the second part of their lives. Often they are still working, and may have adequate financial resources, but are anticipating changes in their household/family composition, health, or finances. Just as senior centers do not appeal to many senior citizens, the conventional leisure retirement communities in resort areas do not appeal to some of these people. Their aim is to create a meaningful and supportive living situation with others who share common values and interests while they have the income, health, and energy to commit to the process.

The results take different forms. Two or three older women, each of whom has a small nest egg, pool their resources to buy an urban townhouse. Single parents in their early 40s, couples anticipating the "empty nest" stage or planning for retirement, mature singles who are no longer part of a couple, buy a house together in the suburbs or the country. The groups we have seen initiating these types of plans seem not to be utopian schemers, but prudent, reflective people seeking pragmatic resolutions to some anticipated problems. Banks are becoming more accustomed to receiving mortgage applications from unrelated people pooling their resources and credit; some real estate developers are responding to this market by building homes with two master bedrooms to allow more privacy and equal sharing of resources by such households (Kennedy, 1981).

Other versions of shared housing have been developed within the last six to eight years, usually by nonprofit local community service organizations. Consistent with the recent focus on developing living options oriented to social more than to medical needs, these shared living arrangements often serve somewhat older elderly, who cannot live alone or do not wish to. Typically, two or three people share an apartment, or five to twelve people share a larger house. Some supportive services (such as heavy housekeeping chores, cooking, transportation) can be provided if they are needed by the residents.

Several different models have been developed. Some aim primarily to reduce housing cost and improve the quality of housing for relatively well, independently functioning elderly. Some focus on the potential for companionship and mutual aid, even using the metaphor of the "family" for those primary group aims. A few, offering more services, explicitly consider shared housing an alternative to institutionalization. The simplest and least costly model for a sponsor to develop is a "matching service," or clearinghouse, in which individuals who have space to offer in their own homes and others who need places to live are screened and helped to make initial contact, in order to work out their own arrangements for sharing.

Shared housing seems to offer several advantages: In an era of steep inflation in food, fuel, taxes, and rental costs, it offers relief from economic pressures. It is one way to avoid the isolation that may develop with mobility restrictions or loss of members of a social network. It provides a vehicle for receiving the services needed for continued community living in a small-scale, domestic setting. The evaluation studies available on particular models of shared housing indicate that it can have significant positive impact on residents' well-being, in terms of better perceived health, more activities participation, improved morale and security, and more close friends (Brody et al., 1975; Brody, 1978; Streib and Hilker, 1980; Van Dyck and Breslow, 1978).

Several advantages improve its feasibility for the sponsor as well. Because of its small scale and use of existing housing stock, it requires less capital outlay and shorter planning and organizational time compared with larger government-subsidized housing projects. A small organization can serve its local community, even where the numbers of people to be served and available staff are not large.

There is evidence of gathering momentum in willingness of agencies, local housing authorities, and state social service departments to consider and sponsor some form of shared housing. Some associated policy and planning issues are being discussed. At present, no federal programs support such projects, but many sponsors feel there is little need for governmental involvement. One policy question is whether low-income people receiving SSI or food stamp benefits should be penalized for living in shared housing by the disincentives in program regulations. There can be difficulties with local restrictive zoning codes, but these too have been surmounted. In some locales, sponsored shared households have been declared *legal* families by the court, city council, or state legislature for zoning purposes. Of course, a common question is whether such forms of cooperative living suit the American penchant for privacy and individualistic independence. This chapter's first author is currently studying the strategies developed in these sponsored shared living arrangements to manage sharing of the household and to ensure sufficient privacy for residents.

(4) Reverse Annuity Mortgages. A combination of substantial house values and the absence of mortgage indebtedness places a portion of the elderly in a strong asset position. About 4 million elderly households, over 50 percent of all elderly homeowners, own houses valued over $25,000 free and clear of a mortgage. The capital gains exclusion of up to $125,000 on the sale of a home by persons over age 55, intended to encourage intergenerational turnover of family-sized housing, is one way for homeowners to realize income from this asset. Reverse annuity mortgages allow

older homeowners with low incomes but assets in accumulated home equity to tap that resource for income without having to sell their homes and without receiving a subsidy.

Equal monthly payments are made by financial institutions to the homeowner, as a loan or annuity against the equity in the house. In the more common and more acceptable version, no repayment of this loan is expected until the property changes hands. In a lifetime annuity, probably the most satisfactory version, the household receives an annuity based on the value of the property and the life expectancy of the entire household. The annuity income is usually modest. For example, a widow aged 70, with a $20,000 equity base estimate for a mortgage based on the appraisal of her house and life expectancy, would receive a $42 per month payment for the rest of her occupancy of the house with no repayments (Struyk and Soldo, 1980). HUD would be involved only as insurer if the household members outlive the actuarial expectancy or the asset value of the house is altered unfavorably. When the house changes hands, a lump sum settlement is made to the lending institution and to survivors or to the household, who receive the remaining reserves after the loan is repaid.

Reverse annuity mortgages may be one way for a homeowner to postpone some changes in lifestyle. Home maintenance may be facilitated since there is increased income, and preserving the housing stock raises the potential mortgage value. Such an approach may be useful as part of a plan to defer a move until health changes require an assistance move.

Although reverse annuity mortgages seem to offer some potential, many questions need to be explored in demonstrations before they are widely implemented. Will homeowners be reluctant to give up the "free and clear" status of their homes for what may appear to be a very small amount of additional income? Some may have strong wishes to leave assets to children. One suggestion might be, to avoid the involvement of financial institutions and loss of assets to interest, obviously, is that children or other potential heirs could make modest monthly payments to parents, structured as loans or direct payments for equity. Informally and formally such arrangements have always existed, but the existence of the new alternative may provide an incentive for more open consideration of such family plans.

Reverse annuity mortgages are not yet widely used, but are increasingly being discussed, with alternative versions proposed to remedy drawbacks and to make them work for lower-income households. However, in a high interest climate, homeowners for whom the yield is substantially reduced are not likely to be enthusiastic. Lenders are likely to be cautious about such arrangements for a number of reasons. From the point of view of lending institutions, they cannot depart from the usual conservatism in lending, so realistic appraisals with large margins for error may make them look as though they are exploitive. Similarly, if lifetime annuities in some average sense are the basis, then some may be expected to survive more and some less than the average. The risks must be understood by the homeowners and their heirs. Possibly the risk could be conceptualized as a purchase and leaseback agreement. Suppose, for example, that someone is willing to buy the property and lease the property back to the former owner. Then the price of the property can be its actual market value at purchase if the lease will be at a rate that will permit a fair yield on the money invested. This is straightforward, and if this is to be done, presumably the purchase price could be invested by the owner to produce income to pay the lease. (More commonly owners sell to rent smaller quarters elsewhere, of course, provided affordable rental housing is available.) If the former owner is to occupy the sale-leaseback arrangement, then the purchase price and the income that sum would have earned must equal, to simplify, the sale price of the property when the former owner dies. This sum will obviously be much less than the market value of the home when the agreement is made if it is to be a reasonable investment for the buyer.

The Mini-Conference on Housing for the Elderly (October 22-24, 1980, Washington, D.C.) recommended attention to development of mechanisms for home equity conversion into income while retaining residence in the property. The Administration on Aging supports the Home Equity Conversion Project in Madison, Wisconsin, which designed research and development in this area. Interest appears to be moving in this direction as the size of the relevant constituency is recognized. Still, the problem of equity conversion has to be seen in the broader perspective of housing. The objective is to assist homeowners to utilize their available resources, not to give them something they do not already have. The value expressed by some, that owners have the right to stay in their own homes even when they no longer can afford the costs, has to be balanced against equivalent rights for others who have not owned homes. Such problems are now being placed in a broader perspective (Scholen and Chen, 1981).

(5) Housing Allowance Supply Experiment. Between 1972 and 1979, approximately 19,800 low-income households in an Indiana county and a Wisconsin county received direct cash payments for housing expenses in an experiment to test the effects of housing allowances. All income-eligible homeowners and renters in the 2 counties were allowed to enroll, but receipt of the payments was contingent upon living in a dwelling unit that met minimum standards for safe, decent, and sanitary housing. If the dwelling did not initially meet the standards, residents could either bring them up to standards or move to a new dwelling.

During the program (HUD, 1981), about 11,000 dwellings, approximately 8 percent of the housing stock in the 2 sites, were repaired by or for enrollees seeking to qualify for the allowance payments. Among recipients whose preprogram housing did not meet program standards, 86 percent made repairs usually within 3 months of enrollment. Repairs and improvements were usually quite modest, primarily because they were done by residents, friends, or landlords at no labor cost.

The housing allowances, averaging about $1100 per year per household, did not have the effect of driving up housing prices in the area, a major concern prior to the study, but they did improve the housing conditions of the participants and reduce excessive housing expense burdens from an average of 40 percent of income to roughly one-third of income.

Elderly singles and renters were considerably more likely to participate than elderly couples and homeowners. This was attributed to greater reluctance of elderly homeowners to move, to renters' history of mobility, and to the greater housing expense burden of single-person households. Participation of elderly was higher in the county that had been undergoing rapid growth and development in its urban center, where housing was in good condition, but the market was very tight. Elderly participated relatively less in the county that had an excess of central city housing, which was in poor condition. Although, in general, mobility rates of participants were not greatly affected, single older women, particularly, did become more mobile, moving into more integrated neighborhoods to improve their housing.

The costs of this program are approximately half those of conventional subsidy programs (Struyk and Bendick, 1981), but the program improves residents' living conditions, reduces their housing expense burden, and contributes to the maintenance of the housing stock. It is important to note that this program was not targeted particularly for elderly. Elderly participants did not have to move into age-segregated complexes in order to improve their housing situation. As the results of this study are more finely analyzed and discussed, housing policy may develop that is based more broadly on need than on age status.

ADDITIONAL QUESTIONS AND STRATEGIES FOR RESEARCH

It is not necessary to assume that the aged are different from other age groups, but, because social relations are geared to a life cycle, the presence of the aged may direct focus to particular circumstances. Older couples, for example, may not have housing needs that are particularly different from those of younger couples. They may find new apartments that are efficiently designed, compact, and well-located, just as attractive as those found by younger couples. However, the use of the facilities may be influenced by the circumstances associated with the stage of the life cycle.

By comparing the experience of young and old, thus, we can see immediately that if the young have not had the time to accumulate many possessions, then they do not have the problems of disposing of them or finding a place to keep them. Forming a new family unit, a couple may come together with some possessions and then have to look forward to accumulating others to meet with some expectations of the style of life to which they aspire. By contrast, older couples may have accumulations that simply would not fit into an efficiently designed apartment. How does one get rid of possessions? Are they valuable in some sense other than sentimental? Are they costly because they inhibit moving into another style of living? These are questions that involve values, obviously, but they also represent questions that may not have easy resolutions, even if the persons involved are reasonably sure of what they want.

Housing that is designed for the aged, thus, initially need have no special characteristics. However, the circumstances in which the aged may frequently be found suggest alternatives that are appropriately considered in an open market. For example, if there is an assumption that more storage space is needed for older persons, planning housing to attract the aged would go in this direction. It is not unreasonable to suggest that the market will follow need as it is projected through future sales. What is at issue, however, is the question of what future needs will be, a question that is complicated by two or more tendencies in attempting to outline those needs.

First, there is an element of normative expectation that creeps into the consideration of needs. This can occur subtly, in a way one might describe as the architect's bias. The architect, frequently, wants not only to design efficient housing for the intended purpose, but wants to add a unique flair, the artistic expression that presumably takes it out of the prosaic. The client, presumably, should be appreciative and attracted to the thing the architect is doing. Or it can be more obvious, as in the expectation that older persons should be gravitating to particular types of lifestyles, or, particularly, in the expectation that older persons should be acquiescent and really have no special needs that require particular facilities.

Second, and this has already been alluded to above, older persons may not want to be efficient and conserving of resources. Of course, they may not have examined the alternatives. It is already an expression of a particular value to suggest that they should (must) examine the alternatives. It is not a particularly radical suggestion, though, since examination of the alternatives presumably can be done without pressing to convince the older persons that some alternatives are better than others.

Alternatives that can be presented to the older population can be strategically advantageous. Possibly the one point to which most persons who are trying to be helpful have directed attention is the potential economic disadvantage that home ownership may represent if the income of the older person declines. This may arise in two important ways. First, in retirement, older persons most frequently are on fixed incomes. Second, the owned home may have appreciated value due to inflation. Thus, progressively, the rental value of the home may represent a larger and larger proportion of the fixed income. Since taxes, insurance, and other costs are tied to the value of the home, the actual cash costs to the owner may also be increasing materially. The economic situation for the owner may be made more difficult to manage by having property that is more valuable. Such changes occur independently of initiative on the part of the owner, who may view the newly developed situation as a personal invasion and an unfair attack on the economic welfare.

Responses to this kind of situation have often been humanely but peculiarly oriented. To help the homeowner, for example, it has been suggested that there should be special tax abatement for older persons. This leaves open, obviously, the question of why one special group should be favored over another. Why shouldn't other persons who are unfavorably affected by such change also be helped? Why should homeowners be helped when renters are not? And so on. As in the allocation of any benefits to specially defined groups, there are no simple answers, and what prevails often is the special public-supported charity that legislators favor. It is possible to challenge the notion that older persons "deserve" to stay in the homes they own, simply because they have owned them. From both their perspective and a broader perspective, other arrangements could be more desirable. For those who go through a transition of large family to small family, having a large house may not be cost-effective or pleasurable, even though it is what one is "accustomed to." What should be recognized is that policy decisions in this area are frequently based on local sentiment and in response to vested interest groups, even when the interest groups are conceived as deserving, nice, old people.

When housing policy for older persons is considered, it must be in a more general context of policy about housing for all people. The special needs of the older generation may be appropriately considered, but such needs should not be seen in stereotypic or sentimental terms. The history of housing policy in the United States is not particularly impressive, and obviously the political persuasion of the observer will have some bearing on how the past is judged. But still, some observations appear fairly general. For example, housing directed to the poor has often proved to be far superior to housing available to marginally economically independent persons. Housing designed to maintain persons in their neighborhoods has resulted in maintenance of segregation by housing, something that has been confirmed even by U.S. Supreme Court review. Housing has been developed for which appropriate support services have not been provided, leading to ultimate destruction of the housing. Housing has been developed in which the cost factors to the residents have not been appropriately anticipated, so that residents have had expectations that could not be fulfilled. And generally, in the nature of bureaucratic ventures, housing construction costs and subsidies associated with federal standards appear constantly to put the federal government in a position of sponsoring expensive housing while trying to provide for the lower end of the socioeconomic continuum. Philosophically, many issues become involved that may challenge the whole experience of federal policy. For example, the strategy of housing allowances places a completely different emphasis (from the dominant one of being the landlord) on the place of government in the housing market. Even more generally, issues of entitlement versus welfare orientations in the society raise heated debates about what the federal government should be doing.

If one examines the kinds of concerns that people have as they approach retirement, the categories are not grossly different from what might have been important in prior years. However, the attention society focuses on age at retirement may alter how some things are viewed. From the multitude of studies on retirement needs, clearly, economic questions are foremost for older persons and underlie many other things. Economic feasibility for a style of life means attention to postretirement income, both in terms of benefits and in terms of management of assets. Specific questions focus on taxes, potential supplements to income in employment or by other personal resources, the impacts of inflation, and so on. Income and economic concerns, however, have important implications for other areas, including housing. Other areas of concern, such as medical and health, diet, travel, hobbies, and the like, may be equally conditional on the question of economic expectations, but they are also part of the same social fabric as housing. Essentially, concerns about housing cannot be dealt with in isolation, but only as a part of the whole social environment. Issues of social relations, relations with spouse, with children, with relatives, and so on, may be seen equally to be parts of the consideration of housing, and of the other aspects of the social environment.

When, then, is there need for special consideration of the elderly as a group? Ultimately, it is when it is necessary to attach an adjective to the identification of the age group, such as the frail elderly, the failing elderly, or the dependent elderly. The policy considerations under these categories, then, do not have to do with the elderly, as such, but with classes of people who are defined as needing special protection and attention. In considering, for example, the area of long-term care, it is obvious that it is one in which the elderly are the most common clients. They are not the only persons needing long-term care. They do, however, by the numbers involved and the recurrence of problems they have, represent a focus for attention and development of resources.

Policy with regard to housing, additionally, can be directed intelligently to exploration of development of resources for the transition period between being healthy and requiring protection. Thus, if dependency is viewed as a problem that requires attention and support in society, structuring the situation to encourage persons not to become dependent appears a likely focus. Indeed, much of the attention of policy in recent years has been directed to the idea that institutionalization may not be the best alternative for persons with problems, and has been oriented to finding ways to keep people operative in their own homes, in shared housing, and under various forms of foster care. Such approaches generally appear to be cost-effective in comparison to institutionalization, but often have other favorable aspects as well.

Providing information that is appropriate for future planning is one aspect of policy that should receive little resistance. Still, as with so many aspects of life, there seems to be an implicit expectation that, since all know what their future is, emphasis on planning ahead is not necessary. It is no different with other aspects of life in the United States: We do not put much emphasis on the training of adolescents for their entry into occupations or family, nor on their preparation for child rearing and other equally important aspects of the social process. Still, there is in the United States an emphasis on general education, and there has been a supportive movement for more adult and extension education that may assist planning for the later years. There is fairly strong evidence that persons who have planned for their retirement may get more out of it, but these studies are not without ambiguities. There is a reasonable expectation, however, that as the society becomes accustomed to the idea that more and more persons will live to older age, the needs of older persons and their requirements for special housing will be considered in the marketplace.

REFERENCES

APPLEBAUM, R., F. W. SEIDL, and C. D. AUSTIN (1980) "The Wisconsin community care organization: preliminary findings from the Milwaukee experiment." Gerontologist 20: 350-355.

ATCHLEY, R. C. and S. J. MILLER (1979) "Housing and households of the rural aged," in T. O. Byerts et al. (eds.) Environmental Context of Aging. New York: Garland.

BAER, W. C. (1980) "Empty housing space: an overlooked resource," in R. Mont-
gomery and D. R. Marshall (eds.) Housing Policy for the 1980's. Lexington, MA:
D. C. Heath.
BARSBY, S. L. and D. R. COX (1975) Interstate Migration of the Elderly. Lexing-
ton, MA: D. C. Heath.
BIGGAR, J. C., C. F. LONGINO, Jr., and C. B. FLYNN (1980) "Elderly interstate
migration: impact on sending and receiving states, 1965-1970." Research on
Aging 2: 217-232.
BLONSKY, L. E. (1975) "The desire of elderly nonresidents to live in a senior citizen
apartment building." Gerontologist 15: 88-91.
BOKSER, K. (1979) "Need for housing alternatives." Presented at the Conference on
Shared Housing for Older Persons: Research and Action, City University of New
York Graduate School, December 12.
BRODY, E. M. (1978) "Community housing for the elderly: the program, the
people, the decision-making process and the research." Gerontologist 18:
121-128.
——— M. H. KLEBAN, and B. LEIBOWITZ (1975) "Intermediate housing for the
elderly: satisfaction of those who moved in and those who did not." Gerontolo-
gist 15: 350-356.
CANTOR, M. H. (1975) "Life space and the social support system of the inner city
elderly of New York." Gerontologist 15: 23-27.
CARP, F. M. (1976) "Housing and living environments of older people," in R. H.
Binstock and E. Shanas (eds.) Aging and the Social Sciences. New York: Litton.
——— (1975) "Long range satisfaction with housing." Gerontologist 15: 68-72.
——— (1966) A Future for the Aged. Austin: University of Texas Press.
DONAHUE, W. T., M. M. THOMPSON, and D. J. CURREN (1977) Congregate
Housing for Older People: An Urgent Need, a Growing Demand. Washington, DC:
Administration on Aging.
EGGERT, G. M., J. E. BOWLYOW, and C. W. NICHOLS (1980) "Gaining control of
the long-term care system: first returns from the Access experiment." Gerontolo-
gist 20: 356-363.
Federal Council on Aging (1978) Public Policy and the Frail Elderly. Washington,
DC: Office of Human Development Services.
Federal National Mortgage Association (1979) Forum III: Housing for the Retired.
Washington, DC: Author.
FLYNN, C. B. (1980) "General versus aged interstate migration, 1965-1970."
Research on Aging 2: 165-176.
——— J. C. BIGGAR, C. F. LONGINO, Jr., and R. F. WISEMAN [eds.] (1979) Aged
Migration in the United States, 1965-1970: Final Report. Washington, DC:
National Institute on Aging.
FOX, R. (1979) "Senior home renovation program." Presented at the Conference on
Shared Housing for Older Persons: Research and Action, City University of New
York Graduate School, December 12.
General Accounting Office (1980) Section 8 Subsidized Housing—Some observations
on Its High Rents, Costs, and Inequities. Washington, DC: Author.
——— (1979) Entering a Nursing Home—Costly Implications for Medicaid and the
Elderly. Washington, DC: Author.
GOLANT, S. M. (1979) "Central city, suburban and nonmetropolitan area migration
patterns of the elderly," in S. M. Golant (ed.) Location and Environment of the
Elderly Population. Washington, DC: Winston & Sons.

――― (1977) "Spatial context of residential moves by elderly persons." International Journal of Aging and Human Development 8: 279-289.

GUTOWSKI, M. F. (1978) "Integrating housing and social service activities for the elderly household," in R. P. Boynton (ed.) Housing of Independent Elderly. HUD Occasional Papers in Housing and Community Affairs: Volume 1. Washington, DC: HUD.

HENIG, J. R. (1981) "Gentrification and displacement of the elderly: an empirical analysis." Gerontologist 21: 67-75.

HOCHSCHILD, A. R. (1978) The Unexpected Community. Los Angeles: University of California Press.

HODGSON, J. H. and J. L. QUINN (1980) "The impact of the Triage health care delivery system on client morale, independent living, and the cost of care." Gerontologist 20: 364-371.

HUGHES, J. (1981) "Huge–and untapped–rental reservoir." Wall Street Journal (February 25): 31.

KENNEDY, S. G. (1981) "Houses get two masters, two master bedrooms." New York Times (July 19): C-1, 10.

LAWTON, M. P. and J. COHEN (1974) "The generality of housing impact on the well-being of older people." Journal of Gerontology 29: 194-204.

LAWTON, M. P., E. M. BRODY, and P. TRUNER-MASSEY (1978) "The relationships of environmental factors to changes in well-being." Gerontologist 18: 133-137.

LAWTON, M. P., M. GREENBAUM, and B. LEIBOWITZ (1980) "The lifespan of housing environments for the aging." Gerontologist 20: 56-64.

LAWTON, M. P., M. H. KLEBAN, and D. CARLSON (1973) "The inner-city resident: to move or not to move." Gerontologist 13: 443-448.

LEE, D. (1959) Freedom and Culture. Englewood Cliffs, NJ: Prentice-Hall.

LONG, L. H. and K. A. HANSEN (1979) "Reasons for interstate migration: jobs, retirement, climate and other influences," in U.S. Bureau of the Census, Current Population Reports, Series P-23, No. 81. Washington, DC: Government Printing Office.

LONGINO, C. F., Jr. (1979) "Intrastate migration of the elderly," in C. B. Flynn et al. (eds.) Aged Migration in the United States, 1965-1970: Final Report. Washington, DC: National Institute on Aging.

MOORE, E. G. and M. PUBLICOVER (1979) "The use of public microdata in local studies of the elderly," in S. M. Golant (ed.) Location and Environment of the Elderly Population. Washington, DC: Winston & Sons.

NEWMAN, S. J. (1976) "Housing adjustments of the disabled elderly." Gerontologist 16: 312-317.

NOTO, N. A. (1980) "Tax and financial policies for owner-occupied housing in the 1980's," in R. Montgomery and D. R. Marshall (eds.) Housing Policy for the 1980's. Lexington, MA: D. C. Heath.

OLSEN, E. O. and D. W. RASMUSSEN (1979) "Existing: a program evaluation," in Section 8, HUD Occasional Papers in Housing and Community Affairs, Volume 6. Washington, DC: HUD.

ROSOW, I. (1967) Social Integration of the Aged. New York: Macmillan.

ROWLES, G. (1980) "Growing old inside: attachment to place in an Appalachian community." Colloquium, City University of New York Graduate School, October.

SCHOLEN, K. and Y. P. CHEN (1981) Unlocking Home Equity for the Elderly. Cambridge, MA: Ballinger.

SHERMAN, S. R. (1971) "The choice of retirement housing among the well elderly." Journal of Aging and Human Development 2: 118-138.

SHERWOOD, S. and D. S. GREER (1973) The Highland Heights Experiment: A Final Report. Washington, DC: Government Printing Office.

SMITH, B. W. and J. HILTNER (1975) "Intra-urban location of the elderly." Journal of Gerontology 30: 473-478.

SOLDO, B. J. (1980) "America's elderly in the 1980's." Population Bulletin 35: whole issue.

——— (1978) "The housing and characteristics of independent elderly," in R. P. Boynton (ed.) Housing of Independent Elderly. HUD Occasional Papers in Housing and Community Affairs: Volume 1. Washington, DC: HUD.

SPINK, F. H., Jr. (1980) "Housing and the maturing population." Urban Land 39, 2: 3-4.

STREIB, G. F. and M. A. HILKER (1980) "The cooperative 'family'—an alternative lifestyle for the elderly." Alternative Lifestyles 3: 167-184.

STRUYK, R. J. and M. BENDICK, Jr. (1981) Housing Vouchers for the Poor: Lessons from a National Experiment. Washington, DC: Urban Institute.

STRUYK, R. J. and B. J. SOLDO (1980) Improving the Elderly's Housing: A Key to Preserving the Nation's Housing Stock and Neighborhoods. Cambridge, MA: Ballinger.

TABER, M. A., S. ANDERSON, and C. J. ROGERS (1980) "Implementing community care in Illinois: issues of cost and targeting in a statewide program." Gerontologist 20: 380-387.

Tri-State Regional Planning Commission (1981) Legalizing Single-Family Conversions. New York: Author.

U.S. Bureau of the Census (1978) Current Population Reports, Series P-23, No. 85. Washington, DC: Government Printing Office.

——— (1977) "Geographical mobility: March 1975-1976," in U.S. Bureau of the Census, Current Population Reports, Series P-20, No. 305. Washington, DC: Government Printing Office.

U.S. Department of Housing and Urban Development [HUD] (1981) Conclusions: The 1980 Report. Washington, DC: Author.

Urban Systems Research and Engineering (1976) Evaluation of the Effectiveness of Congregate Housing for the Elderly. Washington, DC: HUD Office of Policy Development and Research.

VAN DYCK, M. W. and R. W. BRESLOW (1978) Evaluation of the Jewish Council for the Aging Group Home Program. Rockville, MD: Jewish Council for the Aging of Greater Washington.

WISEMAN, R. F. (1980) "Why older people move: theoretical issues." Research on Aging 2: 141-154.

8

HEALTH CARE DURING
THE RETIREMENT YEARS

Leslie S. Libow

Geriatric medicine currently is receiving considerable attention from the health care establishment, the government, and the media. This represents a refreshing change, and the reasons for this remarkable shift of focus lie in many imperatives, including those imposed by demography, economics, morals and ethics, and science.

The elderly, who constitute only 10 to 11 percent of the population of the United States, utilize 27 to 50 percent of the U.S. health dollar. They occupy between 30 and 60 percent of acute hospital beds in our nation. There are only 1,000,000 acute hospital beds, but there are 1,300,000 long-term care beds, of which the elderly occupy 95 percent.

Of an internal medical specialist's time, 40 percent is devoted to the elderly; 20 percent of a family practitioner's time is so devoted. This group includes the majority of patients in the practice of physicians such as orthopedists, opthalmologists, urologists, and podiatrists. The elderly utilize 25 percent of all the prescriptions dispensed in this country.

The young or middle-aged patient is acutely hospitalized for an average of 7 to 9 days, but the elderly patient is likely to be hospitalized for up to

AUTHOR'S NOTE: This chapter was originally prepared for the Columbia Journalism Monograph Number 3 (1979). The editors record their appreciation for the right to include Dr. Libow's article in this volume.

twice as long. A typical health bill for the elderly is between $1700 and $2000, of which only two-thirds is covered by Medicare. Thus, approximately $600 to $700 must be paid out of modest income and fixed reserves. The population over the age of 75 now constitutes one-third of the "elderly," and this group is the fastest growing element of the aged population. Although only 5 percent of those over 65 are in nursing homes, this small percentage utilizes an enormous proportion of the health care budget. Of all older people, 20 percent will at some point in their later years, spend time in a nursing home.

Ethical issues, of which there are many, raise such questions as: Should treatment be denied because of age? Are we using age as a reason for economizing on some areas of health care? Should the individual physician make decisions involving ethical issues on behalf of the individual patient, or leave it to society at large to debate these issues?

A brief review of conditions that most commonly afflict elderly patients shows that some of them are already fairly well understood, while others are in urgent need of further research that will make improved diagnosis and treatment possible.

DISEASES OF THE HEART AND ARTERIES

Between 15 and 30 percent of the white elderly and somewhere between 20 and 50 percent of black elderly individuals are hypertensive. It has been demonstrated that sensible treatment of hypertension will reduce morbidity resulting from strokes and heart failure. Although more of the elderly hypertensives should be treated, caution should also be used in such treatment to ensure that the side effects of the medication do not seriously interfere with the lifestyle.

A new type of hypertension, called "systolic" hypertension, has recently been clarified. In the past, physicians have given greater emphasis to diastolic hypertension, which represents the second number in the sequence 140/90. We do not know if treatment and lowering of systolic pressure will reduce the relationship between increased systolic blood pressures and increased morbidity from strokes, heart failure, and coronary heart disease. Research sponsored by the National Heart Institute and National Institute on Aging is now under way to examine this question. In the meantime, it seems appropriate for physicians not to treat systolic hypertension.

The coronary artery disease problem that is manifested by angina pectoris and/or myocardial infarction is quite prevalent in late life. Excellent treatments are available to reduce the chest pain syndromes. One of the beneficial medications, propanolol, has certain hazards for the elderly that are not as significant in the middle-aged. Though it reduces chest pain frequency, propanolol also has a tendency to produce heart failure in the elderly. This relates to the mechanism of the drug and the fact that the ability of the aged heart to deal with increasing stresses is less than that of the middle-aged heart. This highlights the importance of not simply extrapolating from medical approaches in middle life to determine approaches in late life. The 75 year old is not simply the 40 year old 35 years later. Special prescribing approaches are necessary for the elderly, and more research to determine the relationship between age and the effects of drugs is urgently required.

When the chest pain of angina pectoris is so severe and debilitating as to make pain intolerable, or to seriously impair style of life, cardiac surgery is available. This remarkable advance has been applied at various centers and has been shown to be quite a successful procedure. There is a modest morbidity and mortality associated with this procedure. The mortality rate is somewhat higher for the elderly than for the young, but it is still relatively low—in the range of 3 to 5 percent. Older people should not be deprived of this surgery when it is appropriately indicated.

Decreasing heart rates, in the range of 30 to 40 per minute, are not infrequent in the elderly. This is often the manifestation of either heart block or the sick sinus syndrome. These low heart rates are frequently accompanied by fainting or dizzy episodes, or by mental deterioration. The usual treatment is the implantation of a pacemaker. It is estimated that approximately 1,000,000 elderly persons now have pacemakers. What is not well appreciated is the fact that the causes of this heart block and the sick sinus syndrome are unknown and are not related to either hardening of the arteries or to arteriosclerotic heart disease. Further research is necessary into this very prevalent problem.

Pacemakers are a great advance and, in many cases, have prolonged life and provided excellent quality of life. It is thought, however, that there may be an excessive use of pacemakers. If such excess exists, it is not related to any type of unethical prescribing but rather to overzealous use of an outstanding advance. Although it has not been clearly determined that there is excessive use, further clarification of the criteria for the installation of pacemakers is required.

A valvular disease of the aortic valve, which is not seen in early years, is very typical of late life. The cause of this valvular disease is unknown. It manifests itself by a degeneration of the aortic valve, leading to a hardening of the valve, fibrosis, and often to calcification. This is often called aortic sclerosis and leads to aortic stenosis. When the valve change is severe, there is an obstruction to the exit of blood from the left ventricle into the systemic circulation to brain, limbs, and other organs. This is often accompanied by dizziness, fainting, chest pain, or congestive heart failure. The treatment is surgery. Very large numbers of elderly people, particularly men, have been treated for this syndrome with the appropriate operation and have obtained subsequent relief of symptoms.

Stroke, or cerebral vascular accident, reaches its greatest prevalence in later life. The most common cause of stroke is thrombosis, or occlusion of a vessel to the brain. Frequent but less common causes include hemorrhage into the brain and little clots (emboli) reaching the brain vessels from sources such as the heart or arteries of the neck.

Stroke often follows earlier symptoms. If the condition is diagnosed early, it may be corrected. Early symptoms may include recurrent episodes of momentary losses of speech, for example, or transient (minutes or many hours) weakness or numbness of limbs on one side of the body. These so-called transient ischemic attacks are often the prelude to a later stroke. When discovered, they may be quite treatable either by medical means or by surgery of the arteries of the neck. Furthermore, high blood pressure is a significant risk factor with regard to tendency to stroke. Discovery and treatment of hypertension appears to reduce the risk of stroke.

Further research is necessary into the causes of stroke, the methods of preventing it, and its treatment. It is startling that this damaging, costly, and prevalent illness has not been researched to a depth appropriate to its incidence. The key research would be on prevention, earlier detection, and application of appropriate treatment.

Arteriosclerosis, or hardening of the arteries, is a diffuse disease of the arteries in all parts of the body. It is the leading cause of morbidity and mortality in the Western world. The cause is unclear, and considerable research is now being directed toward determining this cause. What has not been studied properly is the linkage of the passage of time (aging) with the development of arteriosclerosis. Arteriosclerosis does not appear to be an inevitable consequence of aging. For example, approximately 25 percent of people over 80 have no significant arteriosclerosis of their coronary arteries. The disease is linked in some way to diabetes, hypertension, cigarette smoking, and possibly to obesity. Research on its linkage with age, hopefully, will give us a greater clue to the understanding of this serious and epidemic illness than do other approaches to its study.

Hardening of the arteries to the lower extremities is a common problem. It causes pain in the calf upon walking, with attendant coldness of feet or toes, discoloration, and ulceration. At times, the inevitable result is need for amputation. Early detection may lead to appropriate medical/surgical treatment.

Arteriosclerosis of the artery to the heart, the coronary artery, is a major component of the diseases called angina pectoris and myocardial infarction. As described earlier, there are medical and/or surgical treatments for these illnesses. Preventive measures in earlier life include appropriate diet (low cholesterol, moderate calories), exercise, treatment of hypertension, no smoking, and resolution of certain midlife emotional characteristics that are associates with a tense and stressful life tone.

Hardening of the arteries to the brain may lead to stroke. Preventive measures in earlier years are somewhat similar those listed above for coronary artery disease and are referred to in the foregoing discussion of stroke.

CANCER AND DIABETES

Many cancers increase in prevalence with each ensuing decade, reaching their peak in late life. This is true of cancer of the prostate, cancer of the colon, and some other cancers. Cancer of the breast has a peak prevalence in early life and then peaks again in late life.

The elderly make more visits per year to the physician's office than do the middle-aged (an average of 7 versus 4 visits per year). This affords an opportunity for earlier cancer detection. On the other hand, older people are not yet as oriented to self-examination for neoplasms, such as the breast cancers, as are younger people.

When present in the elderly body, many cancers behave differently from those in the young or middle-aged. For example, there is a tendency for some cancers to be less malignant in the elderly. If we knew the reasons for this, it could give us insight into the entire biology of cancer, and in particular into the linkage between aging and cancer. This insight could have implications for treatment. For example, aggressive chemotherapy may be inappropriate, since its side effects are severe and there is a possibility of disturbing the balance between age and cancer.

Diabetes mellitus, which relates to the body's handling of sugar and to some genetic predisposing factors, is quite prevalent in late life. Some of the criteria employed to make the diagnosis in the younger patient may not, however, be applicable to the elderly. For example, the "oral glucose tolerance test" is abnormal in about two-thirds of the otherwise healthy elderly. It is doubtful that the bulk of these subjects have diabetes mellitus.

The majority of diabetes patients, needing neither insulin nor oral medications, can be managed with dietary and weight control. Most will not experience serious complications in their lifetime if they observe sensible precautions with regard to diet and foot care. Nevertheless, there are some who have a tendency for infection and who experience the well-known complications that involve the eye, heart, and hardening of the arteries.

VISUAL AND HEARING PROBLEMS

Eye problems increase with age. Cataracts, therefore, are found mostly in the elderly. Not all cataracts require surgical removal. This depends on the degree of visual and social/functional interference. The patient, the primary care physician, and the ophthalmologist should coordinate their input into this decision-making process.

Standard surgical treatments for cataracts are excellent, with success ranging around 95 percent. Recently, the permanent lens implant has come to be considered an ideal procedure for the old-old (over 75 years) and, perhaps, for the young-old (65 to 75) as well. Adverse effects of long-term eye implants have not yet emerged. It should be noted, however, that the procedure is relatively new and is being performed by only a limited number of eye surgeons.

Glaucoma, also, is rather prevalent in late life and is quite treatable if detected early. Frequent eye evaluations are important, and may be done by the primary care physician or by the ophthalmologist. Both medical and surgical procedures for treating glaucoma are available.

Macular degeneration is of unknown etiology, and its treatment is not yet well established. This degenerative retinal disease was previously recognized infrequently, but ophthalmologists surprisingly find it to be one of the most common causes of severe visual problems in late life. Research is needed in this area of age-related illness to define the mechanisms involved.

Diminished hearing is certainly a significant problem in late life. This problem may contribute to the isolation of elderly persons at home or in institutions. Anyone who has any suggestion of hearing difficulty should be evaluated, because many could benefit from hearing aids. A major issue is the right of older people to return hearing aids and receive a refund if, after a few weeks of use, they experience no benefits.

SENILE DEMENTIA AND OTHER MENTAL ILLNESSES

At present, the majority of patients with the tragic disease known as senile dementia are untreatable. A differential diagnosis exists, however, which reveals that somewhere between 5 and 15 percent of all such diagnoses are incorrect, and that the patients are really suffering from reversible illnesses called "reversible brain diseases" or "pseudo senility." The National Institute on Aging is in the process of informing the health care professions of the prevalence of this reversibility and of the proper approaches to uncovering the reversible illnesses.

The approach to the diagnosis and treatment of the irreversible dementias, which constitute the remaining 85 percent, needs to be improved. Contrary to popular opinion, the bulk of these illnesses, about 60 percent, are not caused by hardening of the arteries, and are of unknown origin. Possible causes of this major category include: slow viruses, metabolic defects, genetic factors, toxins such as aluminum, immunological abnormalities, and abnormalities of the neuro-transmitters.

Although approximately 2 to 4 percent of persons over 65 experience senile dementia, there is another group of 5 to 10 percent who have more than minimal memory loss but who do not suffer from significant social dysfunction, impressive disorientation, or intellectual deterioration. Some clinicians have referred to this as "benign memory loss." It has not been clearly established whether it is a precursor of a later onset of senile dementia. The major point here is that within any age group the functioning of memory is not clearly understood. Further research into memory change in late life would not only be of potential benefit to the quality of life for the elderly but would also give us greater insight into brain function at all ages. Several drugs are now being tested with the hope of improving memory loss.

Mental depression is at least as prevalent in late life as it is in middle life, and perhaps greater in late life. The risks of depression include suicide, family dysfunction, and the need for institutionalization. In older men, in particular, there is a considerable risk of suicide. Any mention of suicidal tendencies by an older person should be taken seriously, with a follow-up of professional advice and support. Some depressions are so severe in the elderly that they produce a dementia—a "senility-like" syndrome. Depression is eminently treatable and should be diagnosed as early as possible.

There is no doubt concerning the linkage of brain and bodily functions. For example, more than 50 percent of elderly patients who develop acute heart failure have had a significant emotional trauma within three days of this acute illness. And, as Dr. Robert Butler has pointed out, there are 25,000 excess deaths in surviving spouses during the first year following death of the other spouse.

The first 12 months following forced retirement appear to be accompanied by increased illness and/or mortality. The reasons for this linkage are unclear, but research studies from the National Institute of Health have demonstrated a significant positive relation between a varied, complex lifestyle of a 70 year old and his or her future survival. This would appear to confirm commonsense observations. Isolation and/or diminished use of willpower are not conducive to a positive late-life experience. Vigor and variety probably help reduce decline of the older individual. Luck and money help, too.

How to utilize the insights regarding psychosomatic mechanisms to prevent certain problems in late life is unclear. Certainly, we should all begin preparing for retirement as soon as possible, and the utility of various social support systems should be tested.

Sexual dysfunction, a major concern of the elderly, has often been thought to be caused mainly by psychological factors, although this view is now less prevalent. Suffice it to say at this point that sexual dysfunction is often treatable, and is a problem that is often overlooked by physicians.

GENERAL OBSERVATIONS ON MEDICATION
AND SURGERY FOR THE ELDERLY

The older person is the leading consumer of medications in this country. There is a tendency to receive medications from various sources, including multiple physicians and hospital clinics, as well as over the counter (in the case of nonprescription drugs). Increased public awareness should be directed to the fact that these medications can interact with one another to produce unexpected effects, such as blackouts and dizziness, sexual impotence, confusion, a senile-like syndrome, and so on. There is also a need for an improved manner of dispensing medications so as to assist correct self-administration. Older people with a need for multiple medications have been shown to make a significant number of errors in self-administration, especially in regard to sequence. Similarly, the child-proof safety tops of medication vials are often a significant hindrance to the elderly.

With the excellent development of anesthetic and surgical skills, older people do fairly well in most *elective* surgery situations. Emergency surgery produces an approximate doubling of the mortality rate for most procedures. Thus, there is a tendency to think of elective surgery as "preventive." Surgery presents obvious risks of morbidity and mortality at any age, however, and more than ever in late life.

Prior to surgery, it would be wise to seek a second opinion. Some believe that there is a tendency toward "too much" surgery in the elderly, but this is not clearly proven. The role of surgery in the treatment of many illnesses of the elderly requires further study.

More attention should be given to preventive measures. These include vaccinations against viruses (influenza) and bacteria (pneumonias), as well as social preventive measures, such as preparation for retirement and for support after loss of spouse. The preventive aspect of health care for the elderly has been relatively neglected by the health care system.

Fractured hip is one common and destructive condition whose incidence might be reduced by appropriate preventive measures. It occurs mostly in white, elderly women, and is rare in both black women and black men. Its cause is unknown, but seems to be linked to osteoporosis, or a weakening of the bones, which may be preventable with medications that include calcium and Vitamin D. Other preventive approaches are not clear, but seem to include adequate nutrition, a physically active life and, of course, avoidance of falls. Treatment of the fracture includes surgery, often involving hospitalization between 10 days and 12 weeks. This disease has been estimated to cost annually approximately one billion dollars (or .5 to 1 percent of the total United States health care budget).

Some claim that there is excessive institutionalization in the United States. Certainly, we have an unusually high ratio of nursing home beds to acute hospital beds. It is unusual, however, to see abandonment of the elderly, and it is also unusual to find an elderly patient who is desirous of living in a nursing home and thereby "malingering." For most, the nursing home is a last resort.

Institutionalization could be reduced by research on:

- early detection of senility and the development of new social or medical treatments;
- ways of preventing falls and accidents;
- improved treatments for incontinence; and
- economic or other incentives for family or surrogates to care for patients at home.

EDUCATION OF HEALTH PROFESSIONALS IN CARE OF THE ELDERLY

Specific education in geriatric medicine has long been missing from medical schools, resident training programs, and nursing and social service schools. For the past seven years, with increased emphasis during the past two or three years, there has been a remarkable change for the better. Medical schools have been establishing geriatric medical programs and, consequently, geriatricians are now being trained. The impetus has come from the "imperatives" mentioned at the start of this chapter, and from the efforts of the National Institute on Aging, the Administration on Aging, and other government agencies. Combined, these are all providing support and vital leadership. The first two resident training programs for the training of geriatricians which have been established in the United States have served as role models and as sources for the procreation of some university faculty leaders.

There is every reason to be optimistic about the prospects for a good life in later years. This can become a reality if research support continues to grow, if physicians and other health professionals continue their commitment to this issue, if family and friends are vociferous regarding their concern, and if the elderly themselves are persistent in making known their desires.

9

AGING AND DISABILITY

Lorraine G. Hiatt

INTRODUCTION AND DEFINITIONS

Does the term *disabled* conjure up images of frustration and pity, more recently coupled with hope and triumph? Whom do we picture as disabled? The veteran at meaningful, productive work? The child alongside more physically able students, playing as a group? Young adults driving with the aid of technology? Other adults speaking on the phone, operating controls with eye movements? Or a group of activists wheeling up the ramp of a recently renovated community center?

Are there similar images involving older adults? If so, what are they doing? Ask some of them and you might conclude that all older people are disabled.

Two issues emerge from these reflections:

(1) What are the consequences of the changing physical abilities associated with aging for people who have spent much of their lives as relatively able-bodied?

(2) What is the outlook for future generations of elderly people in terms of their relative capabilities and disabilities?

Though much has been written about stereotypes and images of older people, the social structure appears to be slow to adopt new images or to make use of existing information or technology with regard to coping with diminished functioning (Francher, 1973; Freeman, 1979; Butler and Lewis, 1973). The purpose of this chapter is to examine some issues associated with aging and disability, in an effort to suggest how people of all ages and abilities might better experience the good life in old age.

In Table 9.1, highlights from contemporary definitions of impairment, handicap, disability, and rehabilitation have been singled out for comment.

Rodin and Langer (1980) have described the potent effects of social labeling on the independence and behavior of memory-impaired and emotionally disturbed older people. Quite likely, labels describing physical functioning/dysfunctioning may similarly serve to elicit self-fulfilling prophesies and societal expectations of physical decline (Comfort, 1980; Baltes and Labouvie, 1973; Palmore, 1973; Merton, 1957; Kuypers and Bengston, 1973). This is not to say that social attitudes and behavior cause all impairments of old age, but rather to suggest that both positive and negative expectations may account for the degree of handicap and of disability experienced. It is ironic that we have no well-developed labels or attributes for older people who maximize their abilities or master daily life despite chronic impairments.

The terms outlined in Table 9.1 have come to affect how health of older people is evaluated (though several reflect characteristics of younger population groups as part of their operational definitions). They also influence the types of services provided and paid for, the statistics collected, and the training of caregivers. Rehabilitation professionals have differentiated among "impairment," "handicap," and "disability," because it has been important to place emphasis or responsibility for incapability and rehabilitation on a total system (Haber, 1967). Increasingly, the literature of aging suggests that the experiences of disability are a function of physical, psychological, social, religious/phenomenological, environmental, and cultural factors (Pyrek and Snyder, 1978). Biological explanations alone are inadequate to explain the behavior of people who are impaired (Fozard and Popkin, 1978; Parr, 1980). Yet, a great deal of contemporary intervention has been aimed solely at the individual, without regard to social and cultural contexts and the physical environment (Willems, 1977). The implication of "whole person-system" models is that while the individual and the system may share responsibility for causes, they may also complement each other in terms of improvement. For older people, just as for people of any age, the whole person-system models suggest that all elements have the potential for change.

HOW DISABILITIES AFFECT OLDER ADULTS

We do not really know how disabilities influence the lives of older adults as they age. In fact, while there are relatively good descriptions of the impairments of old age, there is precious little information on the

TABLE 9.1 Definitions and Critique: A Look At the Terminology of Rehabilitation and Its Implications for Age

Term	Definition (Source)	Example	Comments
Impairment	An objective patho-physiological condition (Wolcott, 1978).	A person who does not see as well as her peers, based on standardized measures of visual acuity, can be termed visually impaired. The origin might be changes in the lens structure (which are usually not specified), cataract, or lens shape (nearsightedness, for example).	We have only limited objective techniques for measuring many chronic impairments of older people. Baseline standards have not been developed which are tied to daily performance requirements of older adults. As a result, standards set for younger people have been used as bases for comparison for vision, hearing, and mental function of older people. In other areas, no measures are available, though the condition is common (e.g., losses of agility, endurance, diminished speed of response).
	Usually comparative, based on losses of use relative to one's potential or peers.		
	An impairment may or may not result in a disability (Wolcott, 1978; Jochheim, 1979).		
Handicap	The extra burden an individual must overcome or circumvent to avoid significant reduction of a specific functional ability (Wolcott, 1978).	Mrs. J. may use corrective lenses, magnifying glasses, and increased lighting levels to overcome a reading handicap resulting from visual impairment.	Despite the impairment, she does continue to function. Her handicap may affect close-work activities, but may not accurately be generalized to her mental condition or some other areas of daily living.

(Continued)

TABLE 9.1 Continued

Term	Definition (Source)	Example	Comments
Disability	Failure to function at a level reasonably expected for a given individual, with or without obvious defects (Wolcott, 1978).	Mr. K. may have diminished night vision; he could be characterized as disabled with respect to night driving. Miss L. avoids using or manipulating numbers; even though she has no evident mental or physical deficits, she could be described as disabled in numerical skills.	Currently, there are no baseline standards for functioning with respect to skills one might "reasonably expect" for older people—and people at different ages within the general definition of "elderly." It may be important to differentiate disability from obvious physical impairment from those which derive from ignorance about the effects of activity (reading, use of arthritic joints) on long-range competence. In the absence of such information, we may find older adults forgoing activities or exercise on the mistaken assumption that they are preserving strength or abilities.

Rehabilitation	The restoration of the handicapped individual to the fullest degree of mental, social, vocational, and economic usefulness (Wolcott, 1978). Reduction of any trend toward decline (Kane and Kane, 1978).	The individual has a stroke and loses some facility with the left hand; his speech is also impaired. Through physical therapy, practice, and time, much of the use of the hand is restored. Through practice and speech therapy, most of the communication skills are restored. A person with diminished sight is taught techniques of visual efficiency through low-vision services. While her vision is not fully restored, some useful sight is returned.	The emphasis of most rehabilitation legislation has been upon (1) employable individuals ("usefulness to society"); (2) school-aged children and young adults; (3) acute conditions, such as stroke, where the prognosis is good and results can be anticipated fairly quickly. Yet, most of the disability experienced by older people is from chronic conditions. Few financial incentives are available to individuals regarding rehabilitation. Even fewer incentives/programs are available to *prevent* chronic disability (as through public education, exercise, visual/auditory screening, and the like). Could it be that society (young and old) does not believe that older people are capable of improvements?

combined impact of slight changes in vision, hearing, muscle tone, or response rate on older people (Brotman, forthcoming; Marsh, 1980; Birren and Schaie, 1977). One of the major shortcomings of existing epidemiological data on aging is that impairments are listed singly and separately, and degrees of severity are based on the single impairment quantified (Berkowitz et al., 1979; Kirchner and Lowman, 1978).

For example, suppose that an individual is slightly vision impaired all through life, though not greatly handicapped by this condition. With aging, it may be that the lens of the eye will change in shape and transparency (Marsh, 1980). It may yellow, and muscles that control pupil dilation may become more sluggish, affecting light-dark adaptation, accommodation, and certain responsiveness to light (Fozard et al., 1977). While many researchers suggest that these chronic impairments affect the majority of older people, we have no statistics to bear this out. Without statistics, it may appear that these changes are not significant or that intervention is not appropriate. Yet, such visual changes may influence attention span, concentration, mobility, reading, vulnerability to falling, and ascribed mental function (Cullinan, 1978a, 1978b, 1979; Cullinan et al., 1979; Daubs, 1973; Waller, 1978; Hiatt, 1980; Snyder et al., 1976; Berkowitz et al., 1979). Furthermore, much can be done to compensate for these impairments (Rosenbloom, 1974; Faye and Hood, 1976; Padula, 1981). Part of the problem may arise from how vision or other impairments are assumed to be caused and, therefore, how they are evaluated. Most clinical measures of vision are based on the presence or absence of eye disorders and diseases (National Society to Prevent Blindness, 1980). The objective is usually to determine whether people can see well enough to read, whether they need refraction or correction (visual aids ranging from glasses to magnifying devices), and/or whether problems might be alleviated through surgical procedures. Disease labels and chronic conditions are seldom translated into suggestions for how one might comfortably engage in close work, participate with peers, drive, ambulate, or even prompt one's memory. Even professionals involved in direct care who are not vision experts have difficulty interpreting the results of most vision examinations for themselves or for older people (Snyder et al., 1976). The example becomes more frustrating when we factor in the likelihood that most visually impaired older people are impaired in one or more other functions (66 percent of all visually impaired older people, compared with about 43 percent of all other age groups, are multiply impaired; Kirchner and Peterson, 1980).

Similar shortcomings in evaluation, statistical accounting, and intervention have been described in terms of other disabilities: hearing (Flood, 1979; Powers and Powers, 1978); tactile sensitivity (Thornbury & Mis-

TABLE 9.2   Percentage of People 65 and Over with Various Impair-
             ments, with Implications for Effects

Impairment/Condition	Percentage Reported	Possible Implications
Arthritis	44	Limitations in fine motor coordination, agility, and range of motion (Rodstein, 1971) which may be diminished through lifelong exercise (Butler, 1975).
Hypertension	30	Endurance, activity, and occasionally mobility reduction. Effects may be reduced through learning techniques for management of stress and through diet, exercise, and medication.
Hearing Impairments	28	Participation may or may not be diminished; communication may be handicapped (Mills, 1978; Powers and Powers, 1978; Flood, 1979). The environment can frequently be adapted to maximize hearing, as by reducing background noise (Comalli, 1967).
Heart Condition	27	May result in reduced mobility and agility, and diminished endurance. May be prevented by limiting/ceasing smoking (or exposure to certain noxious substances) and through physical exercise.
Visual Impairments	12	Fine motor coordination may be limited, which may affect activities, self-care, and participation. Orientation and mobility may be affected. Print reading may be limited. Some visual impairments (such as glaucoma) can be prevented or arrested; others may be minimized through low-vision training or other rehabilitation services. (Marsh, 1980; Fozard et al., 1977).

SOURCE: Brotman (forthcoming).

tretta, 1981; Kenshalo, 1977); communication (Ordy and Brizze, 1979; Cohen, 1979); and motor behavior (MacDonald and Butler, 1974; Waller, 1978).

Table 9.2 summarizes some data on impairments of older people, with suggested implications for handicap and disability. (For more detailed tables, the reader is referred to current issues of U.S. Senate, *Developments on Aging,* and to Jacobs, 1980; U.S. Public Health Service, 1980). Ideally, greater attention should be paid to the implications of impairments, as has been done in a review of psychological disabilities including depression and dementia (Pfeiffer, 1977). In addition, it would be most instructive to develop some comparative measures on how many older people do maximize vision or hearing, agility, fine and gross motor skills, communication, endurance, response rates, and stress, for example, despite varying baseline degrees of impairment. We would also want to know how disability and handicaps are minimized.

In the process of developing more useful measures of disability, we would be well advised to consider the context, that is, environment and use, in which people function or do not function. Willems (1977) and Germain (1977) have suggested that evaluations of older people involve ecological assessments. Returning to the example of vision, one finds increasing evidence that measures of vision taken in clinical settings bear little resemblance to those taken in the household where one lives (Silver et al., 1978), and that one may see better in some clinics than in some homes. We might expect hearing measures to be better in acoustically designed environments than in notoriously noisy public areas, senior centers, or even working environments. If the objective is really to maximize functioning, then clinically "true" or "pure" measures must be contrasted with ecological diagnoses and evaluations. In this way, we may also obtain useful information about how stimuli and environments could be adapted to compensate for chronic disabilities associated with the later years of life (see Brody et al., 1971; Lawton, 1977; Windley and Scheidt, 1980; Fozard and Popkin, 1978).

REHABILITATION AND PREVENTION

Rehabilitation is yet to be a reality for many older people as a means of coping with declining abilities associated with aging. In some cases, restoration may be unlikely or an unending battle. However, there are many ways of maximizing some of the changes which become disability, especially if intervention is instigated early and coupled with prevention (see Kane and Kane, 1978). Rehabilitation is the primary objective of many health programs serving younger people. For the older person, access to ongoing rehabilitation seems more limited: Both the programs and the clients are viewed as "exceptional." Why would it appear that an age distinction is made? What societal structures might work to support differential rehabilitation emphases? Before we assume that only exceptional older people can experience positive outcomes from restorative efforts (affecting them, their activities, or their physical/social environments), some systematic ethnographic and epidemiological documentation is essential.

The following appear to be some of the contrasts found in the ways rehabilitation and prevention have been conceptualized for younger and older people.

(1) Imagery. Images of younger disabled people often refer to visible, acute, or chronic conditions (Wolcott, 1978; Bruek, 1978; Goldenson, 1978). Disabilities of later adulthood may be less visible or dramatic and are typically chronic in nature (NCOA, 1978; Wolcott, 1978). Without the drama of the acute, there may be less public or professional interest in making improvements (Eisdorfer, 1969; Hess, 1976).

(2) Prevalence. Disability among younger people is rare, depending upon the condition, affecting fewer than 5 percent of the population. Disabilities increase with the age of the population studied so that only 15 percent of those 85 and over are free of limitations (Brotman, forthcoming; Butler, 1975).

(3) Causes. Disabilities among younger adults typically arise from a single cause—disease, accident/calamity, or birth defect. Disabilities of older people may result from multiple, unspecified causes and have less specific effects (Marsh, 1980; Comfort, 1980). It may also be that we have not adequately looked for causes of disability among the old, presuming age itself to be a satisfactory explanation (Birren, 1980).

(4) Objectives and Intervention. Rehabilitation is often the focus of intervention, especially for younger populations. But intervention may also refer to prevention, palliation, or the development of compensatory abilities or skills. Emphasis in rehabilitation for younger people has taken several directions.

One emphasis has been that of education, preferably along with able-bodied peers in appropriately designed programs (Lapidus, 1980). In contrast, much of the literature in aging focuses on grouping or separating older people of different abilities and degrees of impairment (Brody, 1970; Kahana and Coe, 1975; Lawton et al., 1980). Another area of emphasis has been employment in meaningful, lucrative, competitive work. In contrast, much of the emphasis in aging is on leisure or recreation, giving only lip service to employment-related skill retention or retraining (Lawson, 1979; Baugher, 1978; Merrill, 1967).

Independence in community living has also been emphasized, such as housing (Battelle Columbus Laboratories, 1977; McGuire, n.d.; Pastalan and Moyer, 1969), transportation (Bruek, 1978; Gordon and Shirasawa, 1979, Carp, 1971; U.S. Department of Transportation, 1977), accessibility (Cory, 1978; Garee, 1979; Wittmeyer and Stolov, 1978; Bruek, 1978), and social involvement (Goldenson, 1978; Marden and Burnight, 1972). The goals of rehabilitation of older adults, while similar, have often been directed more generally toward minimization of dependency and institutionalization and have often failed to directly involve the older person in lieu of the caregiving professional.

Prevention of disability in old age has been extremely slow in having an impact on either the public or professional consciousness. But prevention is difficult to sell to people of nearly every age. For example, despite the fact that physical exercise might maximize capability among people of a full range of abilities and ages, little emphasis is put on the topic (Butler, 1977-1978). In health care facilities for older people, physical therapy is provided for some, but exercises are seldom standard fare. It is often easier to obtain surgery or even optical aids than it is to obtain preventative vision examinations (Snyder et al., 1976).

(5) Entitlements. Rehabilitation is an entitlement of younger adults. Among the old, judging from legislated programs such as those falling under the Older Americans Act (Estes, 1979) or Medicare and Medicaid (Kane and Kane, 1978), rehabilitation is not conceptualized as an entitlement (see also Cohen, 1978). Unfortunately, these distinctions between policy and public emphasis may serve to polarize older and disabled people (and professionals or volunteers who work with them), creating competition for programs, space, services, and finances.

INDICATORS OF PROGRESS

There are indications, however, that there may be a greater set of options for older disabled people in the future, especially if certain efforts are encouraged and expanded. Some of these are listed below.

Senior Centers and Disabled Adults. The National Council on the Aging and the National Institute of Senior Centers have seeded a national effort directed at serving people who have a full continuum of abilities through neighborhood senior citizen centers, and utilizing these centers as more than social or recreational sites for the most able or gregarious (Jacobs, 1980). The success of many such programs appears to be a function of public education, for not all older people are accustomed to "mainstreaming" or comingling with people of varying levels of physical and mental competence. Transportation availability and outlook of staff and volunteers toward the clientele are also factors in a successful program.

Increased Interest in Older Workers Among Employers and Labor Organizations. Lawson (1979) and Baugher (1978) are among recent observers who have suggested that older workers are neither a detriment nor a threat to industry. Some ten years ago, Streib and Schneider (1971) reported that retirement itself causes neither a decline in health nor death. Yet the employer-employee working context has not adequately dealt either with issues of retirement or those of maximization of the skills of older men and women workers (Shepherd, 1976). As the emphasis of the 1980s moves from governmentally sponsored to private industry or local level programming, it is urgent that each sector maximally utilize (including retraining, counseling, or adapting the context) the older worker and the disabled worker of any age. The evidence regarding performance competitiveness exists; however, it may have to be presented and advocated, as minority causes of all types can become lost in the process of decentralization. To the individual, the work place may be a familiar source of social learning (Howell, 1978) and may offer continuity between middle ages, when some chronic impairments first occur, and later years of life.

Financial Incentives. Economic models for evaluating the financial as well as social costs and outcomes of rehabilitation of older individuals have been scarce (Albrecht and Harasymiw, 1979; Bennett, 1980). Some, such as Kane and Kane (1978), have argued for financial incentives in long-term care, which might also be extended to adult day health care that would operate to encourage greater attention to rehabilitation. At present society and social policy demand no more than basic shelter, safety, sanitary conditions, and amenities of subsistence. We recognize and reimburse pharmacological interventions, but drug abuse continues to escalate as a source of nonfunction (if not disability) among older people (Zawadski et al., 1978; Green, 1978). Once rehabilitation is viewed as a plausible intervention for older people at some levels, financial incentives should be reordered. For some, it may take the reordering of those financial incentives to bring about interest in prevention and rehabilitation efforts.

Self-Help and Group Support. Much has been written in recent years about the significance of self-help and mutual assistance among people of similar abilities or impairments (Lieberman et al., 1979; Gartner and Riessman, 1977; Butler et al., 1977-1978; Hess, 1976). While social support groups have been sponsored for a wide variety of public issues and personal chronic health conditions, the concept is just beginning to take hold among older people. Similarly, older people have been relatively less vociferous than other constituencies about those issues that hamper their lives (Butler, 1976). There is nothing so compelling as self-advocacy as a means of kindling public support, in counterdistinction to advocacy groups which may also have their own conflicting interests with which to contend. Actually, rehabilitation opportunities and prevention programs for older people suffer from a lack of consumer demand. Many of the efforts of advocacy groups have recently turned toward public education of consumers to develop self-help and self-assessment (health activation) skills and to represent their needs in a systematic method. At the American Foundation for the Blind, for example, there is a current program directed at uses of self-help to compensate for sensory losses in old age. Similar efforts are evident on behalf of Alzheimer's disease (a major cause of dementia), arthritis, stroke rehabilitation, and hearing recovery, to name a few.

Innovation for Selected Disabilities. A cursory review of some common functional disabilities suggests that in many areas there is a growing body of knowledge about how capability can be maximized.

(1) *Communication.* Cohen (1979) has outlined a series of techniques for improving verbal and nonverbal interaction with speech- and/or hearing-impaired older people, ranging from word emphasis and inflection to lowering one's voice, speaking more slowly, and being more conscious of the older individual's body positioning needs (see also Snyder, 1975; Bollinger, 1974; McCartney, 1979).

(2) *Audition.* Corso (1977) and McCartney (1979) have described changes occuring in auditory perception which would suggest the removal of distractions from the environment. Distractions mask voices, given that the sources of sounds are more difficult to separate and, therefore, are more confusing. Acoustical problems may pose obstacles as problematic for older people as were stairs for wheelchair users. While there are some suggestions for improving the acoustical environment, few have been widely adopted (*American Rehabilitation,* 1980). Several workable strategies are suggested for alerting the public to the potential for the auditory environment to support behavior. These include: publicizing "model" settings in existence; documenting examples of renovated and improved facilities; and developing incentives (financial and psychological) for acoustical improvements affecting community and public buildings.

(3) *Response styles and technology for older people.* Some years ago, Lindsley (1964) developed a conceptual outline and program of suggestions for adapting many pieces of equipment and daily activities to limitations in speed, strength, agility, and response styles of older individuals. Not until the past two years has there been real emphasis on the potential of technology for older people. Currently, at least four technology studies are under way: Gerontological Society, Washington, D.C.; Western Gerontological Society, San Francisco; Population Resource Center, New York City; and Case Western Reserve University, Cleveland. The possibilities for using interactive computer systems for memory development or robots to compensate for reduced mobility, maximize staffing, and even motivate exercise among the less stable have yet to become more than fanciful ideas. But, adequately organized to respond to multiple impairments, limited finances, and need for familiarity, technology may be one of several tools for the improved functioning of disabled people in the future.

There are also areas where the concepts are in place but the interventions are awaiting development or implementation. Listed below are some points to consider.

(1) *Mobility.* An extraordinary national effort was undertaken on behalf of people using wheelchairs and wheeling equipment (carts, carriages, luggage racks) during the 1960s and 1970s. As we learn more about posture and mobility of older people, there is a need to encourage ambulation, to design seating which responds to the agility demands of older people, and to provide motivation within housing and community programs to elicit greater or continued mobility throughout the later years of life (see Table 9.3). It may also be that wheelchair specifications and concepts of use which applied to relatively muscular individuals will have to be reconceptualized for older individuals (Fahland, 1976; Hiatt, 1978; Moss Rehabilitation Hospital Rehabilitation Engineering Center, 1978; U.S. Public Health Service, 1980).

(2) *Aging of the population disabled throughout life.* While program developments in senior centers and work places may reach out to people who become blind, deaf, impaired in mobility, or mentally retarded, how will these reach a population that has already experienced some needs (and perhaps seen the benefits of rehabilitation)? Not enough has been done, either by the specific or categorically oriented advocacy groups or by educational centers, to assist other sectors of health, aging, rehabilitation, and related services to understand and meet the needs of these populations. Similarly, professionals in the fields of aging, health, and rehabilitation need to extend education, funds, transportation, and interest to long-established rehabilitation centers, which have traditionally served a narrowly defined population group. Needs may be particularly significant among segments of the population that are living longer and in newer community systems of care, such as the older mentally retarded (Tymchuck, 1979). One might expect that those who have been impaired earlier in life might have different outlooks on rehabilitation, self-care, and mutual assistance. Again, we need to know more, both ethnographically and epidemiologically, about the disabled population as it ages.

(3) *Needs of special populations.* Linn et al. (1979) have conducted one of the few studies of ethnicity and disability. Their work suggests that in some communities disability may be more significant than social class or other considerations in determining one's adjustment to aging. But what about the data that purportedly show that certain minorities are more susceptible to various chronic impairments and likely to receive care from different systems than do their peers (Markson, 1979; Gelfand, 1979-1980; Schafft, 1980)? Other special populations might include individuals

TABLE 9.3   Percentage of Adults with Limitations in Geographic
Range or Mobility

Characteristic	17 - 44	U.S. Adults 45 - 64 Percents	65+
Confined to House	.3	1.3	5.2
Need Help Getting Around	.3	1.1	6.7
Have Trouble Alone	.5	2.4	5.8

SOURCE: National Center for Health Statistics, *Health in the United States*, 1975: 495, 497, 563; National Council on the Aging, 1978: 117.

who do not read or who are illiterate in English (Berg and Hammitt, 1980; Berkowitz et al., 1979). The possibilities for self-care may require different human and media systems according to the needs of special populations, as well as a better understanding of the attributes that translate into workable interventions.

UNWILLINGNESS TO SEEK HELP, PLAN, OR ADVOCATE

A final point to be made concerns images and public information. No system of rehabilitation, for people of any age, will operate for long if it lacks quality. But quality is not the only reason that some rehabilitation efforts, some programs of education or advocacy, fail to hit the mark. Moen (1978) has offered a series of explanations why older people do not avail themselves of assistance or services. These would seem to warrant particular study with reference to disabled populations.

(1) Age may be a prerequisite. It has been suggested that admission of age is admission of weakness (Shanas and Maddox, 1976).

(2) Income information or means tests may be required; these are often viewed as an invasion of privacy. Other income factors may figure into one's "guesstimate" of ineligibility, and may lead to the erroneous conclusion that one is ineligible.

(3) Transportation demands may exceed availability, predictability, finances, or sheer physical endurance.

(4) Study of older people's utilization of Talking Books and other services for print handicapped readers revealed evidence of several other factors (Berkowitz et al., 1979). These included unwillingness or trepidation over identification with the label or cause of "disability" (such as concern over adopting the "mantle of blindness" by visiting a rehabilitation center for the blind, even if that agency in fact serves partially sighted individuals; Genensky, 1978).

(5) Concern over loss of existing friendships and/or affiliation (and implications of interaction) with "disabled" people.

Astute planning at the agency level might create some links among various social settings, build new friendships, and serve to bridge familiar contexts with new experiences.

While the family has been discussed in terms of its willingness to provide care at home for disabled older people, its role in definition, evaluation, intervention, and environmental planning is not well developed. The family would seem to have great support potential for many handicapped individuals, if rehabilitation workers and families alike would be more diligent about seeking each other out for collaboration (see Streib, 1972; Turner, 1975).

The potential exists. We could have a system of care and rehabilitation in place by the year 2000 or slightly thereafter. It may take greater concern with the future and more planning than most people (older or younger) have thus far cared to take on (Kulys and Tobin, 1980; Smith, 1978), but we currently have in hand much of the information and capability required. There is an evident and growing demand. If we can imagine a diversified lifestyle, with options for everyone, despite existing impairments or handicaps, we can perhaps begin to advocate—that is, to *act*—in order to realize a whole person model and contextual supports that will maximize the good life in old age.

REFERENCES

ALBRECHT, G. W. and S. J. HARASYMIW (1979) "Evaluating rehabilitation outcome by cost function indicators." Journal of Chronic Disease 32, 7: 525-533.

American Rehabilitation (1980) "Improving the deaf person's environment." Volume 5, 5: 12-13.

BALTES, P. B. and G. V. LABOUVIE (1973) "Adult development of intellectual performance: description, explanation and modification," pp. 157-219 in C. Eisdorfer and M. P. Lawton (eds.) The Psychology of Adult Development and Aging. Washington, DC: American Psychological Association.

Battelle Columbus Laboratories (1977) Study and Evaluation of Integrating the Handicapped in HUD Housing. Washington, DC: HUD.

BAUGHER, D. (1978) "Is the older worker inherently incompetent?" Aging and Work 1, 4: 247-250.

BENNETT, A. E. (1980) "Cost effectiveness of rehabilitation or the elderly: preliminary results from the community hospital research program." Gerontologist 20, 3: 284-287.

BERG, A. and K. HAMMETT (1980) "Assessing the psychiatric patient's ability to meet the literacy demands of hospitalization." Hospital and Community Psychiatry 31, 4: 266-268.

BERKOWITZ, M., L. G. HIATT, P. DE TOLEDO, J. SHAPIRO, and M. LURIE (1979) Reading with Print Limitations (Volumes 1-3). New York: American Foundation for the Blind.

BIRREN, J. E. (1980) "Vision and aging." Keynote address, presented at Vision and Aging Conference, National Academy of Sciences, Washington, D.C.

——— and K. W. SCHAIE [eds.] (1977) Handbook of the Psychology of Aging. New York: Litton.

BOLLINGER, R. L. (1974) "Geriatric speech pathology." Gerontologist 14, 3: 217-220.

BRODY, E. M. (1970) "congregate care facilities and mental health of the elderly." Aging and Human Development 1, 4: 279-321.

——— M. H. KLEBAN, M. P. LAWTON, and H. A. SILVERMAN (1971) "Excess disabilities in mentally impaired aged: impact of individualized treatment." Gerontologist 11, 2: 124-132.

BROTMAN, H. (forthcoming) "Every ninth American," in Developments on Aging. Washington, DC: Government Printing Office.

BRUEK, L. (1978) Access: The Guide to a Better Life for Disabled Americans. New York: Random House.

BUTLER, R. N. (1977-1978) "Exercise: The neglected therapy." Journal of Aging and Human Development 8, 2: 193-195.

——— (1976) "Why shouldn't providers and consumers (old people and their families) join together in an alliance for older people?" International Journal of Aging and Human Development 7, 4: 343-351.

——— (1975) Why Survive? Being Old in America. New York: John Wiley.

——— and M. I. LEWIS (1973) Aging and Mental Health. St. Louis: Mosby.

BUTLER, R. N., J. S. GERTMAN, D. L. OBERLANDER, and L. SCHINDLER (1979-1980) "Self-help, self-care and the elderly." International Journal of Aging and Human Development 10, 1: 95-107.

CARP, F. M. (1971) "Walking as a means of transportation for retired people." Gerontologist 11, part 1: 104-111.

COHEN, E. (1978) "Civil liberties and the frail elderly." Society 15: 34-42.

COHEN, G. (1979) "Language comprehension in old age." Cognitive Psychology 11, 4: 412-429.

COMALLI, P. E. (1967) "Perception and age." Gerontologist 7, 2: 73-77.

COMFORT, A. (1980) "Geriatric psychiatry: physician-patient goals in mental health of old people," pp. 69-89 in G. Lesnoff-Caravaglia (ed.) Health Care of the Elderly. New York: Human Sciences.

CORY, J. R. (1978) How to Create Interiors for the Disabled: A Guidebook for Families and Friends. New York: Pantheon.

CULLINAN, T. R. (1979) "Studies of visually disabled people in the community." Regional Review 63: 21-25.

——— (1978a) "Epidemiology of visual disability." Transactions of the Ophthalmological Societies of the United Kingdom 98: 267-269.

——— (1978b) "Visually disabled people at home." New Beacon 63, 743: 57-59.

——— E. S. GOULD, J. H. SILVER, and D. IRVINE (1979) "Visual disability and home lighting." Lancet: 642-644.

CORSO, J. F. (1977) "Auditory perception and aging," pp. 535-553 in J. Birren and K. W. Schaie (eds.) Handbook of the Psychology of Aging. New York: Litton.

DAUBS, J. G. (1973) "Visual factors in the epidemiology of falls by the elderly." Journal of the American Optometric Association 44: 733-736.

EISDORFER, C. (1969) "Alternatives for the aging." Torch 42: 35-40.

ESTES, C. (1979) The Aging Enterprise. San Francisco: Jossey-Bass.

FAHLAND, B. (1976) Wheelchair Selection: More than Choosing a Chair with Wheels. Minneapolis: American Rehabilitation Foundation/Sister Kenny Institute.

FAYE, E. and C. HOOD (1976) "Visual rehabilitation in the geriatric population," pp. 123-126 in E. Faye and C. Hood (eds.) Clinical Low-Vision. Boston: Little, Brown.

FLOOD, J. T. (1979) "Special problems of the aged deaf person." Journal of Rehabilitation for the Deaf 12, 4: 34-35.

FOZARD, J. L. and S. J. POPKIN (1978) "Optimizing adult development: ends and means of an applied psychology of aging." American Psychologist 33: 975-989.

FOZARD, J. L., E. WOLF, B. BELL, R. A. McFARLAND, and S. PODOLSKY (1977) "Visual perception and communication," pp. 497-534 in J. E. Birren and K. W. Schaie (eds.) Handbook of the Psychology of Aging. New York: Litton.

FRANCHER, J. S. (1973) "It's the Pepsi generation. . . . Accelerated aging and the television commercial." International Journal of Aging and Human Development 4, 3: 245-254.

FREEMAN, J. T. (1979) Aging: Its History and Literature. New York: Human Sciences.

GAREE, B. [ed.] (1979) Ideas for Making Your Home Accessible. Bloomington, IL: Cheever.

GARTNER, A. and F. RIESSMAN (1977) Self-Help in the Human Services. San Francisco: Jossey-Bass.

GELFAND, D. E. (1979-1980) "Ethnicity, aging and mental health." International Journal of Aging and Human Development 10, 3: 289-298.

GENENSKY, S. (1978) "Data concerning the partially sighted and the functionally blind." Journal of Visual Impairment and Blindness 72, 5: 177-180.

GERMAIN, C. (1977) "An ecological perspective on social work practice in health care." Social Work in Health Care 3, 1: 67-76.

GOLDENSON, R. M. (1978) Disability and Rehabilitation Handbook. New York: McGraw-Hill.

GORDON, S. and K. SHIRASAWA (1979) "Transportation system analysis techniques," pp. 90-112 in V. Regnier (ed.) Planning for the Elderly: Alternative Community Analysis Techniques. Los Angeles: Ethel Percy Andrus.

GREEN, G. (1978) "The politics of psychoactive drug use in old age." Gerontologist 18, 6: 525-530.

HARBER, L. (1967) "Identify the disabled: concepts and methods in the measurement of disability." Social Security Bulletin 29: 1-16.

HESS, B. (1976) "Self-help among the aged." Social Policy 1: 88-99.

HIATT, L. G. (1980) "Is poor light dimming the sight of nursing home patients?" Nursing Homes 29: 32-41.

——— (1978) "Architecture for older people: achieving rehabilitation by design." Inland Architect 23: 6-17.

HOWELL, S. (1978) "Aging and social learning of a new environment," pp. 371-376 in H.O.K. Shimanda (ed.) Recent Advances in Gerontology: Proceedings of the Eleventh International Congress of Gerontology. Tokyo.

JACOBS, B. (1980) Senior Centers and the At-Risk Older Person. Washington, DC: National Council on the Aging.

——— [ed.] (1976) Working with the Impaired Elderly. Washington, DC: National Council on the Aging.

JOCHHEIM, K. A. (1979) "The classification of handicaps." International Journal of Rehabilitation Research (Supplement) 2, 3: 25-31.

KAHANA, E. and R. M. COE (1975) "Alternatives to long-term care," pp. 391-454 in S. Sherwood (ed.) Long-Term Care: A Handbook for Researchers, Planners, and Providers. New York: Spectrum.

KANE, R. L. and R. A. KANE (1978) "Care of the aged: old problems in need of new solutions." Science 200: 913-919.

KENSHALO, D. R. (1977) "Age changes in touch, vibration, temperature, kinesthesis and pain sensitivity," pp. 562-579 in J. E. Birren and K. W. Schaie (eds.) Handbook of the Psychology of Aging. New York: Litton.

KIRCHNER, C. and C. LOWMAN (1978) "Sources of variation in the estimated prevalence of visual loss." Journal of Visual Impairment and Blindness 72, 8: 329-333.

KIRCHNER, C. and R. PETERSON (1980) "Multiple impairments among non-institutionalized blind and visually impaired persons." Journal of Visual Impairment and Blindness 74, 1: 42-44.

KLEBAN, M. H., E. M. BRODY, and M. P. LAWTON (1971) "Personality traits in the mentally-impaired aged and their relationship to improvements in current functioning." Gerontologist 11, 2: 134-140.

KULYS, R. and S. TOBIN (1980) "Interpreting the lack of future concerns among the elderly." International Journal of Aging and Human Development 11, 2: 111-126.

KUYPERS, J. A. and V. L. BENGSTON (1973) "Social breakdown and competence: a model of normal aging." Human Development 16, 3: 181-201.

LAPIDUS, H. P. (1980) "Let's get serious about mainstreaming." Journal of Learning Disabilities 13, 9: 500.

LAWSON, F. H. (1979) "Private enterprise and the older worker: what are the issues?" Aging and Work 2, 1: 7-11.

LAWTON, M. P. (1977) "The impact of environment on aging and behavior," pp. 276-301 in J. E. Birren and K. W. Schaie (eds.) Handbook of the Psychology of Aging. New York: Litton.

——— L. NAHEMOW, and T. YEH (1980) "Neighborhood development and the well-being of older tenants in planning housing." International Journal of Aging and Human Development 11, 13: 211-227.

LIEBERMAN, M. A., D. BORMAN, and Associates (1979) Self-Help Groups for Coping with Crisis. San Francisco: Jossey-Bass.

LINDSLEY, O. R. (1964) "Geriatric behavioral prosthetics," pp. 41-60 in R. Kastenbaum (ed.) New Thoughts on Old Age. New York: Springer.

LINN, M. W., K. I. HUNTER, and P. R. PERRY (1979) "Differences by sex and ethnicity in the psychosocial adjustment of the elderly." Journal of Health and Social Behavior 20: 273-281.

McCARTNEY, J. (1979) "Hearing problems: speech and language problems associated with hearing loss and aural rehabilitation," in M. V. Jones (ed.) Speech and Language Problems of the Aging. Springfield, IL: Charles C Thomas.

MacDONALD, M. L. and A. K. BUTLER (1974) "Reversal of helplessness: producing walking behavior in nursing home wheelchair residents using behavior modification procedures." Journal of Gerontology 29, 1: 97-101.

McGUIRE, M. T. (n.d.) Housing and Handicapped People. Washington, DC: President's Committee on Employment of the Handicapped.

MARDEN, P. G. and R. BURNIGHT (1972) "Social Consequences of physical impairments in an aging population," pp. 445-465 in D. B. Kent et al. (eds.) Research Planning and Action for the Elderly. New York: Behavioral Publications.

MARKSON, E. W. (1979) "Ethnicity as a factor in the institutionalization of the ethnic elderly," pp. 341-356 in D. E. Gelfand and A. J. Kurtiz (eds.) Ethnicity and Aging: Theory, Research and Policy. New York: Springer.

MARSH, G. R. (1980) "Perceptual changes with aging," pp. 147-168 in E. W. Busse and D. G. Blazer (eds.) Handbook of Geriatric Psychiatry. New York: Litton.

MERRILL, T. (1967) Activities for the Aged and Infirm. Springfield, IL: Charles C Thomas.

MERTON, R. K. (1957) Social Theory and Social Structure. New York: Macmillan.

MILLS, J. H. (1978) "Effects of noise on young and old people," pp. 229-241 in D. M. Lipscomb (ed.) Noise and Audiology. Baltimore: University Park Press.

MOEN, E. (1978) "The reluctance of the elderly to accept help." Social Problems 25, 3: 293-303.

Moss Rehabilitation Hospital Rehabilitation Engineering Center (1978) Wheelchair-I: Report of a Workshop, December 6-9, 1977. Philadelphia: Author.

National Society to Prevent Blindness (1980) Vision Problems in the U.S. New York: Author.

ORDY, J. M. and K. R. BRIZZE [eds.] (1979) Sensory Systems and Communication in the Elderly. New York: Raven.

PADULA, W. V. (1981) What Is Low Vision? New York: American Foundation for the Blind.

PALMORE, E. (1973) "Social factors in mental illness of the aged," pp. 41-52 in E. W. Busse and E. Pfeiffer (eds.) Mental Illness in Later Life. Washington, DC: American Psychiatric Association.

PARR, J. (1980) "The interaction of persons and living environments," pp. 393-406 in L. Poon (ed.) Aging in the 1980's. Washingotn, DC: American Psychological Association.

PASTALAN, L. A. and L. N. MOYER (1969) Vistula Manor Demonstration Housing for the Physically Disabled. Springfield, VA: U.S. Department of Commerce, National Technical Information Service.

PFEIFFER, E. (1977) "Psychopathology and social pathology," pp. 650-671 in J. E. Birren and K. W. Schaie (eds.) Handbook of the Psychology of Aging. New York: Litton.

POWERS, J. K. and E. A. POWERS (1978) "Hearing problems of elderly persons: social consequences and prevalence." American Speech and Hearing Association 20, 2: 79-83.

PYREK, J. and L. H. SNYDER (1978) "The human development inventory: a measuring instrument with programmatic implications," in J. Pyrek et al. (eds.) Human Development Assessment and Care Planning. Minneapolis: Ebenezer Center for Aging and Human Development.

RODIN, J. and E. LANGER (1980) "Aging labels: the decline of content and the fall of self-esteem." Journal of Social Issues 36, 2: 12-29.

ROSENBLOOM, A. A. (1974) "Prognostic factors in the visual rehabilitation of the aging patient." New Outlook for the Blind 68, 3: 124-127.

SCHAFFT, G. (1980) "Nursing home care and the minority elderly." Journal of Long-Term Care Administration 8, 4: 1-31.

SHANAS, E. and G. L. MADDOX (1976) "Aging, health and the organization of resources," pp. 592-618 in R. H. Binstock and E. Shanas (eds.) Handbook of Aging and the Social Sciences. New York: Litton.

SHEPHERD, H. L. (1976) "Work and retirement," pp. 286-309 in R. H. Binstock and E. Shanas (eds.) Handbook of Aging and the Social Sciences. New York: Litton.

SILVER, J. H., E. S. GOULD, D. IRVINE, and T. R. CULLINAN (1978) "Visual acuity at home and in eye clinics." Transactions of the Ophthalmological Societies of the United Kingdom 98, part 2: 262-267.

SMITH, J. W. (1978) "You're 35? Time to start retirement planning." Perspectives on Aging 7, 5: 8-9.

SNYDER, L. H. (1975) "Living environments, geriatric wheelchairs and older persons' rehabilitation." Journal of Gerontological Nursing 1, 5: 17-20.

——— J. PYREK, and K. SMITH (1976) "Vision and mental function." Gerontologist 16, 3: 491-495.

STREIB, G. (1972) "Older families and their troubles: familial and social responses." Family Coordinator 21, 1: 5-19.

——— and C. J. SCHNEIDER (1971) Retirement in American Society. Ithaca, NY: Cornell University Press.

THORNBURY, J. M. and C. M. MISTRETTA (1981) "Tactile sensitivity as a function of age." Journal of Gerontology 36, 1: 34-39.

TURNER, J. G. (1975) "Patterns of intergeneralization exchange." International Journal of Aging and Human Development 6, 2: 111-115.

TYMCHUK, A. J. (1979) "The mentally retarded in later life," pp. 197-210 in O. J. Kaplan (ed.) Psychopathology of Aging. New York: Academic.

U.S. Department of Transportation (1977) Transportation and Elderly and Handicapped: A Literature Capsule. Cambridge, MA: U.S. Department of Transportation, Transportation Systems Center.

U.S. Public Health Service (1980) Use of Special Aids: United States, 1977. Hyattsville, MD: U.S. Public Health Service, Office of Health Research Statistics and Technology, National Center for Health Statistics.

WALLER, J. A. (1978) "Falls among the elderly—human environmental factors." Accident Analysis and Prevention 10: 21-33.

WEINBERG, N. and J. WILLIAMS (1978) "How the physically disabled perceive their disabilities." Journal of Rehabilitation 44: 31-33.

WILLEMS, E. P. (1977) "Behavioral ecology," pp. 39-68 in D. Stokols (ed.) Perspectives on Environment and Behavior: Theory, Research and Applications. New York: Plenum.

WINDLEY, P. G. and R. J. SCHEIDT (1980) "Person-environment dialectics: implications for competent functioning in old age," pp. 407-423 in L. Poon (ed.) Aging in the 1980's. Washington, DC: American Psychological Association.

WITTMEYER, M. B. and W. C. STOLOV (1978) "Educating wheelchair patients on home architecture." American Journal of Occupational Therapy 32, 9: 557-564.

WOLCOTT, L. E. (1978) "Rehabilitation and the aged," pp. 149-172 in W. Reichel (ed.) Clinical Aspects of Aging. Baltimore: Williams and Wilkins.

ZAWADSKI, R., G. B. GLAZER, and E. LURIE (1978) "Psychotropic drug use among institutionalized and non-institutionalized Medicaid aged in California." Journal of Gerontology 33, 6: 825-834.

10

PSYCHOLOGICAL WELL-BEING IN RETIREMENT

Arthur Weinberger

The mental health profession has generally assumed that older people could not benefit from psychotherapy. In particular, psychoanalysis, which was the dominant form of treatment until not long ago, was skeptical about the possibility of effecting any positive therapeutic outcome in later life. As a result, little was done to develop a clinical psychology of old age or to promote mental health services for adults past the conventional age of retirement. However, current social, scientific, and political interest and involvement in aging, phenomena no doubt stirred by the burgeoning number of people reaching and surpassing retirement age, are profoundly altering the conception that older people cannot be successfully treated through psychotherapy. Perhaps the most fundamental consequence of this new awareness in the field of mental health is the growing recognition of the following points:

(1) Psychopathology is not intrinsic to aging.
(2) The most frequently seen disorders among retired adults are socially and not biologically induced.
(3) Restoration of mental health is possible and desirable for people who are 65 or over.
(4) Psychological and psychiatric services should be made available to adults during the retirement period.

There can be little doubt that the field of gerontology is in a period of transition and on the frontiers of new knowledge about the relationship between mental health and aging. The purpose of this chapter is to outline a number of basic issues related to mental health during the retirement period, as well as to suggest avenues of needed research.

DEVELOPMENTAL TASKS FOR PRESERVING EMOTIONAL HEALTH

Erikson (1963) was one of the first writers to see old age or the retirement period as a distinct developmental stage, with its own rewards and tribulations. According to Erikson, the psychosocial crisis of this stage could be positively resolved through integration of previous developmental achievements, a process sustaining and promoting emotional health. Failure to accomplish this leads to despair and emotional distress. More recently, a number of investigators have speculated that the principal task of the retirement period is adaptation to loss (Muslin and Epstein, 1980; Pfeiffer, 1977). Muslin and Epstein (1980: 7) have divided this task into three central developmental goals:

(1) acceptance of changes in phase-specific ego ideals;
(2) acceptance of somatic changes; and
(3) accommodation to phase-specific losses.

These authors further note:

These developmental tasks constitute very important phase-specific tasks of the later years that are of major importance in a consideration of the psychosocial equilibrium during aging. A syndrome can be defined that constitutes "resistance to aging" and considers the resistance to the mastery of the developmental tasks of aging as pathogenic, i.e., resistance to changes in ideals and self-system, with resultant lack of acceptance of the limitations, will constitute a specific syndrome of disequilibrium that may result in a variety of psychopathologic phenomena [Muslin and Epstein, 1980: 7].

According to another investigator, successful adaptation during retirement involves replacing some of the losses, remaining active, and making do with less (Pfeiffer, 1977). What are some of the losses to which retirees should adjust? The most frequently cited crises that are related to loss include: widowhood; increased vulnerability to disease, pain, hospitalization, and surgery; loss of income; reduction or loss of status; reduction or loss of physical, sensory, and cognitive functioning; agism—both individual and institutional; and preparation for and preoccupation with death and dying (Butler and Lewis, 1973; Palmore, 1973). Are these changes inevitable? Are lessened expectations the only healthy alternative?

An inspection of the above list reveals that only the first two events are fixed and immutable; everything else is variable and susceptible to modification. More and more evidence suggests that many of the current losses that retirees are asked to bear, and which impair mental functioning, are social in nature and not intrinsic to the processes of aging (Langer, 1979; Rodin and Langer, 1980). Some of the available data also seem to suggest that resisting sociocultural expectations of aging (stereotyped behaviors) is positively associated with mental health. (Bultena and Powers, 1978; Kuypers and Bengston, 1973; Ward, 1977). Consequently, until we can tease out the variances attributable to biological and social factors in aging, the notion that the developmental task in late life is principally adaptation to loss—a response that is essentially passive, and reminiscent of agistic attitudes—warrants at the very least a more tentative formulation. Given that fully a third of adults over 65 consider the retirement period the best years of their lives (Harris, 1975), and that the future aged are going to be better educated and healthier than those who have gone before, a more balanced social perspective can be anticipated.

PREPONDERANT SYMPTOMS FOUND
DURING THE RETIREMENT PERIOD

Pfeiffer (1977: 651-652) states that

the psychiatric syndromes characteristic of old age are a mere handful of relatively simple forms of psychopathology, including prominently among them the depressive reactions, hypochondriasis, paranoid reactions, and transient situational disturbances as well as chronic anxiety states. In fact, the symptoms just outlined ... account for the vast majority of psychopathology that is not based on brain disease or loss of brain tissue.

The explanation offered for the prevalence of these disorders is that they are reactions to some of the crises frequently encountered in old age. Depression, for example, which is by far the most frequent complaint, is understood as a typical reaction to loss. Paranoid reactions are thought to be facilitated by social isolation and sensory deficits, and to serve as a defense to make the environment more secure and manageable (Pfeiffer and Busse, 1973). Attention to various forms of stimuli are excluded or minimized as a way of maintaining control (Weinberg, 1951).

All too often, in the past, many of these symptoms were attributed to the processes of aging, and, seen as inevitable, they were accepted as "normal," even by the aged. It is therefore expecially important to realize that there are no data to indicate a so-called neurosis or psychosis of old age (Muslin and Epstein, 1980: 3), with the possible exception of one or two organic brain syndromes. Consequently, psychological disequilibrium

TABLE 10.1 Nonorganically Based Symptoms Commonly Found in Adults of Retirement Age

Functional Psychotic Reactions	Neurotic Reactions	Character Disorders
depressive	depressive	"criminal" behavior
manic	anxiety	(gambling, vagrancy,
paranoid	phobic	disorderly conduct)
	hysterical	prescribed drug abuse and misuse
	obsessive compulsive	alcoholism
	hypochondriachal	

NOTE: For a discussion of these disorders, see Pfeiffer (1977) and Simon (1980).

is not intrinsic to aging, nor is it the modal response. Thus, psychothera-
peutic treatment is indicated for self-referred and other-referred elderly
experiencing or exhibiting psychological distress and turmoil.

METHODS AND MODIFICATIONS OF TREATMENT

Given the pessimistic prognosis that has been attached to treating the
elderly, it is most interesting that the various therapies that have been used
with older adults have all been found to be "effective." The various
treatments that have been tried include: cognitive (Sherman, 1979); sex
(Runciman, 1975); group therapy (Leiderman et al., 1967); marital and
family therapy (Peterson, 1973); bibliotherapy and psychodrama (Tuzil,
1978); and yes, even dynamic psychotherapy (Hiatt, 1971). Though the
uniformity in results across these treatments is very encouraging, most of
the work reported in the literature is difficult to evaluate because it is
fraught with conceptual and methodological deficiencies (Kahn and Zarit,
1974; Sparacino, 1978-1979).

The question of whether or not to provide psychotherapy is going to
grow in importance in the coming decades, and really is no longer at issue.
What is at issue is what types of therapy are most appropriate for adults of
retirement age. That is, what sort of therapy is best suited to help the
retired adult who finds himself or herself in psychological difficulty? The
magnitude of this question is better appreciated when one notes that there
are no less than 250 different therapies in use today, each in competition
with the others for relieving psychological suffering (Henrik, 1980). While
the need for studying the comparative efficacy of various methods of
treatment was expressed over 20 years ago (Rechtschaffen, 1959), a recent
review concluded that no such research effort has been developed or
seriously attempted (Sparacino, 1978-1979).

The magnitude and complexity of designing and implementing such a
research program, not to mention the problems associated with funding,
have probably been major deterrents to such an undertaking. Although
nothing can substitute for such a study in terms of experimentally valid
output, more limited approaches should also be considered. For instance,
it would be profitable to investigate what effect the age of the client has
on the efficacy of therapy within each method of treatment. Consider
some of the research questions within the cognitive domain that could
thus be reasonably addressed: Is cognitive therapy, or particular cognitive
techniques, as effective with 70 year olds as with 20 year olds? Are
cognitive approaches more applicable to certain developmental periods and
problems than to others? Even though this research approach would not
be sufficient for making cross-therapeutic comparisons, it could neverthe-

less greatly enhance our understanding of the influence of age and its correlates on therapeutic outcomes.

Although evidence for a preferred method of treatment is lacking, a number of investigators have proposed and implemented general modifications in therapeutic technique, tailored to meet the special characteristics and needs of adults of retirement age (Butler and Lewis, 1973; Pfeiffer and Busse, 1973; Post, 1965; Wayne, 1952, 1953; Weinberg, 1951). Typically, these investigators recommended that therapy with retired adults be short-term, active-directive, problem-oriented, flexible, and supportive.

These modifications, and others that will no doubt follow, may eventually spawn yet another brand of therapy (retirement therapy?), geared exclusively toward dealing with the vicissitudes of aging and retirement. Retirement therapy, or something analogous, is very likely to evolve, because future retirees, who will be healthier and better educated than their predecessors, will require not only treatment for mental disorders but also means for enhancing personality growth and development.

TREATMENT GOALS IN PSYCHOTHERAPY

Although authorities agree that adults past the age of retirement could gain just as much, if not more, from psychotherapy than younger adults (Blau and Berezin, 1975; Butler, 1975), there is considerable disagreement concerning the themes and goals to be pursued in psychotherapy. Though no doubt the principal aim is to provide relief from psychological and behavioral distress, the exact means to this goal remain undecided. Proposed treatment goals include: adapting the environment to the needs of older adults (Ginzburg, 1950); accepting the processes of aging (Hammer, 1972; Muslin and Epstein, 1980); providing interpersonal contact (Grotjahn, 1955); and providing relief to relatives. (See Götestam, 1980, for a more complete listing.) Differences of opinion also exist on more specific issues. For example, some clinicians endorse insight (Götestam, 1980; Rosenthal, 1959), others eschew it (Verwoerdt, 1976); some recommend the utility of the life review (Blau and Berezin, 1975; Lewis and Butler, 1974), others warn against it (Hamilton and Cowdry, 1976); some favor delving into fears about death and dying (Butler and Lewis, 1973), others caution to avoid these and related topics (Wolff, 1970).

In respect to therapeutic goals, a number of therapists have remarked that, because many of the symptoms exhibited by the elderly serve as defenses and are ways of coping with the environment, they should not be tampered with unless adequate substitutions can be provided (see Muslin and Epstein, 1980, for a discussion of this issue). In this vein it is important to recall that most of the elderly suffer from social stresses. Is it realistic, let alone ethical, to expect the therapist to provide an individual solution to what is in reality a social problem? For example, should the role of the therapist, because of the widespread problem of isolation found among the elderly, be reduced to that of companion? Sadly, an analyst remarked that frequently in the elderly "the neurosis or psychosis was a much better solution to their life difficulties than any that I as an agent could offer" (Jelliffe, quoted in Muslin and Epstein, 1980: 4).

The differences in opinion concerning goals and the sheer number of opinions highlight two important aspects: The field of geropsychiatry is not only an infant, but a neonate, and the goals of therapy reflect a complex issue, an issue probably as much a function of values as of anything else. Because of the current lack of knowledge, but more on account of the wide variability that exists among retired adults, it is absolutely essential that each client be provided with his or her own individual treatment plan (Muslin and Epstein, 1980). This should take into account the specific problem(s) in relation to the client's physical and mental resources, previous history, and most profitable mode of treatment (such as insight, drugs, diet, environmental support, or some combination).

CHARACTERISTICS OF THE THERAPIST

A number of therapist characteristics have been found necessary for effective therapeutic change (Rogers, 1967; Truax and Carkhuff, 1967). Consequently, it is of some pertinence to ask: Are there any therapist characteristics that are of particular relevance in working with retired adults? Of the variables that may be considered in this respect, two are the attitudes and the age of the therapist.

An obvious barrier to successful treatment is the inability of therapists to accept or feel comfortable with older clients. In addition to "free-floating" negative attitudes toward the aged, some reasons that therapists may feel less at ease than with younger adults are because the aged may stimulate in them (1) fears about aging; (2) conflicts about their own parental relations; (3) feelings of helplessness and of "wasting" time; (4) fears that the client may die during treatment; (5) a wish to avoid professional criticism and disdain, possibly ensuing from working with and/or expressing an interest in older people (Group for the Advancement of Psychiatry, in Butler and Lewis, 1973). These factors undoubtedly impair the ability of therapists to help older clients; however, simply knowing this is insufficient for improving mental health services for people over 65. Research and training programs have to be developed that will not only examine how the age of the client modifies the therapeutic process but that will also generate techniques to help the therapist overcome his or her "age spots" when working with adults of retirement age.

While there are no reliable data to support the notion that the age of the therapist should be a consideration for retired adults seeking psychological assistance, the psychogeriatric literature does imply that older therapists may be more interested in and competent to work with the aged (Garetz, 1975). It is rather plausible to assume that younger therapists may not be fully cognizant nor appreciative of the problems associated with aging and, as a result, might not be as capable with this age group as their older colleagues. Transference and countertransference issues further complicate the question. But before this matter is dismissed as simply a case of reverse agism, it should be examined empirically.

CONCLUSION

It is all too evident that there is a tremendous gap between the number of retirement-age adults needing mental health services and those receiving them. Even though adults over 65 constitute more than 10 percent of the population and exhibit a higher incidence of mental disorders than members of younger age groups (HEW, 1979), only 4 percent of the patients seen at outpatient mental health clinics are past retirement age; moreover, it has been estimated that *less than 1 percent* of treatment time is devoted to the aged in these clinics (Cohen, 1980). Although there are some attitudinal barriers to seeking psychological assistance among retired adults (Sparacino, 1978-1979), financial obstacles may be a greater factor in preventing retirees from obtaining help (Cohen, 1980).

During the coming decades, the conflict between ethical and pragmatic (cost?) considerations of treating the burgeoning number of elderly will come into sharp relief. Will economic considerations be tempered with ethical and social values? If we are to plan judiciously, it is imperative that we pause and reflect upon the following questions: How much should therapy cost and who should pay for it? Should the mental health profession offer "senior citizen discounts?" Should the cost-benefit criterion be applied? Should Medicaid and Medicare cover all or most mental health costs?

While the above questions are critical and no doubt reflect the bottom line, the present economic constraints and proposed cutbacks of programs affecting the elderly preclude saying anything more specific than what is already an obvious and legitimate conclusion: *Quality mental health services commensurate with their levels of income should be made available to retired adults.* In acknowledging and working toward this goal, it is also important to recognize that mental health care cannot be a palliative for the rights and needs of retired adults. Until some of the social conditions that facilitate emotional disorders during the retirement years are amelio-

rated, the effectiveness of the mental health profession will be severely
limited. Psychotherapy cannot and should not be a substitute for the
deficiencies of society.

REFERENCES

BLAU, D. and M. A. BEREZIN (1975) "Neuroses and character disorders," in J. G.
    Howells (ed.) Modern Perspectives in the Psychiatry of Old Age. New York:
    Brunner/Mazel.
BULTENA, G. L. and E. A. POWERS (1978) "Denial of aging: age identification and
    reference group orientations." Journal of Gerontology 33, 5: 748-754.
BUTLER, R. N. (1975) "Psychiatry and the elderly: an overview." American Journal
    of Psychiatry 132, 9: 893-900.
——— and M. I. LEWIS (1973) Aging and Mental Health. St. Louis: Mosby.
COHEN, G. D. (1980) "Prospects for mental health and aging," in J. E. Birren and
    R. B. Sloane (eds.) Handbook of Mental Health and Aging. Englewood Cliffs, NJ:
    Prentice-Hall.
ERIKSON, E. H. (1963) Childhood and Society. New York: Norton.
GARETZ, F. K. (1975) "The psychiatrist's involvement with aged patients." Ameri-
    can Journal of Psychiatry 132, 1: 63-65.
GINZBERG, R. (1950) "Psychology in everyday geriatrics." Geriatrics 5: 36-43.
GÖTESTAM, G. K. (1980) "Behavioral and dynamic psychotherapy with the
    elderly," in J. E. Birren and R. B. Sloane (eds.) Handbook of Mental Health and
    Aging. Englewood Cliffs, NJ: Prentice-Hall.
GROTJAHN, M. (1955) "Analytic psychotherapy with the elderly." Psychoanalytic
    Review 42: 419-427.
HAMILTON, J. A. and E. V. COWDRY (1976) "Psychiatric aspects," in F. U.
    Steinberg (ed.) Cowdry's the Care of the Geriatric Patient. St. Louis: Mosby.
HAMMER, M. (1972) "Psychotherapy with the aged," in M. Hammer (ed.) The
    Theory and Practice of Psychotherapy with Specific Disorders. Springfield, IL:
    Charles C Thomas.
Louis Harris and Associates (1975) The Myth and Reality of Aging in America. New
    York: National Council on Aging.
HENRIK, R. (1980) The Psychotherapy Handbook. New York: Meridian.
HIATT, H. (1971) "Dynamic psychotherapy with the aging patient." American
    Journal of Psychotherapy 25: 591-600.
KAHN, R. L. and S. H. ZARIT (1974) "Evaluation of mental health programs for the
    aged," in P. O. Davidson et al. (eds.) Evaluation of Behavioral Programs. Cham-
    paign, IL: Research Press.
KUYPERS, J. A. and V. L. BENGSTON (1973) "Social breakdown and competence:
    a model of normal aging." Human Development 16, 3: 181-201.
LANGER, E. (1979) "Old age: an artifact?" in Biology, Behavior and Aging.
    Washington, DC: National Research Council.
LIEDERMAN, P. C., R. GREEN, and V. R. LIEDERMAN (1967) "Outpatient group
    therapy with geriatric patients." Geriatrics 22: 148-153.
LEWIS, M. I. and R. N. BUTLER (1974) "Life review therapy: putting memories to
    work in individual and group psychotherapy." Geriatrics 29: 165-173.

MUSLIN, H. and L. J. EPSTEIN (1980) "Preliminary remarks on the rationale for psychotherapy of the aged." Comprehensive Psychiatry 21, 1: 1-12.

PALMORE, E. B. (1973) "Social factors in mental illness of the aged," in E. W. Busse and E. Pfeiffer (eds.) Mental Illness in Later Life. Washington, DC: American Psychiatric Association.

PETERSON, J. A. (1973) "Marital and family therapy involving the aged." Gerontologist 13: 27-31.

PFEIFFER, E. (1977) "Psychopathology and social pathology," in J. E. Birren and K. W. Schaie (eds.) Handbook of the Psychology of Aging. New York: Litton.

——— and E. W. BUSSE (1973) "Mental disorders in later life–affective disorders; paranoid, neurotic, and situational reactions," in E. W. Busse and E. Pfeiffer (eds.) Mental Illness in Later Life. Washington, DC: American Psychiatric Association.

POST, F. (1965) The Clinical Psychiatry of Later Life. Oxford: Pergamon.

RECHTSCHAFFEN, A. (1959) "Psychotherapy with geriatric patients: a review of the literature." Journal of Gerontology 14: 73-84.

RODIN, J. and E. LANGER (1980) "Aging labels: the decline of control and the fall of self-esteem." Journal of Social Issues 36, 2: 12-29.

ROGERS, C. R. (1967) "The therapeutic relationship: recent theory and research," in F. W. Matson and A. Montague (eds.) The Human Dialogue. New York: Macmillan.

ROSENTHAL, H. R. (1959) "Psychotherapy for aging." American Journal of Psychotherapy 17: 55-65.

RUNCIMAN, A. (1975) "Problems that older clients present in counseling about sexuality," in I. M. Burnside (ed.) Sexuality and Aging. Los Angeles: University of Southern California Press.

SHERMAN, E. (1979) "A cognitive approach to direct practice with the aging." Journal of Gerontological Social Work 2, 1: 43-53.

SIMON, A. (1980) "The neuroses, personality disorders, alcoholism, drug use and misuse, and crime in the aged," in J. E. Birren and R. B. Sloane (eds.) Handbook of Mental Health and Aging. Englewood Cliffs, NJ: Prentice-Hall.

SPARACINO, J. (1978-1979) "Individual psychotherapy with the aged: a selective review." International Journal of Aging and Human Development 9, 3: 197-220.

TRUAX, C. B. and R. R. CARKHUFF (1967) Toward Effective Counseling in Psychotherapy. Chicago: Aldine.

TUZIL, T. J. (1978) "The written word and the elderly: adjunct to treatment." Journal of Gerontological Social Work 1, 1: 81-87.

U.S. Department of Health, Education, and Welfare [HEW] (1979) Mental Health and the Elderly. DHEW Publication No. (OHDS) 80-20960. Washington, DC: Author.

VERWOERDT, A. (1976) Clinical Geropsychiatry. Baltimore: Williams and Wilkins.

WARD, R. A. (1977) "The impact of subjective age and stigma on older persons." Journal of Gerontology 32, 2: 227-232.

WAYNE, G. J. (1953) "Modified psychoanalytic therapy in senescence." Psychoanalytic Review 40: 99-116.

——— (1952) "Psychotherapy in senescence." Annals of Western Medicine and Surgery 6: 88-91.

WEINBERG, J. (1951) "Psychiatric techniques in the treatment of older people," in W. Donahue and C. Tibbitts (eds.) Growing in the Older Years. Ann Arbor: University of Michigan Press.

WOLFF, K. (1970) The Emotional Rehabilitation of the Geriatric Patient. Springfield, IL: Charles C Thomas.

11

THE FAMILY AND RETIREMENT

Alice Kethley

A look at the gerontological literature provides strong support for using the family as a logical focal point for understanding the needs of the majority of this nation's retired individuals. The Office of Human Development Services of the Administration on Aging reported that in 1978 82 percent of men and 58 percent of women over age 65 lived in a family setting. Perhaps even more significant is the consistent finding that family members provide the majority of the services to the retired population. As Tobin and Kulys (1980) state in a review of the literature on older families: "The myth that families abandon their elderly had been dispelled, and this became the decade for discovery of the family as a resource for its elderly." Widows, the never married, and divorced individuals, as well as those married and living with spouses, receive support from the family network. Based on these findings, this chapter will explore the retired population as members of families and the implications that has for research, policy, and programming.

THE FAMILY

Perhaps the most maligned and misunderstood group in our society has been the nuclear family. As a nation, Americans have been prone to cling to and romanticize the concept of the extended family while underestimating and degrading the important contributions of the nuclear family system. Parsons (1943) describes the U.S. kinship system in its most negative extreme, which, unfortunately, reflects the view held by many today:

> [In] comparison with other kinship systems, the individual in our system is drastically segregated from his family ... both from his parents—and their forebears—and from his siblings. His first kinship loyalty is unequivocally to his spouse and then to their children if and when they are born. Moreover, his family of procreation, by virtue of a common household income, and community status, becomes a solidary unit in the sense in which the segregation of the interests of individual ego from those of the family of orientation tends relatively to minimize solidarity with the latter.

While this description accurately describes the nuclear family, it is an injustice to apply it to the American family as it has evolved. A number of literature reviews provide a much more useful picture of the family and the interaction between generations (Silverstone, 1978; Sussman, 1976; Tobin and Kulys, 1980; Atchley and Miller, 1980). The family is described as a network of nuclear family households with a great deal of contact between households. While each household fits Parsons's husband-wife and possible children description, the extended family network concept recognizes the exchange of financial assistance, emotional support, social activity, and support services between households.

Rodgers (1973) adds the additional dimension of the "family career," which refers to where each family household is in the developmental process (such as child rearing, empty nest, or retired). The family career influences the need of a household as well as its capacity to contribute to the family network.

Out of the literature emerges a composite picture of the extended family network of which most retired persons are members today. The network is one in which each generation (1) maintains its own household, (2) is part of a kin network, (3) has its own family career, and (4) participates in reciprocal transactions with the other member households. Attributes such as ethnic background, financial or economic status, social class, and religious affiliation, which cause variation in attitude toward family and expectations of the generations in the family network, are most appropriately treated as variables and not as prohibitors that make it impossible to utilize the family as central to retired individuals as a population group.

TABLE 11.1   Family Status and Living Arrangements of the Population 65 Years Old and Over, by Sex, 1975

	Males	Females
Number	9,106,000	13,105,000
Family Status	Percentage	
Total	100.0	100.0
In families	79.8	56.1
Head	76.1	8.5
Wife	X	35.0
Other relative	3.7	12.7
Primary individual	14.8	37.3
Secondary individual	1.2	1.2
Resident in an institution	4.2	5.3
Living Arrangements	Percentage	
Total	100.0	100.0
In households	95.6	94.4
Living alone	14.2	36.0
Spouse present	74.0	35.6
Living with someone else	7.4	22.8
Not in households*	4.4	5.6

SOURCE: U.S. Bureau of the Census (1978: 48).
*Population in institutions and other group quarters.

CHARACTERISTICS OF THE
RETIRED FAMILY HOUSEHOLD

A great deal can be learned about the retired family by looking at the data gathered by the U.S. Bureau of the Census (1976). The 1980 data is not available, but the earlier data (from 1975) certainly can be used to formulate a picture of the population group. Table 11.1 depicts the 65 years and over age group by family status and living arrangement. The table is useful in many ways. It graphically shows that most retired individuals over 65 (such data is not available for retired persons under 65) do indeed live in households—95.6 percent of the males and 94.4 percent of the females. It becomes quite evident that females are more likely to live alone, less likely to live with spouse, and more likely to live with someone else. To keep this information in perspective, it should be noted that these data do not provide information on need or existing systems for meeting need.

Facts about Older Americans 1979 (U.S. Department of Health and Human Services, 1980) further describes the 65 and over group. Part of that information is included here to provide a more complete picture. Approximately 13 percent of older people were either in the labor force or were actively seeking work in 1978. Participation by females in the labor force has steadily increased while participation by males has decreased. Households with both husband and wife were financially better off, with 10 percent receiving an annual income of less than $4,000, 20 percent having annual incomes of over $15,000, and median income for all such families being $9,110. Those 65 and older living alone or with nonrelatives were financially less secure, with more than one-half (53.7 percent) receiving less than $4,000 annual income and less than one-tenth (9.8 percent) receiving an annual income of over $10,000. The median annual income of this group was $3,829.

Statistics concerning living arrangements, family status, and income provide information that can help us to understand the capacity of the retired household to function as an active participant in the interactive and reciprocal processes of the kin network. The family career at this stage includes freedom from the labor force, which would imply time to devote to family interaction, with constraints coming from family history rather than the job.

THE RETIRED FAMILY:
RELATIONSHIP TO KINSHIP NETWORK

At this point we turn to the gerontological literature in order to understand how the retired household is relating to other households in the kinship network. With the extension of life such networks usually include three career families: (1) the retired household, (2) the "empty nest" or adult children household, and (3) the young adult and sometimes child-rearing household (grandchildren). For many, the kinship network moves beyond these nuclear family households to include siblings, nieces, and nephews. As noted above, Tobin and Kulys (1980), Woehrer (1978), Silverstone (1978), Atchley and Miller (1980), and Sussman (1976) have published recent literature reviews that focus on older people and their families. Those reviews indicate that, at least among those working and doing research in gerontology, there is agreement concerning the crucial role played by the kinship network in relation to the retired population.

The concept that retirement is a family issue is reinforced in a number of ways in the gerontological literature. A national poll sponsored by the

National Council on the Aging (Louis Harris and Associates, 1975) found that of those 65 and over, 81 percent had living children, 79 percent had living siblings, 75 percent had grandchildren, and 4 percent had living parents—an implication that the future may hold 4-generation families. Of more interest from the same source is the finding that 81 percent of the elderly had seen at least one of their children in the last week or two. While actual percentages and numbers vary among studies, it becomes quite clear that there is a great deal of personal contact between generational households when there is proximity of households. Telephone and/or mail contact exists when there is distance. Contact between generational households of the kinship network is significant because it provides social-emotional support for the generations and because contact provides the context in which reciprocal help can be given when it is called for.

The amount of actual service provided for by the various generation or career families within the network varies as investigators have used different measures to define "service." Hill (1977) studied the reciprocity patterns between three-generation households, which he designated as grandparent households, parent households, and married children. The results of the study indicated that help that can be defined as service occurred in five categories: economic, emotional gratification, household management, child care, and illness care. Reciprocity among households in all five categories was reported by all three generations, with the exception of "child care." The family career of the grandparents did not include children, hence receiving child care was inappropriate while giving child care was appropriate. Grandparents received the greatest amount of illness care, while married children households received the greatest amount of child care. Though parent households gave more to both grandparents and married children than they received, each of the households was involved in reciprocal actions that were viewed as mutually beneficial.

A study was conducted by the General Accounting Office (GAO) for the purpose of providing Congress with information about the impact of federal programs on the elderly (Comptroller General of the United States, 1977). Respondents were asked if a primary source of help was available in the event of illness or disability and 87 percent reported in the affirmative. When asked to identify the primary source of help or services, respondents reported children (42 percent), spouse (27 percent), sibling (10 percent), other relative (10 percent), and friend (8 percent), which indicates that, of those who identified a person as primary source, 89 percent named a family member. Of further interest is the reporting that, of the agencies surveyed in the same study, the greatest number were providing information and referral, while the smallest number were providing continuous supervision. In an attempt to compute the economic value of the services,

TABLE 11.2   Average Monthly Cost or Value of Services by Family
and Friends and by Agencies per Older Individual at
Levels of Impairment

Impairment level	Family and Friends	Agency	Total
Unimpaired	$ 37	$ 26	$ 63
Slightly	63	47	110
Mildly	111	65	176
Moderately	181	78	259
Generally	204	100	304
Greatly	287	120	407
Extremely	673	172	845

SOURCE: Comptroller General of the United States (1977).

it was found that the value of cost of services provided by family and
friends to community elderly at various levels of impairment exceeded the
value of services provided by agencies. Table 11.2 is taken from this
report.

A number of other approaches have been utilized to express the
importance of the family to the retired population. Some of the studies
involving institutionalized elderly have focused on the family. These
studies emphasize the importance of the family to the retired population
as they age. The *1976 Survey of Institutionalized Persons* (U.S. Bureau of
the Census, 1978) reports that, of those 65 years of age and over residing
in institutions, 29 percent had lived with family before admission. Newman (1975) found that more older people moved to a child's or other
relative's home, to a better home, or to a home closer to a child or relative
than moved into institutions. Studies involving institutionalized elderly
indicate that the family is a crucial variable in the entire process, from
prevention to the actual placing of the individual in the home, and that the
process has a negative effect on all who are involved (Tobin and Kulys,
1980).

In short, the gerontological literature supports the premise that retirement is a family issue. Retired individuals live out their retirement years as
part of a family network, even if they are widowed, divorced, or never
married. The family network usually includes three-generation households—retired household, adult children or empty-nest household and
child-rearing household—plus a variety of other households, which may
include siblings, nieces, nephews, and so on. The importance of the
households in providing reciprocal support and help is central to all
generations, but especially to the retired family.

The number of studies involving the elderly and their families, of which only a small portion have been discussed here, verifies that gerontological researchers and clinicians are well aware of the role of the family as it relates to older individuals. The results of past efforts have led to a recognition of the family as the primary provider of service to the elderly and a call for a change in current social policy when it is punitive toward families that attempt to care for their elderly. Past research has taken a case management approach focusing on health, financial need, and social problems of the elderly, with the family cast as a service provider, much like a case manager with responsibility for acting as a broker between the elderly and the formal service systems (bureaucratic structures providing financial assistance, social services, and health care). The results of such efforts have been beneficial in reversing the myth of the negligent family, in providing basic data on the needs of older individuals, and in pointing out the weaknesses of current social policy, which promotes the proliferation of bureaucratic service systems and may discourage some aspects of interaction among families. Policy can make it economically beneficial to *not* care for the elderly. Unfortunately, some policy efforts have had the detrimental effect of contributing to an already negative view of older individuals as frail and dependent upon society and family.

COMMENT

While there is agreement among some gerontological researchers and the service provider community concerning the important role of the extended family network to the retired family household, there has not been sufficient research effort in the area. Despite knowledge concerning the extension of life and increasing numbers of elderly and extreme elderly in the coming years, there has not developed a reasonable research strategy that would provide information to account for the complexity of the issue. Studies involving family generations, while more costly, would provide much needed data on social, biological, and psychological change with age. It would be a departure from current research strategy that involves identifying a population with a particular pathology (poverty, dementia, isolation, chronically ill, or the like). The establishment of family registers to be studied over time in a longitudinal methodology, or even cross-sectional studies, would provide a more comprehensive framework for recommending social policy.

There are a number of issues that need to be studied particularly. A national study of three- and four-generation families is needed. To consistently study the already retired without including the younger cohort groups, who will be the future retirees, eliminates the opportunity to identify trends of change.

There needs to be an effort to understand the full impact of the extension of the retirement years. A cross-sectional study of existing cohort groups of both retired and preretired could be used to generate a complete set of social, psychological, and physical data, which, with the present level of sophistication in computer models, could be translated into computer simulations of aging populations possessing a variety of characteristics (family size, disease pattern, work history, socioeconomic class, and so on). The combining of cross-sectional study with computer simulation would be an effective way of involving multigeneration families in studies of population trends for developing social policy.

Knowing that women outnumber men and that the disproportion increases with age is of little value unless one takes into consideration other family issues that affect the female in the later years. What effect will the current trend of the increasing participation of women over 40 in the work force have? At this point the popular trend is to editorialize that the effect will be a negative one, when in fact it could indeed result in a new generation of older women who are better prepared financially and socially to maintain independent living.

Just as some individuals manage stress better than others, so do some families. What are the indicators of a family that is successful in establishing reciprocal relationships between generational households? Is it possible that the service system could make the difference between success or failure? Without knowledge concerning the key variables that facilitate family success, it is impossible to know if the thrust of policy should be financial incentives, entitlement programs or services, or elaborate programs with means testing involving some services and some financial assistance. Research models involving families should include siblings, nieces, and nephews, since it is frequently family size that enables the family to share the responsibilities of dependent populations, both young and old.

An extension of the family network has been the formation of self-help groups, such as Stroke Clubs and ASIST (Alzheimer Support, Information and Support Team). Such groups seem to provide strong support for families that have members with a medical problem in common. The support groups supplement a family network's weaknesses through information giving, emotional support, and even sharing of support services. A study of such organizations could indeed reveal information concerning the types of services most valuable in supporting the family.

With the increasing percentage of marriages that end in divorce, it is historically appropriate to begin studying the impact of divorce on families in retirement before the larger group of divorcees reach retirement. What are the implications for pensions that are tied to legal marriages for eligibility? What is the implication of stepfamily members for the kinship system? Who remains part of the normal reciprocal patterns between generations in non-divorce families? Does the existence of a significant number of divorced females currently in their early middle years have any implication for future retired generations?

Families play a crucial role in the lives of individuals at all stages of life, and to the retired the family network seems to be even more significant. Due to the reciprocal relationship between nuclear families within the family network and the trend for younger families to model the mature families in their networks, it is important that the family become a central consideration in research on the retirement years and in the formulation of social policy for the retirement years.

REFERENCES

ATCHLEY, R. C. and S. J. MILLER (1980) "Older people and their families," in C. Eisdorfer (ed.) Annual Review of Gerontology and Geriatrics, Volume 1. New York: Springer.

Comptroller General of the United States (1977) Report to the Congress: Home Health—The Need for a National Policy to Better Provide for the Elderly. Washington, DC: General Accounting Office.

Louis Harris and Associates (1975) The Myth and Reality of Aging in America. Washington, DC: National Council on the Aging.

HILL, R. (1977) "Decision making and the family life cycle," in C. R. Allman and D. T. Jaffe (eds.) Readings in Adult Psychology: Contemporary Perspectives. New York: Harper & Row.

NEWMAN, S. (1975) Housing Adjustments of Older People: A Report of Findings in the First Phase. Ann Arbor: University of Michigan Institute of Social Relations.

PARSONS, T. (1943) "The kinship system of the contemporary United States." American Anthropologist 45: 22-38.

RODGERS, R. H. (1973) Family Interaction and Transaction: The Developmental Approach. Englewood Cliffs, NJ: Prentice-Hall.

SILVERSTONE, B. (1978) "Family relationships of the elderly: problems and implications for helping professionals." Aged Care and Services Review 1: 1-19.

SUSSMAN, M. B. (1976) "The family life of old people," in R. H. Binstock and E. Shanas (eds.) Handbook of Aging and the Social Sciences. New York: Litton.

TOBIN, S. S. and R. KULYS (1980) "The family and services," in C. Eisdorfer (ed.) Annual Review of Gerontology and Geriatrics, Volume 1. New York: Springer.

U.S. Bureau of the Census (1978) 1976 Survey of Institutionalized Persons: A Study of Persons Receiving Long-Term Care. Washington, DC: Government Printing Office.

U.S. Department of Health and Human Services (1980) Facts about Older Americans. HHS Publication No. HHS 80-20006. Washington, DC: Government Printing Office.

WOEHRER, C. E. (1978) "Cultural pluralism in American families: the influence of ethnicity on social aspects of aging." Family Coordinator 27, 4: 329-338.

PART III
AGING AND RETIREMENT POLICY

It is a commonplace that government develops policies in a context of response to apparent pressing problems. From such a reactive perspective broad planning is always difficult, if not impossible. Even blue ribbon commissions established to plan tend to do so within narrowly defined perspectives. Thus policies, once initiated, may often be elaborated *ad infinitum,* without ever being reconsidered in terms of the philosophic bases that originally justified them. Motives underlying policies initated decades ago may no longer be appropriate, but the programs continue on and on. Moreover, we have become conditioned to the entry of the "Lady Bountiful" government into almost every aspect of family life. Sometimes the consequences of social policies are not realistically examined, and sometimes they are not examined at all, to avoid disturbing sacred bovines.

The final section of this volume first takes a hard look at public policies governing retirement and personnel, and predicts that the current institution of retirement, with its supporting policies and programs, will undergo significant change in the years ahead. Issues to be resolved in the future are considered, with passing reference to how other nations have tried to meet the problems of their retirement populations. Chapter 13, "Toward a Policy for Retired Persons: Reflections on Welfare and Taxation," attempts to expose some issues underneath the welter of anomaly and obfuscation surrounding retirement. The vigorous discussion of such central concepts as redistribution of wealth, social security benefits, demogrants, the indexed pension, mandatory retirement, vesting, fringe benefits, and special programs for women should stimulate discussion both from those who are in agreement and those who are not.

The final chapter of the book challenges the set of values about long life which insists that it should be financed outside the productive economy. This chapter stresses the idea that long life can be, and usually is, *good news.* Historians of aging point out that in earlier times, say, nearly to the close of the nineteenth century, aged people as individuals were frequently a problem to themselves and to society. But it is only in the present century that the elderly as a class have come to be considered a problem. Perhaps the 1980s will provide more perspective on an older and possibly wiser tradition.

12

REAPPRAISING RETIREMENT AND PERSONNEL POLICIES

Malcolm H. Morrison

BACKGROUND

Over the past 40 years, retirement institutions and policies have developed in an ad hoc, uncoordinated manner, affecting current patterns of retirement behavior. The most fundamental aspect of these patterns throughout the labor force is increasing early retirement. Because of the general aging of the work force, this retirement pattern is resulting in rapidly increasing public and private pension costs, which will continue to rise even higher because of adjustments required to meet the costs of inflation. Low fertility and improved mortality will significantly alter the age distribution of our future population. Today 16 out of every 100 people are at least 60 years old, and by the year 2030 this figure will escalate to 24 per hundred. The result of this change on the costs of the social security system will be significant. In 1960 there were approximately 5 workers for each social security recipient; today this ratio has declined to about 3 to 1 and will reach 2 to 1 by the year 2030. Thus, if present retirement trends continue, there will be significantly fewer work-

AUTHOR'S NOTE: The opinions expressed in this chapter are solely those of the author and do not necessarily represent the views of the U.S. Department of Labor.

ers available to pay the increasing costs of retirement benefits for a growing older population.

Because of these trends, it is very likely that the current institution of retirement, and the policies and programs that support it, will undergo significant change in the years ahead. It certainly is unlikely that policy makers will accept the projected large increase in the proportion of the government budget allocated to retirement payments without consideration of alternatives to reduce the growth of this allocation. A continuation of current retirement policies will result in very serious economic and social consequences for our society. The continuous increase in the proportion of persons no longer working can be viewed as both undesirable and dysfunctional. However, the combination of demographic changes, high rates of inflation, efforts to control rising retirement benefit costs, the early retirement trend, and the consequences of current pension system functioning will result in significant changes in retirement policies and programs in the years ahead.

In addition to the key policy areas regarding level of earnings replacement from public and private pensions, adjustment of benefits for inflation, financing alternatives, and coordination of retirement systems, a particulary important concern of public policy now emerging is the extent to which older persons can choose to allocate their time between employment and leisure. That is, how should retirement policy be designed in order to provide opportunities for part-time employment with partial retirement, or to allow for a transition between full-time work and full retirement? This question raises the most important underlying issue regarding the future of retirement policy: What should be our long-run goals for the future of retirement in the United States?

While it is clear that we do not at present have one relatively uniform national retirement policy, it is also evident that most of our present uncoordinated policies result in the major trend toward early retirement. This trend is beginning to be perceived as dysfunctional, mainly because of increasing pension costs. Of course, it may also be dysfunctional because it limits the human potential of millions of persons who could contribute to productivity if provided with the opportunity. To a considerable extent, current retirement behavior reflects the incentives provided by current policies. These may be based on the perceived need to remove older workers from the labor force in order to "make room" for younger and middle-aged employees. It is clear that we are approaching the limit of marginal utility for such policies. Every person who retires requires support from the remaining work force. As the tax burden for this support increases, workers suffer reductions in quality of life. Current economic conditions of inflation and declining productivity further reduce quality of life and lower expectations for future growth, with its accompanying economic and social benefits.

A major question that confronts our society is whether we will consciously act to develop and implement a retirement policy that emphasizes more balance in utilizing the capacities of the available work force, or continue our present approach of reacting to limited aspects of the problem with stopgap measures designed to remedy temporarily the most immediate problems. Thus far, the reactive approach has led only to proposals for shifting the financial burden of retirement support from reliance on one method of taxation to another. Such measures, of course, will not resolve the growing financial crisis and are based primarily on acceptance of current retirement policies. A more comprehensive analysis of our emerging retirement crisis demonstrates that dealing only with the income support aspects of the problem will not alter the basic dilemma—the appropriate utilization of human capital. In order to create a new retirement future, the issue of encouraging the employment of older workers must be satisfactorily resolved. Therefore, national policies must be devised to:

(1) modify public pension systems to provide for partial retirement options;
(2) encourage the utilization of pension system incentives for developing transitional retirement programs for employees;
(3) encourage employers to adopt personnel policies permitting greater flexibility for older workers;
(4) create more balance in the sharing of income support for the retired; and
(5) encourage the development of programs involving flexible work-life approaches that are not based on the traditional linear life plan of education, work, and retirement.

FLEXIBLE DISTRIBUTION OF
WORK, EDUCATION, AND LEISURE

Over the past 75 years, industrialization, accompanied by significant economic growth, has resulted in a substantial reduction in the proportion of time spent at work. For the most part, this reduction has resulted from a substantial decline in weekly hours worked. In fact, the average American workweek has declined from approximately 60 hours to 39 hours over the past century. Over the last 40 years, however, the workweek has remained quite stable and most of the reduction in working time has been in the form of vacations and holidays. In addition, the growth of nonwork time has expanded to encompass increased periods of *education* (usually early in life) and *retirement* during the later years of life. The result of these patterns has been the development of the linear life pattern—going to school in youth, working during middle years, and retiring in old age. To some extent this pattern of life scheduling can be viewed as a result of the natural requirements of the life cycle and a response to conditions of industrialization. However, it appears that the continuing rigid adherence to the linear life pattern is primarily the result of expansion of nonwork time and competition for work between age groups. To a considerable degree, the compression of work activity primarily into midlife is the result of factors of advanced industrialization which have resulted in job shortages and the creation of policies to preserve job opportunities for persons in the middle of the life cycle.

The linear life pattern may in fact be dysfunctional for several working age groups—young, middle age, and old—who must share the available job opportunities. Of course, the basic shortage of jobs in the United States continues to result in serious employment problems for youth and for older workers, who are most seriously affected by the linear life approach. Also, the availability of employment for older workers is severely constrained by early retirement policies and the lure of presumably sufficient pension benefits. In addition, serious negative attitudinal barriers influence employer hiring and job retention policies, neither of which are structured to benefit older workers.

Several serious problems now exist coincidentally with the strong linear life pattern. Among these are: (1) severe competition for jobs by members of the postwar age cohorts, trained minority group job seekers, and women labor force reentrants; (2) continuing job shortages; and (3) increasing desire of all age groups for job equality despite present inequities. If the current linear pattern of distribution of work, education, and leisure continues, the above mentioned problems are likely to increase in intensity with the likely exacerbation of problems of youth and older workers. The various inequities in work distribution related to the linear life pattern are already resulting in a growing support burden (particularly for retired and disabled workers) on the remaining work force. The retention or enhancement of the present regularized linear education/ work/retirement pattern with extensions of periods of nonwork will result in even higher support costs for workers and increased tensions between groups of workers. A pattern involving more flexible distribution of education, work, and leisure which would redistribute the extended periods of nonwork time now spent in youth and older age to the middle years of life (for pursuing education, leisure, or part-time employment) is a reasonable response to the dysfunctional aspects of the current linear life pattern (Best and Stern, 1977).

There are indications that such a nonlinear pattern would meet with support from various types of workers, especially students, women, and older workers, who could most benefit by implementation of alternative work patterns. Studies by Best and Stern (1977) also indicate that prime-age workers prefer additional flexibility in work scheduling, with the most popular approach being a modified cyclic life pattern with extended periods of free time in midlife and tapered or phased retirement.

While in principle many workers appear ready to alter the current rigid work-life patterns, there is no general agreement as to the best approaches to take in creating more flexible work-life options. Recommendations include approaches to redistribution of work through shorter workweeks, job sharing, part-time employment, public service jobs, short-time compensation programs, and flexible retirement programs. Recommendations also suggest new approaches to leisure through extending vacation time, more liberal leave-of-absence provisions, and flexible retirement programs. They also call for new approaches to education through voucher plans, paid or unpaid educational leave, work sabbaticals, and utilization of unemployment insurance to support education and training. Obviously these proposals are not mutually exclusive; a change in one area will effect a change in the others.

Many of the above policies do not yet enjoy any broad measure of public support, particularly from organized labor interests, who fear that such piecemeal redistributive steps might be harmful to full-time regular employees and might be utilized by business firms to reduce employment and/or fringe benefits. In addition, while the idea of providing more flexibility in work-life through a more equitable distribution of work, leisure, and education between young, middle-aged, and older workers is appealing, the development of a national policy to restructure and redistribute employment opportunity is quite unlikely. Fortunately there is far less opposition to the creation of modified work-life patterns for older employees, many of whom wish to retain some connection to employment. For this reason a number of major companies are now experimenting with a variety of flexible options designed to encourage *later* retirement. (See the section on personnel and pension policies, below.)

RETIREMENT PATTERNS

The gradual institutionalization of retirement has resulted in making retirement policy an issue of major national concern. Attention is now focused on the problems of maintaining the financial stability of the social security system, regulating the provision of private pension benefits through the Employee Retirement Income Security Act (ERISA), and assuring the right to employment for older workers through the Age Discrimination in Employment Act (ADEA). The recent Age Discrimination in Employment Act Amendments (1978), which prohibit mandatory retirement before age 70 for most private sector employees, serve to intensify concern about future labor force participation by older workers. The changing composition of the United States work force and the influence of this new legislation are being widely discussed with relation to adjustments in corporate personnel and pension policies. Despite the continued prevalence of the early retirement trend, there are a number of factors that are likely to result in later retirement for a growing proportion of the older work force in the years ahead. Among the most important of these are the gradual aging of the population and work force, longer life expectancy, and the concomitant increasing financial support burden for a growing older population.

In most countries with mature pension systems, the continuous aging of the population, accompanied by increasingly earlier retirement by many workers, is already resulting in serious economic pressure on shrinking work forces to finance expanding retirement benefit payments. Over the past 20 years, most industrialized countries have introduced a variety of so-called flexible retirement provisions in public pension systems. Almost all of these policies allow for early retirement (before the normal retirement age) in order to provide benefits to workers who have had hazardous employment or prolonged unemployment, or who suffer health problems. Such early retirement policies have been based on the presumed need to provide job opportunities for younger labor force entrants. They demonstrate one aspect of the linear life pattern approach, namely, extending the period of retirement. Continuation of the trend of lowered retirement age will increase the financing problems of pension systems. Some have predicted that this will result in a slowing of the early retirement trend as more experimentation with later retirement takes place.

Thus far few countries have responded to this problem by developing flexible public retirement pension policies that encourage continued employment of older workers, nor have many business and governmental organizations developed pension and personnel policies that reflect this objective.

Due to the relatively recent recognition of the problems of aging work forces, the concept of flexible retirement has not as yet been clearly defined nor relevant policy options identified. In fact, the amount of research and experimentation conducted thus far has been quite limited. There remain many unanswered questions where empirical research data are lacking. We do not, for example, have comprehensive data on American or foreign firms providing flexible retirement options, nor do we know how many employees have access to or would take advantage of such options of they were available. We have only limited information on the potential response of United States workers to the legislation raising the age for mandatory retirement to 70. Furthermore, there has been little if any policy analysis in the area of creating more flexibility through modification of public and private pension policies. Obtaining answers to these questions will require substantial research effort. Some initial research on discrimination, involuntary retirement, and part-time employment opportunities is under way, but the development of public retirement policy and corporate personnel and pension policy to expand flexible retirement options will require more focused research studies examining both institutional policies and individual preferences.

Despite these informational limitations, it is useful to review recent evidence concerning the preferred form of labor force participation by older workers, examine various flexible retirement policies and programs now functioning, and suggest how managements can best prepare organizations to adapt to the upcoming aging of the work force.

OLDER EMPLOYEE PREFERENCES

Evidence has demonstrated that, while increasing numbers of older employees are choosing early retirement, many older individuals may desire to continue to work on a part-time basis. While the early retirement trend is clearly predominant, there is some question as to whether the expressed part-time employment preferences of older employees are being actualized through employment. Current evidence regarding the *employment preferences* of older workers indicates that between one-third and one-half of those nearing retirement or those retired suggest that they would prefer to be employed at least on a part-time basis (Louis Harris and Associates, 1979). At the same time, surveys of actual job-seeking behavior by older persons indicate that these preferences are rarely actualized (Parnes et al., 1979). Studies now in progress are beginning to investigate the preferences of older employees for employment on a part-time basis. However, far more research is necessary, particularly because employee preferences may be changing in response to newly emerging employer personnel and pension policies permitting various more flexible retirement patterns for older workers.

The evidence suggests, therefore, that although more older persons wish to work part-time, many cannot locate such employment. They either retire completely, lose their jobs, and experience great difficulty in finding subsequent employment, or, in a small number of cases, continue to work full-time. Some have speculated that raising the age for mandatory retirement, increasing social security benefits if retirement is delayed, and worsening economic conditions will lead to increased part-time employment of older workers, but the emergence of such a trend is far from certain. Early studies of the consequences of a higher mandatory retirement age indicate that the early retirement trend is continuing unabated.

Current evidence from the National Study of Mandatory Retirement indicates that few workers are modifying their *planned* retirement age and that most still intend to retire before age 65. However, some evidence indicates that a small number of employees who are aware of liberal corporate retirement age policies (no mandatory age or age 70) and informed about the ADEA law choose to modify upward their planned age of retirement (U.S. Department of Labor, 1979). Also, a few recent corporate studies indicate that for the small number of persons still working at ages 63 and over, between 30 and 40 percent intend to remain beyond age 65 (Hewitt Associates, 1980; Travelers Insurance Company, 1980). To a considerable degree these studies both imply and demonstrate that older employees will respond positively to corporate flexible retirement initiatives.

One possible approach to limiting or, at a minimum, "spreading out" the cost of future retirement payments would involve a shift of the traditional full retirement pattern toward *transitional* or *phased* retirement, where older workers might gradually reduce working hours over a period of years before becoming "fully retired." Such an approach might be coupled with the development of a partial pension system, which could supplement wages earned from part-time employment with partial pension payments. Both of these approaches, of course, represent a substantial departure from current policies and are more complex than such adjustments as raising the minimum age for receipt of social security benefits or shifting the financing of retirement payments from payroll to general revenue taxes. Yet adjusting the linear life plan to create retirement flexibility would be a far more significant reform which could clearly benefit millions of middle-aged and older employees and assist the economy in adjusting to fewer younger labor force entrants in the years ahead. Movement in the direction of flexible retirement programs requires that older workers be provided with opportunities and incentives to stay in the labor force. Any significant modification of the early retirement trend will involve: (1) the actual availability of older employees for employment at least on a part-time basis; (2) the provision of incentives for continued employment through public (and possibly private) pension systems; and (3) provision of flexible work work arrangements by employers.

PART-TIME EMPLOYMENT

Most older persons probably leave their full-time jobs because of mandatory retirement and economic reasons, such as pension eligibility or declining health. The crucial question is whether they are interested in continued employment on a full- or part-time basis. Unfortunately, clear research evidence on this question is lacking. Of particular importance is the lack of data as to the proportion of older persons who leave the labor force and do not in fact desire work of any type.

At present about 14.5 percent of all nonagricultural wage and salary employees (11 million workers) work part-time by choice in the United States. Only 5 percent of such workers are 65 years of age or over. However, among all older persons working part-time, whether by choice or not, nearly 50 percent are voluntarily employed part-time, the highest percentage of any age group. Of persons over age 60 and not in the labor force desiring employment, half perceive that employers will consider them too old and an additional 25 percent think there are no jobs available. Thus, nearly 80 percent of persons who desire employment believe they cannot get jobs and presumably reduce their job search activities. These beliefs are, in fact, supported by mandatory retirement policies and negative stereotypes of older employees held by employers. The clearest indication of older worker preferences comes from national opinion surveys conducted by Louis Harris and Associates in 1974 and 1979. The results indicate: (1) large majorities of current and retired employees and business leaders are opposed to any mandatory retirement age; (2) about half of all current employees say they would prefer to work either full- or part-time as an alternative to retirement; (3) about half of current retirees say they would prefer to be working; and (4) most older workers still plan to retire between ages 60 and 65. These preferences imply that, while workers apparently intend to retire initially, a significant number anticipate a subsequent return to work. While these preferences cannot be assumed to reflect actual behavior, they indicate a significant desire by current and retired workers for flexible employment opportunities.

Despite the seemingly irreversible trend toward early retirement, several recent developments here and abroad suggest that retirement policies may gradually be modified to encourage and accommodate more flexible retirement. In some countries, mainly in Europe, public pension systems are being modified to provide increments in final pension benefits and establish partial pension programs that allow a gradual transition to retirement. In a few instances, particularly in the United States, private pension coverage has been extended beyond the usual retirement age by business firms. Such inducements to remain employed are likely to become more prevalent as the cost of supporting an increasing retired population rises. Decisions to remain employed at least part-time are likely to increase due to the interaction of individual preferences and wider employment opportunities. Public pension policy may also be further modified to provide additional inducement to stay in the labor force through an increase in the age of eligibility for receipt of benefits or the establishment of a partial pension option for older workers who wish to work part-time.

FLEXIBLE RETIREMENT OPTIONS

In order to develop options for flexible work opportunities for older persons, experimentation with a variety of approaches is desirable. Programs can be introduced easily by employers and unions without disrupting usual employment practices, creating real options for older employees. Such options should not be introduced without giving careful consideration to effects on employee benefit programs and personnel policies. It is important to recognize that, since major public pension policy changes are unlikely in the near term, developments in flexible retirement options will be more influenced by innovations in personnel and private pension plan policies than by government regulatory requirements.

The following major retirement options can be suggested as providing a meaningful approach to flexibility: (1) early retirement; (2) retirement at the "normal" age at which full benefits are available from public and/or private pension systems; (3) transitional or phased retirement, involving a period of permanent part-time work before full retirement; and (4) a continuation of employment (full- or part-time) beyond the regular retirement age.

PERSONNEL AND PENSION POLICIES

Throughout the world, business organizations have generally taken the lead in developing flexible retirement approaches. While the current level of development can only be considered experimental, these policies and programs serve as models for future expansion and modification. In the United States, for example, the results of recent surveys demonstrate that employers are in the process of initiating changes in personnel and pension policies which may introduce more flexibility in the retirement process.

In a national mail survey of 1636 firms and a telephone survey of 256 larger (more than 500 employees) firms contacted in the spring of 1979, Copperman et al. (1979) reported that between 50 and 60 percent of firms *permitted* pension benefit accruals after the normal retirement age for workers continuing employment. This may be a general pattern in industry. However, despite the availability of such benefit accruals, very few employees remain employed beyond the normal retirement age of pension plans and thus few utilize this option. They further found that about 11 percent of all firms had or were implementing flexible work hours (flexitime) programs, 17 percent had permanent part-time employment programs, and 5 percent had phased retirement programs. Overall, 15 percent of all employers surveyed had or were implementing some type of alternative work schedule policies. It is important to note that while most employers expected a small number of their employees to continue to work past the age of 65 in response to the new ADEA age 70 mandatory retirement age, 90 percent of the employers expected that such continued employment would be quite minimal. It is interesting to note, however, that when queried about potential effects of continued inflation on retirement behavior of employees, 23 percent of all firms expected that more employees would forgo early retirement and 48 percent expected that more employees would wish to continue working past the normal retirement age.

Similar findings resulted in a survey conducted in August 1979 by the Bureau of National Affairs. A total of 267 medium to large size organizations were surveyed about retirement policies and programs. This study indicated that 15 percent of the employers had established some type of phased retirement program for all employees or specific groups of employees. In addition, 52 percent of all firms used retirees as consultants and 62 percent recall retired employees to work for short time periods. Again, in this survey most firms (86 percent) reported no or very little effect of the change in the mandatory retirement age. The study suggests that the reason for this is that thus far few employees have actually been affected by the change. However, about 20 percent of the firms have experienced an increase in the number of workers staying on beyond the normal retirement age. Finally, almost 30 percent had made changes in their retirement programs over the last two years, and an additional 32 percent expect to make changes in the near future. Modifications most frequently involve improved insurance benefits for retirees, medical insurance, life insurance, and so on. Recognizing their importance, more and more firms are also developing and implementing retirement preparation programs.

Examples of recent corporate policy modifications affecting older workers are: (1) experimentation with flexible work schedules and part-time employment for older workers by Lockheed Aircraft and Schering-Plough Corporation; (2) establishment of extra vacation time (or cash in lieu of vacation), extra pension credits, and fringe benefits for older employees by Teledyne Incorporated; and (3) establishment of transitional and trial retirement programs by the Polaroid Corporation.

The studies conducted thus far have not been representative of all American employers. They have not investigated employee plans, attitudes, and behavior in responding to the new mandatory retirement age, changes in Social Security law, and continuing inflation. The major national study of age discrimination and involuntary retirement now being conducted by the U.S. Department of Labor (1979) will establish definitive baseline information on a uniquely linked and nationally representative sample of 6000 employees and their employers. The results of this study will, therefore, provide the most definitive information on current and planned employer personnel and pension policies, and employee plans and preferences regarding retirement. While it is unlikely that this study's major findings will significantly differ from the surveys reported above, the amount of detailed information developed will be far greater and the basis for assessing changes over time in employer policies, employee preferences, and actual retirement behavior will be established. Preliminary results from the study indicate that few older workers are currently changing their retirement plans as a result of the increased mandatory retirement age under the ADEA Amendments of 1978. However, most employers formerly setting mandatory retirement at age 65 (about half of all U.S. firms) have now moved this requirement to age 70 to conform to the new law. It is difficult to predict the longer-term consequences of the law due to its relatively recent enactment. The possible response of employees to gradual retirement policy modifications by employers is also difficult to predict.

The major methods now used by American employers to provide flexible retirement options include: (1) reduced workweek schedules (four-day or three-day week) prior to retirement; (2) extra vacation time in years prior to retirement; (3) reduced hours of work; (4) job transfer programs; (5) employee consultants; (6) temporary or permanent part-time work for retired employees; and (7) payroll transfer programs (rehiring an older employee through a private employment service). Flexible retirement programs developed in other countries include: (1) special job allotments for older workers; (2) job redesign and special unemployment allowances in West Germany; (3) various work hour reduction programs in France (including days off per week, extra vacation time, and paid leave); and (4) establishing older worker quotas, with government subsidies for hiring, and extended unemployment benefits in Japan.

Some other innovations, such as mobility allowances, retraining programs, and specialized employment services, are utilized particularly in Scandinavia and West Germany. Some of these types of programs are beginning to be experimented with in the United States—such as reduced work hours approaches—while others, including job allotments, retraining and mobility allowances, government subsidies, and specialized employment services, have received little attention. To a considerable extent, the pervasiveness of the early retirement trend, coupled with severe youth unemployment difficulties, has resulted in only limited United States government attention to the problems of older workers. However, the increasing aging of the population, accompanied by dramatic increases in retirement support costs, will undoubtedly result in a gradual reallocation of employment and training resources toward middle-aged and older workers.

CONCLUSION

In the United States and abroad, the aging of populations has been accompanied by a major trend toward early retirement. Now, however, various flexible retirement approaches are being discussed and in some cases implemented. Generally, these allow for increased choice as to the time of retirement and provide for various forms of continued employment for older workers.

In this country, approaches by business, government, and educational institutions include eliminating a mandatory retirement age and establishing specialized programs such as part-time employment, payroll transfer, reduced work hours, and retirement assessment. In Europe, innovations such as mobility allowances, employer subsidies, retraining, older worker quota systems, specialized employment services, and phased-retirement programs are in use. Both here and in Europe, some forms of flexible retirement (usually early retirement) are mandated by public pension programs.

These recent initiatives represent the beginning of an overall adjustment to changing demographic trends and economic conditions. In the future, larger numbers of older persons will be in good health and interested in continuing in some form of employment. Though the supply of such workers is likely to increase, gradually at first, as time passes more will desire to continue employment. Moreover, as pension costs continue to escalate, public policies are likely to mandate a later retirement age to reduce economic burdens on younger workers and to finance retirement pension payments.

All these developments require that much more attention be devoted to examining new work arrangements for older persons, including part-time work, job sharing, partial retirement, midlife sabbaticals, job adjustment, shifting, and retraining—all useful personnel practices with great potential for older workers. To implement any of the programs in a particular organizational setting, a review of work force characteristics and current personnel and pension policies is usually necessary. Requisite to successful implementation of flexible retirement policies is accommodation to the employer's needs, the employees' preferences, and the particular work environment characteristics of the organization.

REFERENCES

BEST, F. and B. STERN (1977) "Education, work and leisure: must they come in that order?" Monthly Labor Review (July).

Bureau of National Affairs (1980) ASPA-BNA Survey No. 39, Retirement Policies and Programs. Washington, DC: Author.

COPPERMAN, L. F., D. G. MONTGOMERY, and F. D. KEAST (1979) "The future labor force participation of older workers and the employment environment." Presented at the annual meeting of the Gerontological Society of the United States, November.

Louis Harris and Associates (1979) 1979 Study of American Attitudes Toward Pensions and Retirement. New York: Johnson and Higgins.

Hewitt Associates (1980) Compensation Exchange Survey on the Age Discrimination in Employment Act. Lincolnshire, IL: Author.

MORRISON, H. H. [ed.] (1981) Economics of Aging: The Future of Retirement. New York: Litton.

PARNES, H. S., G. Y. NESTEL, T. N. CHIRIKOS, T. N. DAYMONT, F. L. MOTT, D. O. PARSONS, et al. (1979) From the Middle to the Later Years: Longitudinal Studies of the Preretirement and Postretirement Experiences of Men. Columbus: Ohio State University Center for Human Resources Research.

RHINE, S. H. (1980) America's Aging Population: Issues Facing Business and Society. New York: Conference Board.

Travelers Insurance Company (1980) The Travelers Pre-Retirement Opinion Survey. Hartford, CT: Author.

U.S. Department of Labor (1979) Studies of Involuntary Retirement and the Effects of Raising the Retirement Age Limit. Washington, DC: Author.

13

TOWARD A POLICY FOR RETIRED PERSONS: REFLECTIONS ON WELFARE AND TAXATION

Edgar F. Borgatta
Martin B. Loeb

There is an old saying that a camel is a horse that was designed by a committee. If this is the case, and one thinks of the federal government as an extremely large committee that has been working on the problem for a long time, then the welfare and taxation policies that exist are understandable. The policies, however, must be seen as having so varied and such poorly defined objectives, so often confused and conflicting, that the system borders on chaos. There are continuous demands for reform, but these hardly are directed to creating a more coherent system.

Nowhere is there any clear statement of policy as to what the objectives of taxation should be, although there are myriad statements and implications of a purpose of some redistribution of wealth and minimum economic support for all. How this concern for the redistribution of wealth and the support of all within the system is to be implemented is something on which there appears to be no general agreement. The principle that seems to have governed the development of policy is the introduction of the least objectionable (least costly) programs, based on an implicit morality of caring for the dependent and worthy needy. "Least costly" is rarely a product of study or design. It is, more pragmatically, what is left of proposed legislation as it proceeds to enactment. In the variety of demands resulting from the many ways in which people can be needy, a competitive situation frequently is created with regard to who will get how much of what. There always appears to be a situation of limited resources, and attention is given first to one type of needy person and subsequently to others, and the priorities will vary.

The complexity of the situation is due not only to the variety and intensity of needs that are advanced, but also to the historical development of those who are to be the providers of services. In more distant history, largesse by the wealthy was coincident, in one way, with government largesse, since often the rich and the rulers were the same. In more recent history, as government forms have changed, wealth has resided also in professional, commercial, and industrial families, and so the notions of public and private charities have grown separately. The emphasis on private charities, however, has diminished in the last few decades as government has been organized as more stable in the position of providing services for the needy.

One of the interesting issues that grows out of examination of the historical antecedents to our current welfare program is that the press for *income testing,* determining that persons are indeed needy, is constantly defended on the basis of limited resources. This seems to emphasize making sure that resources are not provided to those who presumably could get along without them. There appears to be an implication that if the redistribution system gives something to people who are not in need and who could get along without the allocation, there is something immoral involved. This notion is inconsistent with so many ways in which redistribution and allocation of resources already occur in American society. For example, we have services that are provided by various levels of government where it is clearly considered that the services are not equally distributed, but that they are important to the system. Such services occur in the forms of such pervasive systems as the legal system that establishes property rights, the services of developing and maintaining road systems, and protection at the level of national armies and other levels, such as police and fire departments. It does not take broad knowledge to recognize that some of these services are provided by local governments and others by the federal government, and that historically the involvement of the federal government is more recent for some services than for others.

However, the services mentioned so far do not deal with the support of individuals directly in the way providing welfare services implies. Still, in such an important area as education, with minor qualification, the delivery of services has been universalistic, without income testing. We are well apprised of the aberrations that have occurred historically, but in the current era there is no question that the educational policy of the federal government is for provision of equal opportunity, if not the somewhat stranger concept of equality of outcome. In a naive sense, presumably each person in the United States should have equal access to a minimum of education as made available through various governmental resources. What we are emphasizing here is not the notion that those who are needy are entitled to such education, but the fact that the many who could afford private education are not excluded from the general resource. Education is noted by way of example; there are many areas in which public provision of services occurs where alternate services are available for those who can afford them.

The focal point to which we are moving is the notion that income testing as a system for redistribution is only one possibility, and, from the point of view of history, may not necessarily represent development of the most efficient or most appropriate system. It is not a characteristic of human history that planning for redistribution looms large in the actual enterprise of government. Thus, attention to some of the philosophical positions that have been advanced as alternatives sometimes has been less than dramatic. Since some of the suggestions that arise out of the alternative views of those who are trying to fine tune an imperfect, grown-like-Topsy type of system may potentially be extremely important and practical, in our presentation here we will first focus on one major alternative that is likely to get more attention in the future.

DEMOGRANT

The currently popular word for a universal redistribution system that allocates a minimum amount to each person is the *demogrant*. The idea is obviously not a new one, and it has occurred in many different philosophical and economic writings. However, the concept has reemerged with visibility only in the last few years, and is seen sporadically in the newsletter, for example, of the Institute for Socio-Economic Studies. While others at the University of Wisconsin Poverty Institute have been interested in the issue, Irwin Garfinkel has given particular attention to the issue of the demogrant, contrasting it to welfare systems based on income testing. Garfinkel (1979), in the consideration of welfare reform, addresses this issue specifically: "Now, at the outset of the 1980's, the nation faces critical questions: Should we continue to increase our reliance on programs that restrict their benefits to those with low incomes? Or should we, in future reforms, work to reduce the role played in our income support system by income testing?" He notes that some programs, such as Medicare, do not involve income testing. But in the past few decades there is no clear-cut direction in which welfare has moved. Kesselman and Garfinkel (1978) review the contrast between the negative income tax (NIT) and the credit income tax (CIT), and in process point out that the former explicitly involves income testing, while the latter is designed to be a universal payment program without income testing. The authors point out that

> surprisingly, the argument against non-income-tested programs has never really been elaborated beyond this level. [CITs are inefficient because they are not concentrated where the need is the greatest.] Yet, income-tested schemes have gained wide acceptance in the period following the advocacy of a negative income tax by Milton Friedman (1962). They have been the subject of voluminous, theoretical analyses, cost estimates, field experiments, and legislative proposals.

Kesselman and Garfinkel do an extensive analysis of the income-tested versus the nontested programs with regard to economic efficiency. While the presentation is intriguing and instructive, it is relatively narrow, probably in response to the awareness of how little consideration of a CIT there has been in the United States. Their conclusion, however, is important and will be of use as our consideration moves in the direction of issues with regard to the aged: "Relative to an NIT, a CIT offers the potential of minimal distortion of labor-supply and other private economic decisions, minimal public cost of tax-transfer administration, and safeguards on the balance between adequate transfers and excessive taxation. Thus the CIT would appear best suited to insuring a floor under individual incomes while causing minimal disruptions of laisez-faire principles."

The idea of a CIT has been given particular attention in the state of Wisconsin, possibly through the interest of the Poverty Institute at the University of Wisconsin. A report presented by a special panel to the Wisconsin Health and Social Services Department recommended an earned income tax credit, but went on to recommend substantial additional changes having the impact of non-income-tested programs, such as a universal child support tax program (Socio-Economic Newsletter, May 1979). The development of a CIT at less than the federal tax level does not seem plausible, but interest in it at the state level may herald more serious consideration. Here we will not enter the myriad issues, but only point out a few interesting suggestions. For example, with a demogrant system certain kinds of current protections may not be necessary, such as unemployment insurance designed to provide minimum support. Possibly raising more interesting and emotionally charged debate would be the suggestion that if a demogrant exists, then the utility of minimum wage legislation would be questionable. While the reader ponders this possible consequence, we note that some possible effects on labor force participation by older Americans are noted subsequently.

The emphasis to which we have been moving is the notion expressed here of "insuring a floor under individual incomes" that ostensibly can operate to substitute for many of the welfare programs that are devised and advanced under the concept of income testing. Among advantages which have been noted for the CIT, but even for the NIT, is the fact that such programs would be administered through the tax system, and thus would eliminate many of the bureaucracies that exist for other types of welfare in-kind and income support programs. A massive bureaucracy that would become duplicative, as suggested later, would be the Social Security Administration. One does not need to be cynical to suggest that consideration of movement in this direction might meet with tremendous opposition, since many bureaucratic positions could be eliminated through such simplification. With a small bit of cynicism, we are reminded that there are two classes of direct beneficiaries in any welfare program—those who receive the services and those who administer the services.

The practicality of a suggestion such as the development of a demogrant through the tax system is hardly explored. Dismissal of the idea is easy for those who wish not to think about it, but the fact of the matter is that if we are providing services and income to all members of American society at this point in time, and presumably there is some notion that this is at least a partial reality, then alternate systems would cost more or less only on the basis of their structure in providing for the redistribution of wealth. What is clear, however, and is pointed out by Garfinkel (1979), is that the current system is less than efficient, and may indeed violate some very basic American values. We will not enter the details of this discussion, but will rather mark something with which most persons who have looked at welfare programs are familiar.

In particular, there is an element of an "all or none" threshold in development of income-testing programs. Thus, those who are indeed without income may be eligible for programs, while those who are just above the threshold may find that benefits are withheld from them so arbitrarily by rules that they are in more dire conditions than those who are ostensibly less economically productive. Similarly, there are many analyses to suggest that we have a major system akin to the well-known principle that "no good deed goes unpunished." Thus, marginal taxes for those who attempt to work and are at the bottom of the heap are so massive at the threshold that they demoralize and discourage persons from attempting to move into a more productive status. A common example of the high marginal tax is the operation of social security benefits, where, beyond a given amount of earned dollars, the social security benefits are reduced by one-half of every dollar earned—50 percent is a high marginal tax rate.[1]

One of the problems of the working poor is the obverse of this, that is, the disqualification from benefits if one attempts to move up the economic ladder and does so in small increments. A more general phenomenon has been reflected in terms of the participation of the persons at lower income levels who are unable to take advantage of programs open to those who are below them in the scale of economic productivity. These facts, and the relative difficulty that large segments of the American population have experienced in recent economic times, suggest that rethinking the whole basis for the redistribution of resources is not an impossibility.

The reason that such issues are of relevance here is that the development of programs for those who are growing older and are moving in the direction of retirement, for those who come to retirement, and for those others who simply grow older and do not go through that rite of passage which implies moving from a productive work status to a period in which productive employment is not essential as such, are affected directly by the way that tax and welfare policies are formulated. The existence of such *relatively* universalistic programs as Social Security makes for one kind of planning. If it were to revert back to income testing, it would alter expectations radically for a major segment of the American population. Social security and its structure will be discussed in part, and we do not mean to imply that it satisfies in any general way the requirements of a demogrant system. However, it has elements moving toward the demogrant and, we will note, elements also moving away.

Part of what is at issue and will have to become relatively central in the development of policy for older Americans is how they are going to be considered. There has been some movement to treat older Americans as a special class, and this type of simplistic mentality has led to a number of peculiarities in response. However, it must be remarked immediately that such simplistic type of categorization occurs commonly in society, and in this sense older Americans are no different from anyone else. The issue, however, is whether older Americans should be treated as a special interest group, or whether they should simply be treated as other Americans, possibly with a little more attention to making sure they are aware of their rights. The question, simply, is whether or not persons should be given assistance because they are older or because they are in need. If there is a basic notion that all who are in need should be given attention, there is no reason whatsoever to giving special attention to the aged as a class. If the notion is that there should be medical services available for all persons, then older persons are no different from younger persons. If there is a notion that those who are unable to care for themselves should be receiving care, again, there is no reason to make reference to age. Of course, statistically speaking, the aged may more frequently be dependent than some other age groups, such as those from 25 to 30, but this in no way alters the principle.

SOCIAL SECURITY BENEFITS

When Social Security law became effective in 1936, emphasis was placed in public relations on the participatory contributions of those covered, and the notion that one earned an annuity. This idea is still carried by some of the early champions of the system, such as Robert M. Ball, a former Social Security Commissioner (*New York Times,* December 2, 1979). By contrast, in vacating his office more recently as Commissioner of the Social Security Administration, Stanford G. Ross emphasized that the idea that Social Security is a contributory pension plan is simply a myth: "No workers' tax payments are cumulated to pay his or her future benefits, and no worker actually pays what the private insurance plan would charge for the promised benefits" (*New York Times,* December 2, 1979). The point made by Ross can be substantiated reasonably by reference to the reserves that exist. To cover the current obligations of contributing members, for example, according to Treasury Department estimates, reserves would need to be 4.2 trillion dollars in 1979, as compared to the actual reserves in the fund at that time, which were 30 billion dollars, or substantially less than 1 percent of the anticipated liabilities *New York Times,* November 30, 1980). Thus, what appears to be clear is that Social Security is not a funded pension plan but an income transfer system.

As soon as the idea is generally accepted that Social Security is indeed an income transfer system, some of the peculiarities of revisions and reforms do not become necessary. For example, and currently this is a somewhat radical idea, there is *no* justification, other than how the system began with its myths, for the idea that some persons should get more benefits than others. The idea that some people have paid more into the system and, therefore, should get more out of it is a relatively strange one in a society in which ideas of progressive taxation are generally accepted. Remember, this statement is made on the assumption that Social Security is an income transfer system, and not a funded pension system. Thus, it follows that future development should move in particular directions. One direction could easily be in the furthering of the system toward becoming a universal system with no income testing. The development of the

Supplemental Security Income (SSI) in 1972 can be interpreted as a move in the direction of universality by providing a coverage for those who did not contribute enough to become eligible for social security. The second radical comment to be made here, of course, is that if there were a demogrant system, there would be no need for a Social Security system as an income transfer system, nor for any of the other transfer systems designed to take over under presumed special conditions of need, such as unemployment, disability, or the like.

Another policy issue that comes to the fore in examining the operation of the Social Security system is whether or not the federal government knows what its policy on the family is. A great deal of federal tax and welfare legislation has impact on the family, sometimes encouraging one thing, then another. For example, credits and deductions are used to lessen or alter the tax burden for certain family statuses, creating explicit policy on type of family encouraged, although many representatives of government might deny that there is a governmental policy on the family. The federal government often takes positions regulating the family, as with the computation of benefits and taxes for couples, say, depending on whether or not they are married. In a demogrant system, and in any system that is oriented to the protection of individual rights rather than the recognition of groups as having special rights, credits or benefits would be allocated to individuals. Therefore, there would be no tendency to penalize persons because they have found it convenient to pool resources and also to be married. The barrier to marriage for older persons because of possible loss of benefits is well known. What is less often considered is the penalization of persons because they have been married. If persons can operate more efficiently by group living, which is what married persons do, why should policy at the federal and other levels be designed to penalize them? There is some irony in the fact that income tax options to ease the burden of single wage earner households eventually have led to the peculiarity of the "marriage penalty" that some married couples experience, paying more taxes than they would if they were single. Even more ironic is the position of the federal government that persons cannot at their convenience change their marital status to pay the smallest amount of taxes. The extension of this principle can be ludicrous, but, given the way bureaucracies work, it is certain to be advanced at some point.

With regard to Social Security, it is clear that some considerations about equal or fair treatment are sometimes creatures of sentiment and sometimes of the peculiarities of common economic assumptions and theories. For example, in considering the issue of fairness of the Social Security system with regard to women, it is noted that they are more often in the position of making contributions to the system that then are not relevant to their benefits, which may derive from the earnings of their spouses. Equity does not require that women get the same benefits as men; it requires merely that they be treated equally, and the law does this. But in raising this issue we place emphasis on the fact that it is a peculiar tax system, that benefits are not allocated with regard to contribution in some circumstances, and that the suggested alternatives to maintain the system do not cure the problems. For example, one type of possible solution to this problem of spouse benefits has been the suggestion that under concepts of community property the accounts of spouses be credited with payments, thus increasing the individual accounts and making viable benefits that somehow reflect the earnings of the spouse as well. This is convoluting an already poorly conceived system. It also is a continuation of the myth that there is some rationale for the payout being related to the input.

If there is merit to the notion that Social Security is a taxation and income transfer system, and the weight of this position seems overwhelming, then quite a number of things follow with regard to possible change and reform. Without elaborating some of the possible directions too far, the more obvious may be advanced. First, of course, given the fact that the myths have been surveyed by the beneficiaries as well as by the creators of the myths, some attention must be given to transitions and changes so that they do not occur too abruptly and appear to be penalizations. The notion that there can and should be changes is not an innovation presented by present authors so that suggestions may be made. The President's Commission on Pension Policy has advanced some policy changes that are relevant here.

The first and possibly most important suggestion from the President's Commission is based on the observation that tax incentives may not be enough to stimulate low- and moderate-income workers who are covered by pension plans. For this reason:

> the Commission concludes that serious consideration should be given to the establishment of a minimum advance-funded pension system. Such a program could be thought of as an advance-funded tier of social security that would permit contracting out to pension plans that wanted to meet its standards or as a universal, employee pension system with a central portability clearinghouse [President's Commission on Pension Policy, 1980a].

What is important about this suggestion is the notion of a central portability clearinghouse for individuals, and the notion of advance funding. This, then, would be a pension system. Whether it should be universal and mandated is a separate question, and one which raises many issues. The main issue, however, can be stated simply. If the implication is that the underlying social security system is not adequate to maintain participants in the style to which the Commission would like them to be accustomed, why attempt to raise the standard by a universal mandatory saving system which cannot touch all persons equally? Isn't the same effect accomplished by raising the baseline of a universal social security system (presumably a demogrant system)? What is important about a universally available *pension* system is the emphasis on portability, and, as will be noted in the later section on vesting, in the detachment of the pension assets from the control of employers and unions.

The President's Commission in no way presents a coherent, well-organized policy recommendation. For example, we have noted that all but the romantically inclined are willing to recognize the Social Security system as a tax and income transfer system. If this is the case, then another of the Commission's (1980a) recommendations has a little "Alice in Wonderland" showing: "Contributions to and benefits from social security should receive the same tax treatment as do those of other retirement programs." Alas, this suggests that the benefits that are paid (which, by the suggestions made here, should be moved in the direction of tax credits) would be taxed. This is a strange perspective! Presumably, this would have the effect of flattening the returns of the benefits, of narrowing the band, which would be consistent with the idea that in a tax income transfer system the returns for all should be equal and without income test. However, the method is still the same as the income-test welfare procedure that tends to penalize the virtuous. Under the system, those who save for their retirement as compared to those who do not will continue to be penalized. No good deed goes unpunished, once again.

Even more serious, from the point of view of regression to the older mentality of welfare, is the notion that: "As life expectancy increases, it would seem equitable to expect retirement ages to rise" (President's Commission on Pension Policy, 1980a). In the Commission's November 1980 Interim Report, the age is mentioned as 68 years, the outgrowth of some consensus. Part of the problem with the notion of advancing the age is that it reflects the Social Security system continuing in much its current form, the direction of change being more in keeping with the older welfare characteristics of redistribution. Under the notion of demogrant, the age of normal retirement becomes a specious concept. What is important here is that the Commission does not see this as permissive, but as normative. The concern arises from worry about what will happen when "there will be extraordinary growth starting in 2010 as the post-World War II baby boom begins to retire. When this generation retires, funding problems will intensify, particularly if the birthrate remains low" (President's Commission on Pension Policy, 1980a). The proposal is less than imaginative.

Another issue that may be raised with regard to the normal age of retirement concept is whether it fits into the style of life that has been generating over the decades. For example, there has been a vision and some progress toward shorter work hours, shorter workweeks, and possibly shorter work years. For example, according to a report in the ISR Newsletter (Autumn 1977), a survey indicated that a majority of men and women now retire before the age of 65, and 40 percent of working family heads 35 to 63 years of age were planning to retire before the age of 65. In a general way, this is a trend of many nations, and the suggested policy in the direction of extending the years of work has an odd misalignment to this trend.

Possibly this is a good point at which to introduce an issue that is always brought up—political feasibility. Asking whether it is politically feasible to advance the age of normal retirement is like asking what the chances are of getting rid of rent control in a city that is made up of a majority of renters. Not all things are easy for politicians, but, then again, there are some that see their task as defined more broadly than that of simply getting reelected. With regard to increasing the normal age of retirement, the procedure advanced is essentially one of "grandfathering" (grandpersoning?) by making rules applicable only into the future. However, grandfathering is necessary only within bounds. The rollback of double digiting was accomplished in a rational manner, since it was broadly seen as an error and a problem for the administration of Social Security. If it is feasible to plan moving in the direction of advancing the age of normal retirement, it is equally feasible to do other things, although the appropriate circumstances need to be developed. For example, if there is a move to recognize Social Security as a general tax, it can eventually be combined with income taxes, particularly if the notion of the CIT is integrated in such a shift, although this is not necessary. At such a time, the benefits of Social Security could begin to flatten toward the principle of becoming uniform *by applying the indexing for inflation only to the minimum benefit.* With the economic strategies of administrations and their advisors, the inflationary rate would soon have the social security benefits all to the level of the minimum or standard for each individual. There are some ways in which the federal government is efficient, and maintaining inflation seems to be one of those.

As a final reflection on the recommendations of the Commission, it should be noted that an appropriate suggestion is directed to the current earnings test for Social Security. If there is an objective to encourage all members of society to be economically productive, then they should not be penalized for being productive. With a CIT arrangement productivity is not penalized, and the Commission (1980a) at least recognizes the principle in suggesting that "if the Commission recommendation on tax treatment of social security benefits is adopted, then the Social Security earnings test should be removed." This at least recognizes that good deeds should not be punished too severely.

The presentation thus far has been quite broad. From here the discussion moves to some more narrow considerations, although the relationship to these initial comments will be apparent.

MANDATORY RETIREMENT AGES

An issue that has received attention in the recent past and that now appears to be moving into less prominence centers on the question of mandatory ages of retirement. Up to a short time ago, most organizations and institutions could specify a mandatory age of retirement, usually 65 years of age, and not have to justify it other than to note the coincidence and convention corresponding to Social Security and so many other concepts of an appropriate age of retirement. The debate around age of retirement goes in two directions. First, many have noted that individuals who reach the age of 65 may be extremely active and vigorous, in no way showing any physical or mental decline or deterioration. Thus, the arbitrariness of a mandatory age of retirement has been questioned on this basis. Second, with the arrival of the current inflationary period, many have noted that some persons would like to continue working beyond that point of 65 years of age in order to augment income levels or, indeed, to provide for income support in the first place.

The debate around the issue of whether there should be mandatory retirement *at all* has come out of this debate, and some subsidiary questions have been clarified. In particular, since the age of retirement legally moved from 65 to 70 years of age, no massive shift of work-related behavior in the population was found corresponding to this legal change. Much to the surprise of many, it was discovered that people are looking forward to retirement and intrinsically are not feeling that they should be given the opportunity to go on working forever. Some persons, of course, might continue working, particularly in the more highly specialized professions. In any event, some tendency in this direction had been noted. However, for the masses of the population, a great desire to continue working simply has not been manifest, especially if there has been no personal economic pressure.

A second objection to the raising of the mandatory age of retirement has come from people who have been concerned, possibly overconcerned, with the potential blocking of younger people in their upward mobility because older persons would continue to occupy the prestigious and valuable locations in hierarchies. Some, for example, became concerned with the possibility that "a whole generation of the ablest young people would likely be turned away from scholarly careers" (David B. Truman, *New York Times*, October 25, 1977). What is interesting about such positions among educators, of course, is that others can point out directly that old persons can be highly productive and imaginative, but that among the older persons there will be some who have become "deadwood." This concept derives from the notion that they have been in positions for considerable periods of time without keeping up with change and without being productive. Young people, obviously, cannot have had the opportunity to become "deadwood," although certainly they have the potential for getting there at some point in time.

Raising the issue of whether or not people should be fired for relatively unproductive behavior on the job, of course, is a no-no. Firing someone simply because he or she has become inefficient and relatively unproductive is viewed by many as inhumane, and downgrading the individual under those circumstances is almost as bad. Age, however, has nothing to do with this. There are relatively incompetent persons in positions of all types; it does not require much cynicism to reflect on the general applicability of Parkinson's Law or the Peter Principle, or any of the myriad variations of these observations that have been elaborated subsequently. Some may see our employment structures as protecting the least competent employee and intrinsically defining those who produce more than the minimum as "rate busters." Others may question why seniority should have come in more recent times to be equated with higher pay in some areas, particularly the area of higher education, but also in other areas where promotional series have been developed, as is common in civil service. This is a touchy issue, and we would maintain that it has nothing to do with age, except that as people grow older they may lose their competitive concerns. The residual question is whether or not a particular individual has become incompetent. Use of an arbitrary cutoff date in order to protect those persons who should be evaluating and making decisions about termination or downgrading is a solution that should be called into question. There is no reason the value of equal pay for equal work should be canceled by seniority any more than by sex, race, or any other suspect category. But, as we note, this goes both ways.

In an open society, there is no reason to suggest that contracts cannot be made between *individuals* and their employers. Thus, there should be the potential for contracts that last for one year, for five years, and possibly even to a given age, such as 70. The potential for such contracts, however, may not exist in large segments of the labor market. For example, where unions exist, if such contracts were made they would be between the union and the employer, and individuals might not have some options. What would appear to be most at issue is that when such contractual relationships are known and well understood, they should hardly be seen as objectionable.

Finally, it should be noted that statements that are permissive are not the same as those that are mandatory. Suggestions that persons should be permitted to work if they are able and desire to do so do not imply that all persons must, or that all persons should. What is often at issue in examining policies is whether or not they are flexible and permit variation that should be not only permitted but welcomed in society.

VESTING

If the notion is accepted that funds that are to provide for pension coverage are a part of wages, then the idea of *instant vesting* becomes a viable and important principle. That is, the wages that are presumed to be set aside in order to purchase an annuity for the individual should be allocated directly to an account for the individual. This account could be truly individual, much as Keough Accounts or Individual Retirement Accounts (IRA) are actually maintained individually, or as a share in a collectively held fund, such as the Teachers Insurance and Annuity Association (TIAA) or the College Retirement Equity Fund (CREF), where the dollar value is represented directly by purchase price and accumulated earnings (TIAA) or by current value of shares in a variable fund (CREF). With the wages transferred to the individual's account, thus, they cannot be made conditional for delivery to other circumstances, such as demonstration of loyalty by being tied either to a union or an employer for a given period of years. There is a clear distinction that can be made between the benefits that are supposed to be wages and a presumed concept of reward for loyalty to an organization.

Laws are whatever governments pass and what is interpreted by the courts, and while the intentions underlying the initiation of laws need not be questioned as having evil intent, some of the consequences of laws are not what they are supposed to be. For example, with regard to vesting, some dramatic and almost unbelievable cases are found in recent history. The most celebrated of these, possibly, is the one involving John Daniel, a truck driver in Chicago and a member of Teamsters Union Local 705 without any breaks in membership. After 22 years of working and finding a need to retire in 1973 because of health, Daniel found that because of an interruption in his employment in 1960-1961 he was disqualified from a pension. The case went all the way to the U.S. Supreme Court; Daniel died in December 1979, without learning that the application of the law did indeed exclude him from a pension.

The idea of vesting only after a long period of association either with an employer or a union seems to emphasize the idea that a pension is a reward for loyalty and continued service, rather than a payment of wages that are set aside for a special purpose, a form of savings to be available in later years. Some may see virtues associated with the idea of a reward for loyalty and continuous participation with an employer or union, but consideration of these matters has militated in recent years against exploring exactly what the presumed pension plans are designed to do. Some of these issues have been developed as protections to provide individuals with information about plans, and also some specifications have been involved in the development of the Employee Retirement Income Security Act of 1974 (ERISA). Still, anyone who explores the area will find that very little has been done in redefining pensions associated with employers and unions so that they are designed to protect individuals and allocate the presumed wage benefits directly to individuals. Rather, pension plans appear to continue almost without changes as means for controlling the loyalty and mobility of workers.

One of the pension issues that is not explored frequently is the fact that so long as the pension plans are directly in the control of unions and employers, rather than the members who would be owners of their segments of the cumulated funds, the potential for several serious problems exists. For example, if funds are cumulated, and then paid out without regard to the contribution of the member who is retiring, the basis of the funds is that future contributions are utilized in anticipation to pay the current retirees. Such organization of pension funds depends on a stable or growing unit, but to predict this is to have an extraordinary belief in the stability of industrial systems. Centers of production for particular industries have shifted not only within the United States, but also throughout the world, and some previously relatively undeveloped areas have become main producers in some industries that the United States formerly occupied in part or dominated. This has been true of relatively basic industries and of highly technical areas as well. If industry is disappearing, then the labor force is likely to be declining and the potential for being able to support a pension system based on future earnings simply cannot exist. This is a serious danger, and this problem, of course, also represents the kinds of problems that have been associated with the federal Social Security system.

There are already examples of pension plans that are in or border on bankruptcy, and these frequently have even been uncovered in some relatively protected environments, such as pension funds associated with local governmental units. In this circumstance the situation arises when benefits are increased without providing the funding basis for the increases.

Another way of looking at the problem of pensions with regard to vesting is that, as the system now operates in many circumstances, what really becomes the defining feature is that a majority of the employees who may never get any funds are essentially providing the funds for the minority who are favored. Some observers would find this type of all or none system less equitable than other potentially structured systems that allocate benefits directly to individuals. The latter, presumably, could be oriented to giving back value proportional to the contribution. Again, it must be recalled that the consideration of pension plans, both private and public, cannot be carried out without giving recognition to the context within which they exist. If a federal inclusive system of supports already exists, such as a universal Social Security system or CIT program, the underlying base on which additional support could be developed can be received more easily as a matter of option.

In this presentation we have not emphasized the issues of what some of these programs do psychologically to the participants. However, most of us have experienced conversations with people who have expressed sentiments with regard to retirement which indicate their feelings of being locked into a system. The expression of this frequently comes out in the form of a statement that one has put in so many years, and now must put in so many more. Decisions to move, to alter work careers, and so forth, must all be held in abeyance if the requirements of vesting are not yet met.

The notion that pensions represent part of the income of an individual is contradicted also by attempts to administer such funds for the control of behavior of the participants in other ways. For example, a recent case (1979) arose in New York City, when a school teacher was indicted by a Queens County Grand Jury on counts of obscenity, particularly involving pornographic materials with children as subjects. Aside from the issue of guilt or innocence, the case became interesting because the teacher was ostensibly eligible for retirement, and the chancellor of the school system attempted to block these benefits. The issue was viewed as a moral one of punishing the alleged crime by removing the benefits, in contrast to giving recognition to the pension benefits as a part of the earnings of the individual. The point was made clear that this was not the imposition of a legal fine by a judge after a case was adjudicated, but the attempted manipulation and interpretation of what the basis was for retirement benefits. Clearly, in the view of the chancellor of the school system (and of other officials and several newspapers), the benefits were not earnings that had accrued to the individual and were justly his. They were viewed as benefits, which could be allocated to moral and deserving teachers as they terminated their services and requested retirement benefits.

ARE OLDER PERSONS ADULTS?

Another implication that may be examined after a consideration of vesting deals with the options that should be available for persons with regard to their annuities. Most plans, such as the Teachers Insurance Annuity Association (TIAA), which may be advanced as an example of one of the most progressive of the large plans, require that the benefits take the form of annuity payments. That is, the payments are based on a life table, and are projected to be self-liquidating in a statistical sense so that the average participant gets all of the investment (less costs of administering the system) and its accumulated value back. This is a protective system, but if there is a general universal minimum support system, then there is a good question about the rationale for maintaining such systems as the only alternatives. For example, why should not one who retires have the option of taking all the funds in his or her account and living it up for a few years? This raises the kind of issue that involves the implicit imposition of morality on all, without taking the perspectives of individuals into account. The issue is not dissimilar from the attempt to get colleagues to stop smoking for their health and longer life—to which one shrewdly commented: "I'll stop if you add the years to the middle of my life, not the end." But more obvious circumstances arise with the restriction to annuity payouts. For example, suppose a person knows that he or she will deteriorate and die in a short time. Can one then at least enjoy the accumulation while there is some time, assuming one has not yet retired? Not under most current pension systems, although the person's account has a cash value in a system like TIAA and, if he or she were to die, the survivors could get the whole thing in a lump sum.

If fringe benefits are supposed to be a part of wages, then it would appear reasonable that they not only have the characteristic of portability associated with instant vesting, but that the participant should have some control over the nature of the fund. Thus, for example, we have this in funds when they are individualized as Keogh plans or as IRAs. Not only may the basis of the fund be shifted from one form to another (within limits), but the payout may be controlled. A recent report indicated that 90 out of 546 companies surveyed were found to be offering a lump-sum payment option based on the estimated cash value of the annuity at retirement, available for reinvestment or use by the employee on leaving. The implication is not necessarily that the employee will stop working at this point, but merely that work for the particular company has ceased. Some companies put restrictions on how the funds must be treated, but most do not (New York Times, April 5, 1981).[2]

COST OF LIVING INCREASES

Inflation, reasonably, can be thought of as a national problem. While inflation may result from wage increases in separate industries, or price advances in various categories of goods, or from some other collective procedure of looking at the incrementation of costs that are passed on to consumers, economists frequently point directly to the federal government as the source of inflation. Stated most simply, the argument is that if more money is printed, it has less value. This may not only be simple, but may be overly simple. However, here we are not looking to enter the argument, which can become a great economic debate. Whatever the source, it arises at federal levels of policy and no single industry, labor organization, or other unit can be seen as creating inflation. If it is a collective phenomenon, by definition federal policy either tolerates or encourages it through monetary, banking, tax, and regulatory policies.

The point is that if government policy at the federal level is seen as causing inflation, then it is an interesting question to ask where the remedies for individuals who are affected adversely by that inflation should occur. If the inflation itself cannot be controlled, at least some attempt might be made to remedy the circumstances of those who are adversely affected by it. On this, there is likely to be little argument, although there is the constant argument regarding from where the money is going to come. There is always more government involvement potentially, and we will not labor the point that it might be better to concentrate on reducing inflation rather than providing resources for those adversely affected by inflation.

The issue of inflation often is not considered in a broad context. For example, in the most recent historical period the greatest growth in the union movement in the United States has been in the area of civil service employees. The unionization of teachers, for example, is essentially a post-World War II phenomenon. Similarly, federal employees of various types essentially became a major segment of organized labor only in this post-World War II period. During the depression period, the virtue of civil service positions was that they were "secure jobs" and thus poor pay presumably was compensated for by the element of predictability.

During the 1960s in particular, recruitment for civil service was often difficult because of residual low pay and presumably uninteresting positions, particularly in comparison to growth industries, academia, and other areas. Policy changed in the federal government to move in the direction of paying "equivalent" wages and salaries, although some ambiguities arose about how these categories would be defined. Among other changes there was the development of fringe benefits after relatively liberal patterns, particularly with reference to retirement. There are a number of traditions for early retirement in civil service, particularly if the armed forces are thought of as a form of civil service. Additionally, for fire fighters and police officers in large cities, traditions of early retirement after 20 years of service, not dissimilar from the armed services, often existed as a way of compensating for hazardous and physically demanding duty. These concepts frequently were carried over into other areas, and so, for example, it might turn out that teachers could retire at half pay at a given age (say, 55 years) having only 20 years of service. Civil service and working for the government, of course, are not uniform circumstances, and at the local level there are still many persons working for villages and towns who are not covered by many benefits that are thought of as commonplace for larger units of government. But in larger cities certainly there has been this generalization of benefits and keeping up with salaries in civilian circumstances. One of the discoveries during this post-World War II period was that monies that are associated with taxes are infinitely expandable in the thought processes of legislators. After all, one develops a necessary budget, and then taxes accordingly. Bureaucrats and legislators sometimes determine such things in an apparent vacuum. So, providing for civil servants may become defined as an issue of appropriate attention, and idealistic concerns can be raised, but this may be done without consideration of how other taxpayers may be faring.

Cost-of-living increments have been relatively easy to put into effect in some government units, but once put in place they appear to become forever necessities. Thus, benefits that are attributed to these units may increase over time because they cumulate and are never renegotiated, while circumstances affecting the private taxpayers who are not in these circumstances may be quite different. For example, as business and industry slows down during inflation, it is often very difficult to negotiate cost-of-living salary increases in the private sector, and only strong unions in limited industries have been able to do so as a matter of contract. Rarely do such matters touch the majority of workers, who may go for years without a raise, where the more local employer frequently argues that increases in costs make it impossible for him to give cost-of-living increases.

The major point raised here is that inequities occur, and they are resolved or attempts to resolve them occur in particular local circumstances. Society does not respond effectively, in a uniform way, to problems such as the increasing cost of living and inflation. To the contrary, only some segments are responsive. This in turn raises the question of whether local units should be, as a matter of policy, attempting to resolve the problems of inflation, or whether they should, by contrast, be concerned with developing pressure to have a more universal response on the part of the federal government to deal with these problems.

Some things may be described in relatively crass and harsh terms. For example, in 1980 in New York State a bill to supplement the pensions of city workers who retired prior to July 1, 1970, passed both houses of the legislature. Ten years after retirement, presumably, it is proposed to change the conditions of employment for individuals, ostensibly a cause that everyone should support. Presumably, those retired prior to that time received meager pensions, so it would be a good thing to give them something more substantial. But, the question that becomes immediately evident is why persons should be given this kind of treatment simply because they were employees of New York City. Taxpayers may ask the question of why *they* should not be given some support, assuming that they retired before July 1, 1970. Many taxpayers receive no pension whatsoever. Whenever people are dipping into the local treasuries of governmental units, there is a reasonable question that can be asked as to why one expenditure to support some people is more desirable than one to support others. If the notion is that the poor deserve more support, then this is a form of welfare, and it is unreasonable to suggest that simply because people were employees of the government they should be more deserving than those who were productive workers in other areas. Vested interests become involved, of course, and these are manifest as a political thrust.

SPECIAL PROGRAMS FOR THE GROWING NUMBERS OF OLDER WOMEN

The facts of improved length of life are well known. At the turn of the century, expectation of life at birth was about 50 years, with women having somewhat less than 3 years longer expectation of life than men. In 1977 expectation of life was 73 years, with women having somewhat less than 8 years longer expectation of life. Thus we see, in the period since the turn of the century, a rather remarkable lengthening of expected length of life by a half. The statistics are similar when looked at in alternate ways. For example, length of life has advanced during this period when looked at from the beginning point of 1 year of age, of 20 years of age, or any other beginning point. The advancement is attributed to many things, including, particularly, the control of communicable diseases, but also the control of other diseases. In addition, a major global explanation is often advanced that increase in expected length of life is a reflection of the general improvement in the quality of life historically.

TABLE 13.1 Expectation of Life, by Color and Sex

At Age 65 Years	White			All other		
	Male	Female	D	Male	Female	D
1977	13.9	18.4	4.5	14.0	17.8	3.8
1969-1971	13.0	16.9	3.9	12.9	16.0	3.1
1959-1961	13.0	15.9	2.9	12.8	15.1	2.3
1900-1902	11.5	12.2	.7	10.4	11.4	1.0

SOURCE: U.S. Public Health Service (1980: Section 5, Table 5-A).
NOTE: "All other" were black only in 1900; blacks constitute about 95 percent of "all other" in other years.

Most important from the point of view of social gerontology is the fact that the gap between expected length of life for men and women has been increasing. The gap between blacks (or others) and whites, by contrast, has been decreasing. So, for example, while there was about a 15-year gap between blacks and whites for expectation of life at birth at the turn of the century, the gap in 1977 was about 4.5 years. This is presumed to be associated with relatively greater improvement for blacks while the quality of life was improving for all.

The statistics for expected length of life at age 65 years are summarized in Table 13.1. Note that as survivors, beginning at that point, blacks are not grossly dissimilar from whites, and the small gap that existed at the turn of the century was nearly closed by 1977. Relative improvement for the blacks paralleled that for the whites, only showing a small residual gap for women. However, at this age group, the gap for men and women shows the same pattern of widening noted at other age groups.

The differential in expected length of life is accompanied by other facts, including the increasing proportion of women among older persons, which has received attention in the literature. In terms of views of the growing number of women who are old becoming a social problem, legislative and other responses have been directed to a social policy of attention to these women.

As a response to the fact that women live longer than men on the average, meaning that there are more older women than men, more widows than widowers, and so on, the suggestion commonly arises that a tremendous investment of federal and other resources should go into the study of problems of older women. Presumably, as a consequence, tremendous investments should go into the provision of the services specially keyed to the older woman. This social logic requires examination in terms of the values involved; one of the concerns of policy makers should always be to examine values in a broader perspective of other related values.

One might suggest that an equally appropriate action might be to examine why women live so long, and to remove the factors that lead to this persistence. One will say: "Come on, be serious, we are concerned with preserving life, extending it, and improving the quality of life." The improvement of quality of life has been given in a general way as the reason for the length of life being further extended. It follows, therefore, that in furthering the general improvement of the quality of life of women, presumably they will live even longer, and the gap in years lived by men and women will be increased even more.

This leads, then, to the question of priorities in policy. Should there be an emphasis on policies that further extend the life of women beyond that of men, or should there be emphasis on the extension of life for men so that it approximates that of women? The equitable thing would appear to be, on the face of it, to institute policies that will equalize the average length of life of men and women. Thus, attention should be directed to studies of the problems of men, presumably at all age levels, and the ways in which the quality of life can be improved and subsequently the length of life can be extended for them.

No doubt there will be objections to such a suggestion. What will they be? A notion of biological determinism has little substance, and most explanations of current differences refer to environmental and experience factors. The suggestion that men elect to do things that will make them die younger (rather than older) as a means of dismissing the argument has to be placed in context with an equal argument that women elect their roles in society, and thus there should be no concern with sex-role definitions. Arguments about whether men or women are responsible for society as it is are fruitless, obviously, and the statement that men and women are equally the captives of the culture is hard to contradict. If this last statement is reasonable, then the justification for giving priority to the extension of the average length of life of men would appear quite appropriate. Blaming the victim is a poor logic under most circumstances, and so we arrive at what may be an unexpected suggestion.

From the point of view of policy, the growing number of women living to older ages does not suggest emphasizing female studies in the expectation that they may need special care. Rather, even a casual examination of the value system and society as it operates suggests that the emphasis should be on men, to seek knowledge on how to improve their lot so that they may live as long as women.

CONCLUDING COMMENT

This chapter has traversed some basic issues with regard to the whole organization of taxation and welfare. We suggest that the government (and the people) may sometimes have difficulty in getting perspective. To aid this process we have used as a backdrop the CIT or demogrant as we have focused on specific issues. We have been intentionally provocative. Time passes and the familiar engrosses us all too easily. Certainly there has been shortsightedness in how we have operated, and our economic policy seems to be more a cultural phenomenon than based on empirical science. Here it is suggested that if there is to be perspective added, it has to go beyond the notion of "fine tuning" an amorphous system in a traditional mold. There are alternatives and they do not need to be radical. The CIT or demogrant is really not all that radical, but it would need extensive study and phasing-in culturally, since we have in some ways become a nation of many special interest groups seeking categorical aid rather than concerning ourselves with national well-being and basic support for all.

The second point we have made implicitly is that good intentions do not necessarily make good policy. The overtones of "Lady Bountiful" and the Poor Law of 1601 in so much of welfare policy lead to unintended consequences that seem less than sensible. We need to convince ourselves and others that a more rational system is both easier to operate and more attuned to a universalistic notion of equity.

NOTES

1. The reality of the view of being punished for working for those just above the welfare threshold is seen in real economic terms that are made emphatic even in the most public documents: "For the four-person family with no income [in 1973], benefits from public assistance, food stamps, school lunches, and medical assistance are valued at $5,500. The gross income equivalent is $7,000—equal to 89 percent of the BLS lower level living standard, sometimes known as the city wage earners budget. It represents the gross earnings of a worker earning about $3.80 per hour for a 35-hour week. Housing subsidies bring the gross income equivalent to $8,000 and day care to as high as $11,500" (Joint Economic Committee, 1973).

2. Incidentally, for those who do not use the annuity form of payout this also bypasses the whole issue of whether there should be use of unisex life tables or single-sex life tables for computation of annuities. In the past, life tables for each sex have been used, since women at age 65 live about 4 years longer than men. Thus, if the same life table is used for both, on the average women get a substantially equal total payout only if they get smaller monthly (periodic) payments. The trend

forcefully supported by the Equal Employment Opportunity Commission (EEOC) has been toward equal monthly payments, thus leading to greater total payment, on the average, for women. (In the use of individual-sex life tables, equal monthly payments may also be accomplished by allocating more money for women as part of payment of wages into the accumulation accounts.)

REFERENCES

GARFINKEL, I. (1979) "Welfare reform: a new and old view." Journal of the Institute of Socioeconomic Studies 4: 58-72.

KESSELMAN, J. R. and I. GARFINKEL (1978) "Professor Friedman, meet Lady Rhys-Williams: NIT vs. CIT." Journal of Public Economics 10: 179-216.

President's Commission on Pension Policy (1980a) An Interim Report (May 1980). Washington, DC: Government Printing Office.

——— (1980b) An Interim Report (November 1980). Washington, DC: Government Printing Office.

U.S. Public Health Service (1980) Vital Statistics of the United States, 1977. Volume II. Hyattsville, MD: Author.

14

UNLEASHING THE PRODUCTIVE VALUE OF LONG LIFE

Merrell M. Clark

Americans have adopted a set of values about long life which are proving to be extremely costly. It may prove to be desirable or necessary to continue our current practices of financing long life outside the productive economy. On the other hand, the costs are so extreme that we certainly will need to review all of the assumptions underlying current practices. This process of review may take place over the decade immediately ahead as Congress confronts the trajectory of national expense associated with retirement. Although the aggregate retirement paycheck in 1980 did not quite reach $300 billion, it already had become the nation's top social priority, well ahead of health care, education, or defense. Now we can watch that paycheck grow to $1.2 trillion over the next nineteen years, honoring commitments already made.

The purpose of this brief chapter is to explore several values issues surrounding long life in America. The exploration should open a number of questions for future research. It will be concerned with the fundamental purposes of long life, with the benefits a long living society should expect to receive from its investments in consumption or production by its members, with issues of fairness which flow from segregationist policies, and with unresolved conflicts between the biblical understanding of human worth, current practices, constitutional principles, and public misunderstandings of fact.

THE AMERICAN SCENE

First of all, it will be helpful to review the nature of public misunderstandings regarding long life. In the 1970s, observers of the American scene noted that our federal budget was "graying," our campuses were "graying," our work force was "graying." Hardly an institution in the society managed to avoid a little "graying." The reason for all this "graying" is the "graying" of society. In the United States, long life has become extremely popular. Thanks to medicine, white-collar and professional jobs, easier blue-collar and farm jobs, education and other social interventions, we now can expect to live three-fourths of a century, if we are adult males, and four-fifths of a century, if we are adult females. There are 15,000 of us now living in our eleventh decade; a million of us are living in our tenth decade; 24 million of us already have lived two-thirds of a century.

At the same time, giving birth to children has decreased in popularity. Lately, sanction of chemical and surgical controls on fertility has caused birthrates to plummet to the point where sheer human replacement is barely maintained. Long life has become a prominent feature of our nation even faster than it would have become had birthrates remained high. As a result, all regions, sectors, industries, communities, congregations, families, and other structures of our society and economy are filling up with people who enjoy long lives, while proportionately fewer babies are arriving to keep the society as young as it once was.

One of the passing ironies of this moment in the long history of humankind is the widespread anxiety caused by this demographic change. Americans do not like the idea of becoming "old." "Aging" people are expected to be the victims of their own crumbling systems, the impoverished victims of the competitive forces of society. This expectation is compounded by increasing awareness that "nonproductive" retirees will place a mushrooming economic burden on a proportionately declining work force. All the growth of the older population, to a layman, seems to magnify the fears of becoming "old." The growth threatens not only more decay and abuse, but greater cost as well. The idea that long life can be, and usually is, *good news* strikes many people as an unintelligible idea. In spite of all of the progress in human development that has occurred in this century, the mindless repetition of bad news about growing "old" has worn a hole in the nation's aggregate brain. The great achievement of long life for most people goes largely uncelebrated. Like a corollary to

Murphy's Law ("If something can go wrong, it will"), if something goes right, it will be denied.

AN AMERICAN MIRROR

A 1974 survey of American attitudes by Louis Harris and Associates displayed the contours and scope of this denial. The survey showed that actual conditions of elders are very similar to conditions of younger people in most respects, and that those conditions are generally very good, but the nation labors under consistent misunderstanding and believes older people are different, erroneously, in specific ways. For example, older people and younger people are generally satisfied with their incomes (15 percent of elders claim serious money problems versus 18 percent of youngers), but 62 percent of the public believes age is a factor in poverty! Similarly, few older people claim "loneliness" is a serious problem for them (12 percent), just as do younger people (9 percent), but the public believes, at the rate of 60 percent, that age is a factor in loneliness!

The real differences between elders and youngers are highly focused in two areas. First, the proportion of elders who experience health problems is substantially higher, although only a minority of either young (10 percent) or old (21 percent) populations experience health problems at any point in time. Second, the proportion of elders who allocate major portions of their time to work is substantially less than that of younger people, 10 percent to 51 percent! This largest difference, of course, has been caused by government, not nature. The survey also showed that elders get high marks in public attitudes in one area only. They are believed by younger people to be "warm and friendly" at the extraordinary rate of 82 percent. Not surprisingly, older people themselves do not share in this fantasy. Older people believe older people are "warm and friendly" at a modest rate of 25 percent.

Elders get very low marks, however, in two areas which are crucial to their integration as productive members of the society. Even though older people view themselves as "bright and alert" in proportion to other age groups (68 percent), the public at large is not ready for that notion (29 percent). Similarly, even though older people view themselves as "good at getting things done" in the same proportion as other age groups (55 percent), the public at large gives them a lower score (35 percent). In sum, the Harris survey showed that the public has exaggerated notions of the problems of long-living people, and it underestimates their productive capacity. The public expects older people not to be competitive, and it hopes they will be affectionate.

AMERICAN GOOD NEWS

In contrast to these dismal public expectations, the facts are more cheering:

- The real poverty rate among Americans 65 and older on a per capita basis after subsidy and taxes is lower than for the 18-64-year-old group.

- The median per capita income of Americans 65 and older is higher than the national median.

- Gender and race, not age, are the prime causes statistically of low income in the 65 and older population as well as in the 64 and younger population. (Use of aging household poverty statistics by advocates of increased benefits merely disguises single female survivorship.)

- Older Americans (12 percent of the population) contribute up to 35 percent of the national vote.

- Long-living Americans own nearly 30 percent of the nation's private homes, yet they pay less in mortgage expenses than any other group.

- Work force participation by males of 65 or more years has been driven down from 70 percent in 1900 to approximately 18 percent today, not because of poor health (health has improved radically since 1900), but because of a public policy adopted in 1935 to remove parents-of-parents from job competition with parents, using age 65 as an administratively convenient trigger.

- Approximately 4.6 million Americans of 65 or more years are now engaged on a regular basis in volunteer service. (All government programs designed to pay older volunteers a wage or their expenses account for .3 million of these people.)

- Approximately 3 million Americans of 65 or more years are employed out-of-home (and *report* they are employed despite the enticements of the unreported cash economy). In addition, approximately 5 million females of 65 or more years report that they are employed in the home in the family economy.

- If motivated to do so by sufficient earnings or by a worthy and interesting challenge, an additional 6 million long-living Americans would reenter the paid or charitable work force.

- Of all Americans who were born more than 65 years ago, combining those in their seventh, eighth, nineth, tenth, and eleventh decades of life, 80 percent have no limitations on their mobility.

- A high proportion of the wealthiest Americans are old—a fact of life which probably has been the case throughout our history.

- American retirement systems now are filling rapidly with an unprecedented pool of professional and executive talent. While many nations boast few professionals, our retired population includes thousands of accountants, artists, clergy, educators, engineers, executives, journalists, and even lawyers or doctors who previously were employed by universities or by public or private bureaucracies.

- In virtually every field of American endeavor, many of the leaders are in their seventh and eighth decades of life. Being old and vigorous no longer can be viewed as an exceptional phenomenon. Examples abound in banking, insurance, finance, manufacturing, retailing, entertainment, mass media, religion, government, and many other fields.

- Of American retirees, 53 percent regret having retired.

In sum, although age is believed to be a significant factor in poverty by 62 percent of the public, long-living Americans actually possess or represent an embarrassment of riches in many ways. Not only do more and more Americans manage to last a long time, they also are less prone to illness in their later years than were older people in earlier decades. They are more highly educated, trained, and informed. And, despite the opposite public belief, they are better off financially than any generation of elders in American history. In fact, America has produced the largest population of able, educated elders ever produced by any nation.

Against the background of these facts, it is striking that official policy still is designed to encourage these people to withdraw from productive participation in the economy. It is clear that, in this society's distribution of responsibilities and benefits, we have developed a special place for the long-living members. While showering them with the benefits and discounts, we pay not only the cost of the benefits but also the cost of removing them from responsibility. Never has such a high-quality population been available for employment or service without being asked or encouraged to contribute to the resolution of our most urgent economic and social problems.

With this new abundance of long, able life in our midst, given adequate financing as a matter of law, what is it for? The answer to that question is not forthcoming from existing policies and practices. Indeed, the premise of existing policies and practices is the need to depress the productive value of long life on the economic assumption that withdrawal by elders from the principal economic activities of the nation is necessary in order to permit participation by newer people. It is ironic that the genius of the Social Security system lies in its humanitarian promise of income security as an incentive to leave the productive sector, yet the law is bankrupt with regard to the purpose of life thus financed. Retirement is the antithesis of vocation, albeit a dignified cover for the truly infirm.

A BIBLICAL MIRROR

Such a nonproductive view of human life stands in sharp contrast to the biblical values which undergird American life. Were the God of the Judeo-Christian tradition asked what long life is for, He probably would answer that it serves a number of worthwhile purposes. He might say that it gives one, for example, an opportunity to practice one's capacity to love and to glorify Him and to love one's fellows and enemies. He might say that it gives one an opportunity to perfect one's service to Him by doing His work on earth. He could point out that it provides an opportunity for one to multiply through others all of the resources He has provided, including one's mind, body, spirit, time, and belongings. He might suggest that it gives one an opportunity to fix one's mind on the future and on eternity so as to live obediently, in faith, in the present. In short, long life gives people an opportunity to fulfill their vocations, to be and to do what they were called into life to be and to do.

The idea of retirement is entirely foreign to the Bible. There is in the entire biblical record no sanction, no recognition of retirement. There is not even any mention of retirement. On the contrary, every exemplary servant in scripture dies while active in service. With reference to our biblical heritage, it also is noteworthy that no recognition of seniority is apparent. Children are recognized to be different from adults, but leadership among adults comes from adults of all ages. There are no second-class citizens on the basis of age. People who are considered important sometimes are distinguished by the accrual of many years, apparently as a sign of grace, but long life in itself is neither revered nor demeaned.

As Americans review current policies and practices regarding long life, it will be instructive to do so in light of the values enshrined in the biblical record, despite its distance in economic, social, and intellectual time. That record of a people who lived on agribusiness, trades, merchandising, and humane ministries enunciates a value system regarding long life which is surprisingly contemporary and realistic. The problems of long life are not obscured. Saul's senility, Moses' frailty, Sarah's jealousy, all are explicit. Yet, despite problems, biblical servants survive to make their ultimate, finest contributions: long lives dominated by the ideal of faithful service. They reveal human purpose in a social environment of scarcity, frailty, moral turpitude, and complex internal and external enmities not unlike our own. Of particular importance to Americans is the story of Abraham and Sarah. Many parallels to the American experience may be found in that legend. And now, America also is a nation of long-living people, a nation, if you will, of Abrahams and Sarahs. Despite our expensive laws designed to encourage retirement, as noted above, many of our major institutions continue to be led by faithful elders.

THE PURPOSE OF LIFE

So it is that we find a conflict in values between socialistic retirement ideas and our biblical heritage. The conflict fixes itself on the central question of human value: What is the purpose of long life? While such a question cannot be answered for particular individuals, whose independence requires that they select their own courses, it must be answered for the nation as a whole. Our current policies discourage any association between the costs of financing long life and the benefits derived from that financing. At the present time, the only benefits associated with the costs are withdrawal and survival. That is tantamount to financing dead weight, a social function which is bound to be resented as the weight increases.

On the other hand, the case actually may be worse than stated. The financing of long life by the state, without requiring production, has depressed by 75 percent the productivity of American men over 65. Their capacity to contribute to the support of three generations has been diminished, not increased, and the loss to GNP would approach $100 billion. Once the nation can design a purpose for long life which is worthy of its men and women, then the financing to achieve that purpose will be more productive and more palatable.

How does long life work to the advantage or disadvantage of a nation? Current arrangements make it difficult to develop an unbiased answer to this question. Stimulation to withdraw from the economy seems to rest on the premise that long life is valueless, that long life should become a cost center which yields no productive value to the society. As a result, the more popular long life becomes, the more costly it will become without reference to any value derived.

Who pays for the costs of nonproductivity? We know who pays the costs of retirement income. First they are paid by workers who pay taxes or contribute directly or indirectly to pension funds. Then they are paid by all consumers who must pay the prices of goods and services, which absorb higher costs of labor. But who pays for nonproductivity? It is easy to trace the flow of income, but difficult to calculate the loss of output. All people who produce income and purchasing, or who would like to do so, undoubtedly share in the loss, but it is not easy or possible to isolate particular populations. It is at least safe to say that the younger families of nonproductive elders absorb the loss.

What would happen if the current system of incentives were changed so as to yield similar protection from poverty but to encourage optimal productivity? This could be achieved simply by removing the earnings test, eliminating age factors in taxation, and by placing pension eligibility on an open actuarial basis, year by year, thereby affording at no additional cost a powerful retirement deferral credit. Economists believe this would increase GNP, reduce elder dependency, increase tax revenues and the support of public pensions, and generate additional employment opportunity. Would it also permit Americans to view long life with personal relish and to view the achievement in others with esteem?

What values associated with long life are missing in our culture? What prevents our people from reveling in the fullness of life? Have we built into our system incentives and disincentives that negate human value? Have we given adequate leverage to long-living people, permitting them to optimize their purposes in life and their productive value to society? Unless we develop good answers to these questions, there is no likelihood that we will develop good answers to issues surrounding the financing of long life.

FAIRNESS IN SOCIETY

Since 1935, when the age trigger for all Americans of 65 years was introduced, the society has developed increasingly segregated categories of thought and behavior regarding the old versus the new members of society. Many issues of fairness surround this practice of segregation among adults on the basis of birthdate. Today long-living Americans are heavily regulated by public programs. Not only are personal income and health insurance payments made by law, but special buses, special meal sites, special housing, and special caretaking arrangements also are made available to long-living people. Most older people resist this public beneficence, and special marketing efforts are necessary to find people who truly need and will accept this special treatment.

Why are the same benefits not marketed to needy people among the young? The volume of need for subsidized services of these kinds is even greater among younger people than among older people. Why, for example, should a 55-year-old, low-income grandparent be denied access to a job as a foster grandparent? If special bus routes are generated, why should not younger people who need transportation in the same neighborhoods be afforded seats along with the people 65 and older who qualify? If exactly these same distinctions were made on the basis of race or gender, as they have been in the past, they would be causes for civil disobedience.

The people who framed our Constitution were determined to preserve individual liberty, to constrain regulation with regard to any of the basic freedoms of individuals, and to prevent the development of classes in society. In recent years, the Constitution has been invoked to preserve the rights of individuals without regard to race or gender. Invariably, courts have ruled that individual merit or need must be judged without regard to such accidents of birth as race or gender. Also, courts have favored the dissolution of segregated facilities, arguing that segregation is necessarily a cause for inequality. Despite this tradition, however, we have built a two-class society on the basis of birth date without regard to individual merit or need. Segregation is provided and enforced by law.

What humane values permit this segregation and disregard of individual merit or need? Why should social benefits be accorded to people with birth date X, whether they need them or not, while people with birth date Y who need those social benefits are denied access?

What economic gains and losses accrue to the society as a result of practicing age segregation? How does enterprise profit, for example, from a policy that diminishes the economic status and productive value of long-living people? How does the public benefit from tax forgiveness programs accorded to long-living people whether they are wealthy or not?

Why does this society persist in enticing people away from their normal pursuits and personal vocations, regardless of their excellence or value, purely on the basis of birth date? Is it fair for the young to bear disproportionately heavy taxes in order to finance able elders who have been forced into public dependency against their will by public policy? Put another way, is it fair to prevent long-living people from sharing equally with young people in shouldering the burdens of the society?

THE FUTURE

It is time to get on with the task of resolving these issues, for we truly are caught in an economic and social vice of the first order. On one side of the vice, we are faced with rapidly increasing costs of retirement consumption—now $300 billion and soon to be $500 billion—at a time when the nation desperately needs to increase productive growth in order to remain strong in the world market and in world politics. On the other side of the vice, we are confronted with proportionately declining populations of young people whose labor is stretched merely to keep up with living costs and who also must absorb increasing taxes to finance consumption by their elders. It will not be possible to dissipate this pressure by raising taxes or by reducing benefits to the old. It will not be possible to postpone the crunch by diversifying the governmental pockets of wealth used to finance benefits for the old. It does not matter what governmental pockets are depleted since all pockets are filled by the taxpayer's pocket.

It may be possible to resolve the issues by reevaluating long life in terms of its value to the society and in terms of its eligibility for equal treatment under the law. This need not imply reductions in protection for the poor or infirm. It may not even imply any reductions in retirement income at all. It could imply, however, that equal access to the means of wealth could be restored to elders, that qualification for social benefits could be determined on the same bases of income and disability as those that apply to younger people, and that the incentive to maximize productive value could be restored.

The prevailing notion that long-living Americans are incapable of dynamic leadership, incapable of generating new enterprises and associations, incapable of meeting the nation's needs for faithful service, incapable of filling vacant slots for willing workers, and incapable of fully financing themselves until confronted with disability or death—this notion is an affront to our dignity and a denial of fact. The fear that elders, on the other hand, are fully competitive—the exact opposite of the incapacity notion—and would take jobs from younger people is exactly the basis for all social discrimination, whether the access to wealth is accorded to women, to blacks, or to elders. Such a fear can have no sanction in this society over the long haul. It denies the basic premise of individual opportunity and free competition on which our society is built.

Current aging policies are discriminatory and unaffordable. They assure that the fastest-growing sector of the population will become only a rapidly increasing burden on national resources. These policies are based on a lopsided view of human value and a misunderstanding of labor markets in a free economy. Aging policy now should be tested against the central objective of increasing the productive value of long life. Policies that encourage the use of elder talent to build a stronger nation, to build a stronger economy, and to build greater personal wealth will stand upright in any American future. So will the long-living Americans who benefit. So will all of us. The time is now overdue for us to unleash the productive value of long life.

INDEX

ABOUT THE AUTHORS

ROBERT C. ATCHLEY, Professor of Sociology and Anthropology at Miami University of Ohio, is likewise Director of its Scripps Foundation Gerontology Center. A member of the board of directors of the Western Gerontological Society, he also serves as Editor of Special Publications for the Gerontological Society and chairs the Public Policy Committee of the Association for Gerontology in Higher Education. His *Social Forces in Later Life* went into a third edition in 1980. Among his other books is *Families in Later Life* (1979), with Sheila Miller and Lillian Troll.

EDGAR F. BORGATTA is Director of the Institute on Aging at the University of Washington. Previously, he was Research Director of the Center for Gerontological Studies and a member of the CUNY doctoral faculty in the programs in Sociology and Social-Personality Psychology. While at the University of Wisconsin–Madison, he was Brittingham Research Professor. He has also been a faculty member at Harvard, Cornell, and New York Universities. He has written extensively on sociological methods and statistics, and in many areas of social research. He serves as Coeditor of *Research on Aging: A Quarterly of Social Gerontology.*

MERRELL M. CLARK serves as Director of the Aging Program and Executive Vice President of the Academy for Educational Development. In this capacity, he has been responsible for creating the National Committee on Careers for Older Americans, of which he is Vice Chairman. He is President of ELDERWORKS, an independent public foundation. Between 1972 and 1977 he was Vice President of the Edna McConnell Clark Foundation, where he directed the Program for the Elderly, which has stimulated new projects based on the utilization of elder talent in 50 American cities.

LORRAINE G. HIATT is a National Consultant on Aging for the American Foundation for the Blind. She is an Associate in the Center for Human Environments of the Graduate School and University Center of the City University of New York, where she is completing doctoral work in environmental psychology. She is currently directing an AoA-funded project on "Uses of Self-Help in Compensating for Sensory Losses in Old Age." She has made several national studies of services for older people in housing, reading, and environmental design, and has authored 15 scholarly publications since 1976.

LOLA M. IRELAN is Chief of the Program Population Studies Branch in the Social Security Administration's Office of Research and Statistics. She is a career civil servant, having entered the government service upon completion of graduate work in anthropology and sociology at the American University. Her work has been in fields closely relevant to government policy, including dental manpower and public health, poverty and welfare, and social insurance. The Social Security Administration's longitudinal Retirement History Study has been under her direction since its inception in 1968.

WYATT C. JONES is Professor of Social Research in the Florence Heller Graduate School for Advanced Studies in Social Welfare at Brandeis University. Since 1969 he has held appointment as Research Sociologist in the Veterans Administration Hospital, Brockton, Massachusetts. He serves on the editorial board of several scholarly journals, including *Evaluation Review, Research on Aging,* and the *Journal of Social Service Research.* His most recent book (with H. E. Freeman and L. G. Zucker) is *Social Problems: A Policy Perspective.*

ALICE KETHLEY serves as Deputy Director of the Institute on Aging at the University of Washington. Her primary interests are in the family and intergenerational aspects of research and training in aging and the long-term care of the elderly. At the university she is Director of the Interdisciplinary Gerontological Training Program and Project Director of a model services project, "Community-Based Comprehensive Care for the Elderly."

LESLIE S. LIBOW is Medical Director of the Jewish Institute for Geriatric Care and Chief-Geriatric Medicine at the Long Island Jewish-Hillside Medical Center. He is also Professor of Medicine in the School of Medicine in the State University of New York at Stony Brook. He pioneered the nation's first geriatric medical residency program and is one of the leaders in the movement to include geriatric preparation in the country's medical schools. He is a regular contributor to professional journals on geriatric/gerontology-related topics.

MARTIN B. LOEB is in his twenty-first year as a member of the faculty of the University of Wisconsin—Madison. In 1973 he became Director of the university's Faye McBeath Institute on Aging and Adult Life, a position he relinquished this past year. Earlier, at the University of Chicago, he was a Fellow in the Department of Anthropology and a member of the Committee on Human Development. Professor Loeb has also taught in the School of Social Welfare of the University of California at Los Angeles. He was a founder of the Association for Gerontology in Higher Education, serving as president in 1974-1975. He is Coeditor of *Research on Aging: A Quarterly of Social Gerontology.*

NEIL G. McCLUSKEY is Senior Consultant for the Project in Career Change Options and Preretirement Education of the Academy for Educational Development. He was the founder of the CASE Center for Gerontological Studies in the Graduate School and University Center of the City University of New York. He has held faculty appointments at Gonzaga University, the University of Notre Dame, and the City University of New York. He is among the authors in the Doubleday volume, *The New Old: Struggling for Decent Aging;* the Wordsworth collection, *Gerontology in Higher Education: Developing Institutional and Community Strength;* and the newly revised *Aging: Prospects and Issues,* from the Andrus Center of the University of Southern California. He was coeditor (with Edgar F. Borgatta) of *Aging and Society: Current Research and Policy Perspectives* (Sage Publications) and is currently Coordinating Editor of *Research on Aging: A Quarterly of Social Gerontology.*

ABRAHAM MONK is Brookdale Professor of Gerontology in the School of Social Work of Columbia University. He also directs the university's Brookdale Institute on Aging and Adult Human Development. Before coming to New York, he was a member of the faculty of the State University of New York at Buffalo, and, prior to that, a faculty member in the University of Buenos Aires. While lecturing in 1976 as Fulbright-Hays Senior Scholar at the University of Haifa, he received the Max Prochovnick Memorial Award from the Israel Gerontological Society. His most recent book is *The Age of Aging: A Reader in Social Gerontology.*

MALCOLM H. MORRISON is currently Acting Chief, Research Support Staff, Employment Standards Administration, U.S. Department of Labor. He has primary responsibility for major national studies conducted by DOL to examine the impact of involuntary retirement and the effects of the Age Discrimination in Employment Act (ADEA) on the labor market. These studies will be the basis for DOL reports to the president and the Congress in 1981 and 1982. He has edited a book forthcoming from Van Nostrand Reinhold Publishers, *Economics of Aging: The Future of Retirement.*

KAREN SCHWAB is a Research Analyst in the Social Security Administration. For the past several years she has been analyzing the Retirement History Study, concentrating on retirement patterns of sample members, and is currently completing doctoral studies at Rutgers University.

ARTHUR WEINBERGER was one of the first group of trainees in the CASE Center for Gerontological Studies, and completed his doctorate in the Social-Personality Psychology Program of the Graduate School of the City University of New York. He has written on the influence of agism on helping attitudes and has published in the *Psychological Bulletin, Research on Aging: A Quarterly of Social Gerontology,* and *New York* magazine. Currently he is examining factors associated with discounts for seniors. He also serves in the Burden Center for the Aging as a counselor for homebound elderly.

SHEREE WEST worked two years as a Trainee and Research Assistant in the CASE Center for Gerontological Studies and then became an Associate in the Center for Human Environments of the Graduate School and University Center of the City University of New York. She was the recipient of an Administration on Aging Dissertation Grant for her work on "Sharing and Privacy in Shared Housing for Older Persons." She has served as a consultant on environmental change for geriatric patient orientation at New York City's Bellevue Hospital.